THE WILLIAM COMPANION

Mary Cadogan is well known as a writer, critic and broadcaster. Her biographies of Richmal Crompton and Frank Richards have been much acclaimed, while *You're a Brick, Angela!*, which she co-authored with Patricia Craig, has for some years been required reading for anyone with an interest in popular fiction. Married with one daughter, Mary was born in Ealing and grew up in the Bromley, Kent, area where she still lives, and where Richmal Crompton lived and worked for most of her life.

THE WILLIAM COMPANION

Mary Cadogan

with

David Schutte

and contributions from
Kenneth C. Waller

PAPERMAC

First published 1990 by Macmillan London Limited

First published in paperback 1991 by
PAPERMAC
a division of Macmillan Publishers Limited
Cavaye Place London SW10 9PG
and Basingstoke

Associated companies in Auckland, Delhi, Dublin, Gaborone,
Hamburg, Harare, Hong Kong, Johannesburg, Kuala Lumpur,
Lagos, Manzini, Melbourne, Mexico City, Nairobi, New York,
Singapore and Tokyo

ISBN 0-333-56524-X

A CIP catalogue record for this book is available from the British Library.

Typeset by Macmillan Production Limited

Printed in Hong Kong

Cover illustrations are reproduced by kind permission of the
Thomas Henry Estate and taken from: *William the Bold*, first
edition jacket, 1950 (front and spine); *Happy Mag*, August 1936,
'A Fair Catch' (back top left); *Happy Mag*, November 1925,
'Business Before Pleasure' (back bottom right).

**In memory of Richmal Crompton in her centenary year
and Thomas Henry –
with ever grateful thanks for William**

CONTENTS

Acknowledgements   viii

List of Plates   ix

Source of Illustrations   xi

A Note on References   xiii

Introduction: The World of William   1

THE WILLIAM COMPANION   7

Appendix 1: The William Books   219

Appendix 2: The William Stories in Date Order of
Magazine Appearance   221

Appendix 3: Characters Not Listed Individually in
the A–Z Section   230

Appendix 4: Articles 'By William' (by Richmal Crompton)   239

ACKNOWLEDGEMENTS

Special thanks are due to David Schutte and Kenneth C. Waller for contributing from their respective fields of expertise certain articles to the *Companion*. Their contributions are initialled. I would like also to thank: Richmal Ashbee, Michael Wace, Darrell Swift and other members of the Richmal Crompton Centenary Committee who have encouraged me to produce the *Companion*; my editors at Macmillan, Adam Sisman, Susanna Wadeson and Hazel Orme, for their enthusiasm for this project; Joan Baverstock for her recollections and invaluable help with original material; Winifred Hebb and Lionel Fisher for providing further information on Thomas Henry; Ian Fryer, Alan Whitehead, David Bellamy, Les McLair, Gordon Wright, Ashley McCrery and Terry Morris, who gave free access to material over a long period of time; Professor Graeme Davies, Bill Lofts, Derek Adley and Brian Doyle; and others too numerous to mention individually who gave help along the way. Acknowledgements are due to Macmillan Children's Books for permission to quote from the William stories and to the estate of Thomas Henry for the use of various pictures.

Photographs are reproduced by courtesy of Joan Baverstock (page 2), Richmal Crompton's family (pages 1, 4, 5 above left and right, 8 above), the Thomas Henry Estate (pages 3, 5 below, 6) and Syndication International Ltd (pages 7 below right, 8 below). Henry Ford illustrations are reproduced by kind permission of the Octopus Publishing Group.

Every effort has been made to trace all copyright holders but if any have been inadvertently overlooked the author and publishers will be pleased to make the necessary arrangement at the first opportunity.

(M.C.)

LIST OF PLATES

(between pages 112 and 113)

Richmal Crompton as a young woman in the 1920s.

Thomas Henry in the early 1920s, around the time he began to draw William.

A selection of vintage magazines, which feature colour 'William' covers by Thomas Henry.

Richmal Crompton in middle age.

Richmal's brother, John Lamburn, and her nephew, Thomas Disher, both of whom provided inspiration for the William stories.

A wooden jigsaw by Thomas Henry; one of the comparatively few spin-offs from the 1950s.

The *Just William Magic Painting Book*, illustrated by Thomas Henry and published by BB Ltd, probably in the early 1950s.

Dicky Lupino, the first film William, pictured on the cover of the book of the film *Just William* (1939).

The book of the 1948 film *Just William's Luck* starring William Graham.

John Clark, the first radio William (1945).

The first regular television William, Dennis Waterman, in the 1962 BBC series.

Richmal Crompton and Thomas Henry with some of their fans (Nottingham Book Fair, 1958).

William's most recent appearance on screen was in the 1977/8 LWT series, starring Adrian Dannatt with Bonnie Langford as Violet Elizabeth Bott.

SOURCE OF ILLUSTRATIONS

Page	Source
iii	Happy Mag, Oct 1936
v	Happy Mag, Feb 1927
vii	Happy Mag, Nov 1923
viii	Happy Mag, Jan 1926
ix	Happy Mag, June 1926
xi	Happy Mag, Jan 1926
xiii	Happy Mag, Oct 1925
xiv–xv	Happy Mag, Oct 1936
1	Happy Mag, Oct 1926
1	Home Magazine, March 1919
2	Still William, 4
3	William's Happy Days, 2
3	William and ARP, 4
4	William and the Witch, 5
4	William the Bold, 2
7	William Does His Bit, 4
8	William the Showman, 6
10	William the Bad, frontis
11	William and the Masked Ranger, 5
11	Still William, 5
12	William's Happy Days, frontis
14	Happy Mag, Dec 1928
17	William the Detective, 6
20	William's Happy Days, 10
21	Still William, 9
22	William the Fourth, 13
24	Home Magazine, March 1919
25	William Does His Bit, frontis
27	William the Good, 3
29	William the Conqueror, 1
30	William the Good, 5
31	Just William, 2
33	Happy Mag, Sep 1923
34	William the Fourth, 6
36	William and the Tramp, 1
37	Happy Mag, May 1924
39	Home Magazine, July 1919
42	Happy Mag, July 1925
43	William the Bad, 9
44	William the Good, 8
46	William the Fourth, 9
48	William and the Pop Singers, 1
50	William in Trouble, 9
53	Happy Mag, June 1926
54	William in Trouble, 1
55	William and the Space Animal, 1
56	Happy Mag, Sep 1926
58	William the Fourth, frontis
58	Happy Mag, Feb 1927
62	More William, 6
63	Happy Mag, March 1929
64	William's Happy Days, 6
65	William the Dictator, 2
66	William Does His Bit, 10
67	Happy Mag, March 1925
69	Still William, 14

Page	Source
71	Happy Mag, March 1927
73	William the Good, 2
74	Happy Mag, Feb 1924
74	Just William, 4
76	William Again, 5
77	William Carries On, 8
78	William the Fourth, 7
79	Just William, 11
79	William the Rebel, 1
79	William the Lawless, 5
82	William in Trouble, 2
84	William the Conqueror, 13
87	William's Crowded Hours, 2
89	William the Conqueror, 3
90	William Again, 2
91	Happy Mag, Christmas Extra 1929
92	William in Trouble, 7
94	William the Fourth, 5
97	Sweet William, frontis
99	Sweet William, 2
100	Happy Mag, Nov 1930
102	William the Bad, 7
103	William and the Brains Trust, 9
106	Happy Mag Christmas Extra, 1926
109	William the Rebel, 4
110	William and the Space Animal, 5
112	Woman's Own, 14 March 1947
113	Punch, 22 Apr 1914
116	Happy Mag, Sep 1939
120	Homes and Gardens, June 1943
122	William and ARP, 8
123	William and the Pop Singers, 2
124	William the Fourth, 13
127	William and the Tramp, 2
128	William and the Evacuees, 1
130	Home Magazine, June 1919
133	William Carries On, 7
136	William the Bad, 1
137	William the Pirate, 2
138	William and ARP, 2
140	William and the Evacuees, 8
143	William's Happy Days, 10
144	Sweet William, 10
146	William and the Witch, 5
149	William and the Moon Rocket, 8
152	Happy Mag, Sep 1927
154	Happy Mag, Aug 1925
154	William Carries On, 4
156	Still William, 6
158	William the Superman, 2
159	Happy Mag, May 1927
160	William and the Moon Rocket, 6
161	William's Television Show, 4
162	Happy Mag, Feb 1926
166	Happy Mag, Aug 1926
167	Happy Mag, Feb 1926
169	William and the Pop Singers, 5
171	Home Magazine, July 1919
174	Happy Mag, Jan 1939
175	Happy Mag, June 1929
177	William, 9
181	William in Trouble, 7
182	William and the Brains Trust, 9
183	Just William, 7
184	William Again, 5
186	William the Outlaw, 4
187	Happy Mag, Feb 1927
190	Sunny Mag, Apr 1927
191	William the Fourth, 8
192	More William, frontis
193	Tit-Bits Summer Annual, 1928
195	William Carries On, 8
197	William the Bold, 2
198	William Carries On, 5
200	Happy Mag, Jan 1926
201	Just William, 5
216	William and the Masked Ranger, 4
218	William the Pirate, 1

A NOTE ON REFERENCES

In most instances the full titles of the books referred to in the *Companion* are given, together with the relevant chapter-numbers. However, when many stories have to be mentioned, only the number of the book (see Appendix 1) is shown, followed by the number of the chapter. It should be noted that the pagination of the original Newnes publications and that of the current Macmillan reprints differ; therefore chapter- and not page-numbers are appropriate. In the case of *William – The Detective* two chapters have been omitted from the Macmillan reprint, so the chapter-numbers shown refer to the Newnes edition.

Cross-references to other articles in the *Companion* are indicated by CAPITAL LETTERS.

The *Companion* and its Appendices have been prepared entirely by reference to original source material. They also contain some previously unpublished biblio-graphical information.

Never let yourself get bored is William's golden rule—

—and don't worry if your adventures annoy other people—just keep busy !

INTRODUCTION: THE WORLD OF WILLIAM

Richmal Crompton created William Brown just over seventy years ago. The first published story of his exploits was 'Rice-Mould' which appeared in the *Home Magazine* of February 1919, and this scruffy, belligerent, opinionated anti-hero was to inspire several hundred stories, which have been collected into thirty-eight books. Just a few years after he bounced on to the literary scene, his name had become part of the language, synonymous with robust and riotous boyhood. His career has not only spanned the decades but has also undergone interpretation in a variety of media; stage, screen, radio and television presentations, as well as spin-offs such as toys and games, have consolidated his fame.

All this would have come as no surprise to William, who commented more than once that the world would ring with his name, and that 'sta-choos' would be put up to him. It was, however, a surprise to Richmal, who intended him only as a pot-boiler; her ambition was to establish herself as a serious novelist but, although she produced some forty adult novels and several collections of short stories, William 'took and held the field' (Richmal Crompton, 'Puppet Pulls the Strings', *Books and Bookmen*, December 1957).

As well as creating William, she established a wonderfully colourful and interesting world around him, which encompassed his rather cynical something-in-the-City father, his long-suffering, perpetually sock-mending mother, his gloriously good-looking, flirtatious and work-shy elder sister Ethel, and his susceptible undergraduate brother Robert. William's inventiveness was enhanced and extended by his association with his special friends – Ginger, Henry and Douglas – and with the demure, elusive and dimpled Joan, the only female who was permitted to join their society or gang, the Outlaws. (The redoubtable Violet Elizabeth Bott, despite her celebrated threat to 'thcream an' thcream' until she was 'thick' in order to get her way, never quite managed to gate-crash the group,

although she knew better than anyone how to flatter and batter and generally manipulate William and his friends.)

Richmal established her ever-growing cast of characters in a remarkably elastic and quintessentially English village, where, over the years, William tangled with edgy dyspeptic ex-military men, stuffy spinsters, nervous clerics, 'self-made' social climbers, and batty aesthetes, authors and artists. By the end of the 1950s, egged on by readers' letters which highlighted discrepancies in the stories, Richmal started to analyse and correct the thirty or so William books which had by then been published. She got as far as noting alterations in Ginger's and Joan's surnames and in Robert's age. She also realised that, when collected, the stories had sometimes been published in the wrong order, and that she had, on occasions, confused some of her lesser characters. She listed the relatives of Henry, Ginger and Violet Elizabeth, and some of the places around William's home. After cataloguing twelve of Ethel's admirers and twenty-four of Robert's girlfriends she wisely gave up the correlating process, appreciating that this would take precious writing-time.

About the village itself she was – perhaps deliberately – vague. In the stories it is given neither a name nor a location. In the 1962 *Collectors' Digest Annual*, Gerry Allison records an extract from one of Richmal's letters to him about it:

> . . . I just set down people and houses in places where I want them for the particular story I am writing. The village in which William lives is entirely imaginary . . . a small country village in Kent – or perhaps Surrey or Sussex, within easy reach of London . . .

One reason for producing *The William Companion* is to draw attention to small anomalies; it also aims to provide a background into which Richmal's wide-ranging characters, places, events

and relationships can be slotted. Hopefully it may help enthusiasts to trace some elusive story, incident, protagonist or quotation; to find out if William really paid Joan the compliment of saying that he liked her better than any insect, or just when, in his efforts to be helpful, he told people that Ethel suffered from epilepsy and consumption – and alcoholism. And did William actually kill a cat – or several cats? Did he have a crush on his pretty young teacher? Or on an ageing pantomime star? Did Robert ever take his finals? Did the feud between the Outlaws and the Hubert Laneites ever end – and so on and so on.

sive homes, that these domiciles seem to have been constructed to accord exactly with the comings and goings of neighbours, and the events taking place inside the houses, as described in some detail in the stories (see WILLIAM'S HOUSES and the plan of The Hollies). If we assume (and the text gives evidence for this in each case) that William (at different times) lived in two houses, attended two schools and (daring thought) was on affectionate terms with two Joans, then *almost* everything about William's physical world works out to be meticulously constructed, orderly and 'real'.

As well as Richmal's stories, Thomas Henry's illustrations are well represented in the *Companion*. On occasions when he produced two (and sometimes three) versions of the same incident (see HAPPY MAG) I have tended to use the first drawing that he made. Thus the William who is portrayed here is often redolent of the 1920s and the early books, with his hair and socks looking surprisingly tidy – gummed down, and pulled up, respectively. Sometimes, however, he appears in the far more dishevelled state (spiky hair, with socks falling down, and cap and tie awry) that characterised him from the middle of the 1930s until his last appearance in 1970.

Naturally I hope that the *Companion* will be enjoyable in its own right, as well as in guiding readers old and new into some highways and byways of Richmal Crompton's wonderfully witty stories. I started to prepare it on the assumption that William's world had grown entirely organically over the years, but I have to say that the deeper I dip into the texts, the more I begin to move away from the idea that the village and its characters 'just growed' towards the acceptance of a structuralist approach. Despite Richmal's comments to Gerry Allison about the unfixed location of William's anonymous village, Kenneth C. Waller, drawing only on information available in the narratives, has not only placed but also named William's birthplace and stamping-ground (see WILLIAM'S VILLAGE). He has also produced a map, to be published later this year. It has often been considered, too, that William's homes have been only vaguely envisaged, expanding, contracting and acquiring embellishments according to the needs of individual stories. Yet we can now see, even if Richmal never had a physical plan of William's two succes-

Although the *Companion* has been produced primarily for entertainment, it is interesting to observe the social changes which are reflected in the saga. For example, in between the wars the leisured ladies of William's village not only somewhat orgiastically promoted sales of work and bazaars (see FUNFAIRS AND FÊTES) but also found time to dabble in elitist literary groups and esoteric coteries. The Second World War brought the excitements of social shake-ups, as well as solidarity and the dogged retention of many of the village's traditional activities and values. After the war, the Outlaws find themselves becoming involved with the problems of the National Health Service, civic bureaucracy, protest marchers, interplanetary travel, and so on. Nevertheless, William & Co. remain perpetual embodiments of unpretentious and engaging youth:

'What'll we do this morning,' said Ginger. It was sunny. It was holiday time. They had each other and a dog. Boyhood could not wish for more. The whole world lay before them.

A difficulty which sometimes prevents a full appreciation of events and relationships is that the stories are occasionally presented in the wrong sequence in the books. Thus Jumble, for example, is established in *Just William* several chapters before William first stumbles upon him! The original order in which the stories were published in various magazines is shown in Appendix 2. However, even though this order throws more light on the development of the saga, it *can* be confusing because the magazine sequence did not always represent the order in which Richmal actually wrote the stories!

It has not, of course, been possible to mention every character or incident. To do so, with appropriate commentaries, would necessitate the production of a volume larger than the thirty-eight William books. However, Appendix 3 lists all the named characters who do not have entries in their own names in the A–Z section. Inevitably an element of personal choice is involved in the selection of material. Many of my favourite stories have been resavoured, and used in the *Companion*. I have tried, however, to focus on lesser-known – but intriguing – characters as well as on the luminaries.

MARY CADOGAN

THE WILLIAM COMPANION

Abbot, Rosalyn

A nineteen-year-old 'distinctly pretty' girl 'of limited intelligence', much admired by Robert. Like characters in several other of Richmal's books Rosalyn is influenced a great deal by the cinema: 'She went to the pictures in Hadley twice a week, and on the intervening days moulded her life and emotions on those of the heroine she had last seen.' Rosalyn gives Robert a hard time after William tries to convince her that his elder brother is courting Miss Gloria Gaye, a film-star who is temporarily staying at Honeysuckle Cottage. He isn't, of course – but William thinks the screen actress is the most likely of all the females in the locality to tempt Robert into matrimony. He is particularly anxious at this time to get him married off because Hector, Ginger's elder brother, has become engaged and, preparatory to setting up home with his beloved, has offloaded his bicycle and boxing-gloves on to Ginger (*Just William's Luck*, 3). William hopes for a similar handout if he can make an appropriate match for Robert!

Rosalyn dresses far more glamorously than many of the village girls, unlike her spinster aunt, Miss Abbot, a cat-loving busybody who wears knitted suits and picture-hats which are well past their prime and period of modishness. Rosalyn appears in *Just William's Luck* , 7, and Miss Abbot in 11.

A.F.S.(Auxiliary Fire Service)

Richmal joined this soon after the outbreak of the Second World War in September 1939, and avenged herself on a bossy senior officer by allowing William to debunk his prototype in *William Does His Bit*, 4, which was published in 1941. The Outlaws – 'these plucky boys' – put out a fire started by nasty Section Officer Perkins's cigarette-end. In fact they discover the fire only

because they go to his house to arrange a watery booby-trap for him!

Albert (1)

' " 'E's errand-boy at the grocer's, he is, an' 'e's offen round 'ere. 'E's called Halbert, 'e is." ' Albert, or Halbert, is a member of the impromptu and somewhat dubious secret society formed by William to inflict retribution on his temporary and tyrannical form-master, Mr French. (He is driven to enrol boys whom his mother 'would have designated as "common" ' because Ginger, Henry and Douglas are all at this time laid low with chicken-pox. The other members are Sam (Mr French's gardener's boy) and Albert's daredevil friend, Leopold. Not surprisingly, the avenging society gets out of hand. (*William Again*, 7))

Albert (2)

(This name seems to be favoured by Richmal Crompton for boys of humble origin.) Five-year-old Albert is a dirty and dishevelled child from the poorest part of the village, who is 'a proper trile' to his family, according to his elder sister Gert, a toughly charismatic girl whom William much admires: ' "Always gotter be a-mindin' of 'im, or a-washin' of 'im or a-dressin' of 'im," said Gert bitterly. "Can't do nothink nor go nowheres for 'im." '

William, whose New Year resolution is not to bother with trivialities but to do something really big, decides at one fell swoop to solve Gert's problem and to provide the vinegary spinster MISS MILTON with lasting emotional satisfaction. This determined lady has been passionately urging every well-to-do family in the village to 'adopt' groups of the local poor. William's brainwave is that Miss Milton should adopt Albert, whom he secretly transfers to her home and her bed (boots, grubby clothing and all), thus setting in motion a characteristically anarchic train of misunderstandings and mishaps. (*William – The Showman*, 6)

Algy

Small boy who, with his sister, sees William crawling along in a ditch dressed as an Ancient Briton. William's revealing animal-skin costume does not enhance his appearance. (He has lost his proper clothes.) Algy's sister pronounces him 'a loony' who 'thinks 'e's a frog', and warns Algy that he'll be eaten if he doesn't run away. Algy and his sister run off, screaming, to William's intense irritation. (*William – The Fourth*, 14)

Ambitions

William's career ambitions and fantasies are legion: '. . . resplendent in top hat and dressing-gown, glorious, irresistible, monarch of his kingdom, William the Pirate, the Smuggler, the Red Indian, the Robber Chief, the Ring-master, William the Victorious, William the Ever-Come-Out-On-Top swaggered across the lawn . . .' (*William – In Trouble*, 5). 'His mind ran over the careers that he had at various times decided to embrace – engine driver, explorer, spy, detective, prime minister, space traveller, sweet shop proprietor, speed-track racer, lion tamer, postman, diver' (*William and the Witch*, 1).

Generally speaking, each ambition provides inspiration for one story or chapter of his exploits. One of the most extravagant of his career aspirations crops up almost in passing in *William – The Detective*, 11, after he and the Outlaws have met Miss Carrol, Ginger's mother's second cousin, who, unlike most of their adult relations, turns out to be 'not bad'. They confide their ambitions to her: ' "Ginger's to be an engine-driver, Henry's an acrobat, Douglas's a gangster, and William's a world potentate. . . ." ' Somewhere lower down the power-scale he also has shots at being a dictator and a prime minister.

In a very different field, inspired by his garbled understanding of the life of Francis of Assisi, William decides to become a saint, although he soon finds that the religious life has severe limitations: ' "I'm jus' about sick of bein' a saint. I'd sooner be a pirate or a Red Indian any day" ' (*William – The Conqueror*, 4).

Most consistently he wants to be either a pirate or a tramp. Genuine pirates never cross his path, but he encounters gentlemen of the road with surprising frequency; however dire and dirty the schemes of these itinerant con-men might be, tramps are never, in William's eyes, lacking in charisma. For him they irresistibly embody the spirit of outlawry, of 'glorious freedom unshackled by the trammels of respectability and civilisation . . . the attractions of every other imaginable career paled in comparison. After all, he considered, brightening, once he was twenty-one, no one could stop him being a tramp if he wanted to . . .' (*William and the Brains Trust*, 5).

He also flirts with the idea of becoming a 'high-up detective', a chimney-sweep or 'one of those people . . . what fights bulls. They're called tor – something.' 'Torpedoes,' suggests Ginger.

William's incurable optimism stimulates him to undertake the most complicated and demanding of assignments. In *William and the Evacuees*, 1, he is called upon to right the imagined wrongs of several local children who feel that the little horrors from London who have been billeted in the village get all the fun, such as parties, new clothes, tins of sweets, etc. To add insult to injury, 'the way they swank' infuriates the native small fry. Even Arabella Simpkin (who is generally fiercely anti-Outlaw) approaches William with persuasive sweetness: ' "We thought you'd help to 'vacuate us, William, 'cause you're clever." ' William agrees (and within limits succeeds) but experiences pangs of doubt. He consoles himself, however, with the reflection that the Government had managed to evacuate whole towns in a few hours 'without a hitch. William considered himself as good as the government any day.'

In chapter 2 of the same book William tries to get into films. In *William's Happy Days*, 5, he fancies himself as an artist, mainly because in his opinion this means a career which demands no work, but just lounging about in the fields or woods each day in front of an easel. But he finds painting very dull, and in chapter 12 opts for a more satisfying occupation: ' "I'm going to be a millionaire when I grow up," announced William.' Ginger responds that he thought William was going to be a pirate, Douglas that he expected him to be a lion-tamer, and Henry that he understood his leader would become an engine-driver. ' "I'm goin' to be all those," said William very firmly, "but I'm goin' to be a millionaire first." ' Thus we see that there is, for William, no conflict in the possible realisation of his multi-faceted career aspirations. The world is indeed his oyster: 'His eyes gleamed with the light of the explorer. To William life was one long glorious Romance.'

There are, however, occasions when William feels that no one appreciates his life and labours, and that these are doomed to frustration. In *William – The Rebel*, 1, he bemoans the fact that he has lived for so long and 'not *done* anything yet'. His long-suffering mother points out that he's done quite enough, breaking every window in the house at one time or another, making the geyser explode twice, ruining the parquet by sliding on it, and getting tar all over the hall carpet! William, of course, will not be satisfied until he makes the world ring with his name, and has 'hundreds of statues' put up to him, all over the world.

His gripe is that his useless school-work stands between him and his ambitions, and he suddenly decides to run away: '. . . he'd join a band of pirates', become their chief, discover a new continent, conquer the natives, become king and then conquer the whole world (William was nothing if not wholesale). 'All this would take time, of course, and he hadn't a moment to lose' (*William – The Rebel,* 2). Several years later, in *William and the Witch,* 1, he again feels that life is passing him by: he is 'gettin' older an' older' but has 'done nothin' yet' to make his mark on society. By chapter 4 the Outlaws are still worrying about how their most cherished career-plans might be thwarted. William gloomily reckons that there will be nothing left for them to do when they have grown up. Other people will by then have explored everything from the middle of the earth to the mountains and the moon, and even have 'found the Loch Ness Monster'.

Dreaming up something which even in William's imagination he has never tackled before is no mean task, but in chapter 1 he comes up with a career that is bursting with opportunities for the expression of his talents *and* his misplaced endeav-

ours. He will emulate Mr Summers, a psychiatrist who has recently come to live in Green Lane, Marleigh. As William patiently explains to his friends, psychiatry consists mainly of the patient just lying down and talking: ' "You can't get into a mess with it same as you can with . . . spies and space travellers an' detectives an' things." ' A notice is made to adorn the outside of the Old Barn:

WILLIAM BROWN
SEKKITRIST
MENTAL TRUBBLES KURED
THREPPENCE EECH.

His first patient is the real adult psychiatrist, Mr Summers!

Of course, as well as career aspirations, there are many less significant 'wants' in William's life which are generally fulfilled (after the inevitable preliminary period of chaos has run its course and been resolved). In *William and the Evacuees,* for example, the fairly mundane objects of his desire are a tin hat, a *real* drum and a trumpet. In *Sweet William* he yearns for (and gets) a policeman's helmet . . . and so on.

Amos

'. . . a local ancient who performed occasional odd jobs in the village at his own time and pleasure.' He was apparently unreliable not only about turning up but also in the quality of his work. For example, when assembling a hen-house for Archie he imprisons the unfortunate artist inside it. The only reliable thing about Amos is that, whatever stage his current odd jobs have reached (or not reached), at 12.30 p.m. he abandons them and heads for the Red Lion. Conversationally he is also predictable, his sole contribution being the word 'Ar' into which he can 'put innumerable shades of meaning'. (*William's Television Show,* 5)

that Topsy has thus been 'given away' but still threatens Archie with legal proceedings if he doesn't pay the bill. It is, of course, William who (chasing Ginger's pet rabbit) finds that Topsy has been hidden by Andalusia in her bedroom. Andalusia appears only in this one episode (in *William and the Masked Ranger*, 5) but she is just one of several six-to-seven-year-olds created by Richmal who have the makings of characters which deserve fictional longevity.

Andrews, Bob

A picturesque figure, 'supposed to help with the gardening of the Hall grounds'. Handsome, roguish, white-bearded and work-shy, he is a great friend of William and the Outlaws. He takes seriously their pursuits such as playing Red Indians and collecting cigarette-cards. Sometimes he makes them bows and arrows, boats, tops and whistles. He also likes animals, and maintains as

Andalusia

The seven-year-old god-daughter of Mrs Herriot of Applelea Court, who not only has a strange Christian name (derived from the place where her parents spent their honeymoon) but who also calls her rag doll Boadicea 'after Britain's warrior queen'. Not surprisingly, she is very tough and determined. When her dog-breeding godmother hands Topsy, a black poodle puppy, to ARCHIE MANNISTER, Andalusia suffers an access of rage and batters Mrs Herriot about the knees with Boadicea. She steals Topsy back – which is awkward for Archie because Mrs Herriot sends him a bill for the dog for thirty guineas; she considers his surprisingly harmonious 'family' two squirrels, four dogs and seven cats. No wonder William & Co. are shattered when he informs them that the Hall's new owner, MR BOTT, has given him the sack for skiving and for stealing fruit.

Ginger's despondent ' "*we* can't do anything" ' is unacceptable to William, the leader, who waits and watches and eventually arranges 'a bit of blackmail' to bend Botty to his will. He photographs his early-morning al fresco exercises and so vividly captures the comic element of the portly sauce-magnate's near-naked leaping and skipping and gambolling and splashing that Mr Bott will agree to anything to have the snaps suppressed. The episode ends with Bob lazily taking the air outside his lodge, and singing out to the Outlaws: ' "Bob Andrews is not goin', me bhoys. The sack is withdrawn. Th'aud devil's realised me value, glory be to God." ' (*Still – William*, 5)

Angela (1)

Angela is the six-year-old grand-daughter of old Lady Markham. She buys, as a present for her 'Gramma', a two-and-sixpenny string of beads from a secondhand shop in William's village. Unknown to Angela and Lady Markham, these are Mrs Bott's pearls, worth several thousand pounds. Violet Elizabeth, inspired (in common with the Outlaws) by Robin Hood to steal from the rich and give to the poor, has filched them from her mother's jewel-box and sold them for sixpence (which was given to James Finch, 'the village reprobate', and immediately squandered at the Blue Lion). Lady Markham puts on 'the beads' which Angela has bought for her. She is, at that moment, in her carriage on her way to ask Mrs Bott to help at a forthcoming charity fête. Mrs Bott quickly – and hysterically – recognises the pearls that her aristocratic visitor is wearing. (*William The Conqueror*, 9)

Angela (2)

Not the grand-daughter of Lady Markham this time but the sister of Reggie, who has just begun to attend William's school. 'Dressed in a white sailor suit . . . and a white sailor's cap perched on a riot of golden hair', Reggie seems ripe for ragging. However, he is extremely self-assured and full of rapier-like repartee. The Outlaws hate him and vow to think up some dire scheme to knock the cheek out of him. But Angela begs William to look after her brother, and, because she has a demure face and dark hair that make him think of Joan, he cannot resist her entreaty. 'Alas for the fickleness of man!' – William is prepared to play the anti-Reggie Outlaws false 'at a glance from a pair of dark eyes, at the flicker of a dimple in a pair of smooth cheeks'.

Angela, whose surname is not revealed, completely captivates William. While he is conducting his mundane business (homework, sliding down the banisters, perfunctorily washing his hands and attending family meals) he is holding imaginary conversations with her about his heroic exploits, such as killing a lion with his bare hands or holding at bay a hundred hostile Red Indians armed with poisoned arrows. In reality, he can't even keep his promise to her to coerce MR FERRIS, the temporary headmaster, into letting Reggie off a well-deserved detention which is set for the following day. Fortunately, however, William's honour as a power-wielder is saved by Angela's family's unexpected and instant departure from the neighbourhood. He relishes Angela's parting note: 'Dere William, I think that you are the most wonderful pursun in the wurld. I shal nevver forget you.' (*William's Happy Days*, 8)

Angela (3)

William encounters yet another Angela, a fair-haired schoolgirl – as well as her deadly rival Adela – on the beach during a rather dull family summer holiday. Both girls are collecting shells for their adored form-mistress, Miss Twemlow, and the bored William, with little else to do, painstakingly helps them to build up their separate collections. He has to listen to Angela fulminating against Adela (and vice versa) and to hear endless eulogies from both of them about the marvellous Miss Twemlow. Eventually he is press-ganged into diverting her fiancé from attending the Conservative fête so that Angela and Adela can have more time there with their idol. William devotes his whole afternoon to the task but picks the wrong man. Consequently the two members of 'the unfair sex', reconciled by their disgust at William's ineptitude and the rapid evaporation of their crushes on Miss Twemlow, have no further

use for him as either helper or confidant. (*William and the Evacuees*, 4)

Animals

With the exception of cats and overweight dogs pampered by their owners, William is fond of, and always intrigued by, animals. (INSECTS offer a particular fascination and are dealt with separately, as also are CATS and DOGS.) William's empathy with certain animals seems to reflect that felt by his creator (see JUMBLE). For example, in *William and the Evacuees*, 6, Richmal gives us insights into the thought processes of Farmer Jenks's belligerent bull, Clarence (not to be confused with the milder Sammy who is featured in some other stories): 'Clarence found that it relieved the monotony of life to charge strange people and watch them beat it like rabbits.' His quarry reaches the stile and 'Clarence debated whether to charge. . . but remembering that stiles hurt almost as much as [Farmer Jenks's] sticks, decided not to. Suddenly he saw a small boy half-way through the hedge. It was a providential opportunity for face-saving. He turned and charged violently. Ginger just got back in time . . .'

Cows, on the whole, do not provide William with a great deal of challenge or fulfilment; however, in *William's Happy Days*, 5, a cow detached from its herd temporarily latches on to him and follows him everywhere. After enjoying a brief fantasy of himself as the greatest cattle-farmer on earth, William realises that the animal's apparent devotion raises certain social problems. He is on his way to a farewell tea with the delectable Miss Pollit (see ART AND ARTISTS) and 'it was, he felt sure, contrary to all rules of etiquette to go out to tea accompanied by a cow'.

William is much more at ease with rats, which, after Jumble and the occasional special insect, must be numbered amongst his favourite pets. His

training of them leaves a lot to be desired, however, as illustrated by the behaviour of Rufus, one of a cherished pair of white rats. He disgraces himself (and his owner) by climbing out of William's pocket in church, and electrifying the congregation by jumping up on to Mr Brown's balding scalp, and then running along the rim of the pulpit (*Just – William*, 11). Rufus is one of a succession of ratty pets; others include Cromwell, Omshafu and Whitey. In *William – The Detective*, 4, William is indignantly protecting the local wild rat population from the extermination which is the goal of those who have arranged a 'rat week'. He and the Outlaws make the Old Barn into a rodent sanctuary and feeding-house, and the rats become so attached to William that, when his mother forces him to

attend the Children's (fancy dress) Animal Fête as a reluctant Dick Whittington, they follow him. Even though this precipitates the terror-stricken and screeching flight of most of the guests, the support of the rats brings William the first prize (as the Pied Piper of Hamelin!) from Sir Gerald Markham: ' "How he got his scenic effects I'm not quite sure, but it was a clever idea brilliantly carried out ..." '

Strangely, in the same book (chapter 7) William's relations with rats are shown in a very different light. Wandering with Jumble one afternoon he comes across an enclosure of rats in a farmyard. The owner of a fox-terrier explains that the dog, a champion ratter, will be let loose in the enclosure. William persuades him to let Jumble and the fox-terrier compete in the killing of the rats, and Jumble eventually emerges as the winner, 'to William's frantic joy'. Richmal *does* mention that William 'forgot that he had lately played the part of friend and protector of the rat tribe', but, apart from the fact that Jumble's success makes owner and pet feel like 'super boy and super dog', this gory episode serves no purpose to the chapter's main plot and simply introduces uncharacteristic gratuitous violence. Jumble is finally taken out of the pen 'foaming at the mouth with lust for murder'. (It is significant that the 1986 Macmillan reprint of *William – The Detective* omitted the whole of this chapter – misleadingly entitled 'William and the League of Perfect Love' – because of the unsavoury ratting sequence.)

As well as rats and Jumble, William's pets have included mice, caterpillars, stag-beetles, woodlice and a tortoise (he would claim no stake in the Browns' various felines). In *More William*, 5, published in 1922, he is erecting a rabbit-hutch in the back-garden shed. 'He hoped that if he made a hutch, Providence would supply a rabbit.' In this case, William's incurable optimism seems for once to have been unjustified. However, rabbits still feature in several of the stories: Jumble, rather ineptly, is often scratching and scurrying after them, and in *William Carries On*, 9, William tries to save one particular rabbit from becoming a wartime dinner-dish. His 'deeply hidden vein of chivalry' is brought to the surface by the sight of a small girl (another temporary resident of Honeysuckle Cottage) weeping because her plump grey rabbit, Ernest, is destined for the cooking-pot. William by now dislikes rabbits. 'He particularly disliked Ernest'; nevertheless he undertakes the complicated process of finding a refuge for the threatened bunny amongst those which the peppery General Moult is breeding 'in a big way'. This entails William's having to listen to the retired military gentleman's interminable and detailed reminiscences about the Boer War and the Relief of Mafeking. When eventually it seems safe for

William to return Ernest to the little girl, she has switched her affections to a large and fluffy chinchilla: ' "Mother!" she called, "here's this ole rabbit back we lost. Can we have it for supper?" ' (It is no wonder that rabbits are not amongst William's favourite animals.)

One of the most satisfying animal incidents in the William saga occurs in *More William*, 5. William's godfather, his Uncle George, is paying what turns out to be his only visit to the Browns. His mission in life is to transform his godson into 'a gentle boy of exquisite courtesy and of intellectual pursuits'. Broken by Uncle George's ceaseless homilies on geography, history and other horrible subjects, and with all his noisy toys confiscated because of his godfather's insistence on quietness, William decides to take up taxidermy as a 'quiet hobby'. The only dead animal he can find is a small and shrivelled frog. He has heard something about 'tannin' ' the object which is about to be stuffed, and puts the frog at the bottom of a cup of tea in the drawing-room. Unknowingly Uncle George comes in and drinks this; William appears and angrily asks: ' "Who's meddlin' with my frog?" ' As Uncle George investigates the residual tea in his cup the moment holds 'all the cumulative horror of a Greek tragedy . . . On his face was the expression of one who is going to look up the first train home.'

Anthony

A pleasant young man, who is staying with his aunt at Maple Court, a 'palatial mansion' into whose garden William accidentally stumbles when running as hare to his friends' hounds. William disturbs a horribly genteel tea-on-the-terrace party, but Anthony, bored to the back teeth with this, and with his aunt's interminable preaching, takes William under his wing. He stuffs him with chocolate cake, gooseberries, nectarines and raspberries.

William spins him a yarn about being a Scotland Yard man. Anthony claims to be an international crook. Later a bearded man with piercing eyes asks William the way to Maple Court, and, convinced that he is a detective about to arrest his new-found friend Anthony, William diverts him to a house in Marleigh (where a small crowd awaits a visiting speaker). Mr Chance (the bearded gent) is actually a distinguished literary critic: he delivers a robust lecture on the drinking songs of Britain to his stunned audience – which turns out to be the Marleigh Temperance Society, assembled to hear a talk on the effects of alcohol on the liver. Anthony, who of course is not a crook but a sturdy, sporty university student, apologises to William for allowing his imagination to run away with him. Taking responsibility for the whole affair, he gives William a ten-shilling note: '. . .William did not really regret the incident. Nor did Mr Chance.' (*William's Crowded Hours*, 3)

Anthony Martin

Anthony Martin is an exuberant parody of A. A. Milne's Christopher Robin. Richmal, an ardent classicist, is supposed to have loved *Now We Are Six* because one of its poems took its metre from Horace. This didn't, however, prevent her from sending up Milne's besmocked embodiment of childish charm on several occasions. Outwardly sweet but inwardly awful, Anthony is the 'perfect' boy carried to extremes, and of course the antithesis of the rugged William. He brags to the Outlaws about his mother, who stars him in 'literary stories and poems' that appeal to 'really cultured people'. Examples of this arrogant authoress's output echo the famous 'Christopher Robin is saying his prayers' poem: 'Anthony Martin is doing his sums', 'Anthony Martin is cleaning his teeth', 'Anthony Martin is milking a cow', etc.

William's only interest in this cissified paragon, who comes with his mother to stay temporarily in Honeysuckle Cottage, is that Ginger's Aunt Arabelle, a lesser literary lady than Anthony's mother, yearns to interview the awesome infant for *Woman's Sphere*. (Aunt Arabelle is looking after Ginger during his parents' absence; and William & Co., who have already blotted their copybooks with her, are still hopeful that, if she can be placated, Ginger will receive a generous tip at the end of her visit.) Anthony and his mother decline the publicity value of the *Woman's Sphere* ('a piffling paper'; '. . . it would cheapen our market'), so William has to use his well-trained manipulative powers to bring about the interview for Ginger's aunt. Unknown to Anthony, he manages to record the so-called charming child's beastly bullying of his much-put-upon nurse. As a result of William's unashamed blackmail, obnoxious Anthony, despite a lot of sobbing, stamping, scratching, biting and kicking, is forced to grant the interview, in order to protect his winsome public image. (And Ginger gets his ten-shilling tip!) (*William – The Pirate*, 10.)

A more graceful tribute to the A. A. Milne Christopher Robin saga occurs in *William – The Good*, 3, when William, Ginger and Douglas play a version of Pooh-sticks in the village stream.

Anti-Semitism

In the course of his long saga, William skirmishes with people from wide-ranging backgrounds and beliefs, both religious and political. Generally speaking he becomes irritated with foreigners if they cannot understand his language (see XENOPHOBIA) but is tolerant of and even especially sympathetic towards people whom society has cast in the rôle of the underdog. Any study of the popular novels of the 1920s and 1930s quickly reveals the strength of xenophobic and anti-Semitic attitudes which were then current, and Richmal

ideas about the policies of the Nazis are somewhat vague, and Henry has to enlighten him. He explains that they chase out Jews and 'take all the stuff they leave behind', and when the Outlaws reflect that 'Ole Mr. Isaacs is a Jew' the implications of this become appealing. Isaacs owns the village sweetshop, having recently succeeded a far more sympathetic proprietor, who always generously added a few extra sweets for the Outlaws when the scales had gone down (see MOSS, MR). In sharp contrast, Mr Isaacs displays a meanness that infuriates the Outlaws, who are convinced that he gives them short measure.

At first when the Nasties try to terrorise Mr Isaacs they are singularly unsuccessful. He is angered rather than frightened by their home-made swastika banner and, instead of running away, chases the Outlaws and boxes William soundly on the ear. Henry then finds out what the real Nazis do: ' "They've got people called storm troops an' when these Jews don't run away they knock 'em about till they do." ' Spurred on by thoughts of acquiring the wonderful contents of Mr Isaacs's shop, the Outlaws visit it after closing-time. Douglas, who has been apprehensive all along, continues to cast doubts on the rightfulness of the operation, but William tries to convince them that 'it's not stealin' when you're Nasties' but something that can be done 'by lor'. Nevertheless, he suggests that they should take only ten sweets each. In fact they do *not* resort to physical violence with the sweetshop owner. They think they have locked him in the room that holds his safe, but actually they have incarcerated a burglar. They then stumble on the bound and gagged Mr Isaacs, who, enormously grateful to them, says: ' "Take vatever you vant. You can have as much as you can carry." ' It is recorded that he is surprised at the amount his rescuers manage to carry away with them but, as the episode has changed him from tight-fisted baddie to beaming benefactor, all is well. The Outlaws, who some time earlier had

Crompton's books, for adults and children, swim vigorously against the tide of accepted opinion in this area. It is therefore particularly surprising to come across a Jew-baiting episode in a William book.

Chapter 6 of *William – The Detective*, in which the Outlaws become 'Nasties' (their version of Nazis), might have been triggered off simply by Richmal's attraction to wordplay with a bilingual flavour:

'I'll be the chief one. What's he called in Germany?'

'Herr Hitler,' said Henry.

'Her!' echoed William in disgust. 'Is it a woman?'

And, true to his male-chauvinist principles, William appoints himself as 'Him' Hitler. His found 'a strange distaste for the whole adventure' creeping over them, totally abandon their anti-Semitic activities.

Similarly one senses that Richmal Crompton began to find the story unpalatable even before she had completed the writing of it, and that she rapidly rolled it up and put it out of her mind. Certainly all her future references to Hitler are uncompromisingly hostile, even given their comic context (see WARTIME). (There is just one reference to Fascism which is shrouded in obscurity: *William – The Dictator* was published in 1938, a few years after the Mr Isaacs incidents. William, who is negotiating the purchase of a white rat from a boy, is told somewhat convolutedly by him that ' "He's called Wilfred with the boy I got him from's father's bein' a Fashist [sic]" '. To William, anyway, this remark seems to make sense.)

How Richmal came to write the story 'William and the Nasties' will remain a minor literary mystery. It is of course possible that she actually intended to draw attention to the perniciousness of the Fascist ideologies. The story in question was first published in the HAPPY MAG in June 1934 when there was little awareness in Britain of the real significance of what was happening in Germany. It was reprinted in *William – The Detective* in 1935, but Richmal Crompton's literary executor, Richmal Ashbee, and Macmillan, who publish the current reprints, had no hesitation in dropping this episode from the book. (Apparently, however, Hebrew translations of *William – The Detective* published in Israel towards the end of the 1980s *do* still contain this controversial chapter.)

April Fool's Day

The first April Fool's Day to be mentioned is in the second book, *More William*, 13. Robert sternly admonishes William not to try any fool's tricks on him, and William crushingly retorts that he has other fish (or fools) to fry. Determined to save his friend, the mild Mr Gregorius Lambkin, from the matrimonial clutches of his enemy, the managing Miss Gregoria Mush, he keeps Gregorius from an assignation with her by delivering a phoney message. When Gregoria keeps the appointment (in her garden in the half-dusk) she prattles away confidently to the toga-swathed figure on the seat (she and Gregorius are reincarnationists who occasionally sport Roman attire), until, leaning against her 'lover', she finds him to be 'a broomstick with a turnip fixed firmly to the top'. It bears the legend: 'April Fool'.

Archie (fisherman, not artist)

See HOLIDAYS.

A.R.P.

The twenty-first book in the series was called *William and A.R.P.* and when this was published in May 1939 everyone knew that the initials stood for Air Raid Precautions. (The opening eponymous story also appeared in the May 1939 issue of the HAPPY MAG, some time after the first appeal for A.R.P. volunteers had been broadcast in 1937. Few came forward until the September 1938 Czechoslovakian crisis and the notorious Munich Agreement.) In deference to a new generation of child readers, Newnes changed the book's title in 1956 to *William's Bad Resolution*. The 1987 Macmillan reprint restored the original title, and its contents-page carried the following explanatory note:

A few months before Britain declared war on Germany in September 1939, the Government told towns and villages throughout the country to prepare for the possibility of bombing raids from the air. This meant watching for every plane, organising a warning system, building air raid shelters and so on.

These 'air raid precautions' were known as A.R.P.

For William, as for so many real-life children, the donning of gas-masks and experimentation with fire-fighting equipment suggested opportunities for horse-play, as well as for the expression of somewhat cock-eyed patriotic endeavour. The Outlaws founded

AIR RADE PRECORSHUN
JUNIER BRANCH
ENTRUNCE FRE.

' "They'll come if it's free," said Douglas, with a tinge of bitterness in his voice. "They always come to free things." '

Their first and last meeting, which encapsulates techniques practised by the adult A.R.P. such as bandaging and decontamination, ends in chaos: 'Ginger's mother . . . came upon the disgraceful scene – a wild medley of naked boys on the lawn, wrestling and leaping about in the full play of the garden hose, manipulated by Ginger. Their clothes, which they had flung carelessly on the grass beside them were soaked through . . .'

William is left to ponder bitterly on the 'jolly good times' which adult A.R.P. workers are allowed to have, playing a macabre form of 'peep-bo' in their respirators, perhaps, and generally throwing their weight about. (Both Ethel and Robert are attending A.R.P. classes; once war was declared each switched to another form of national service.)

At the beginning of the war, Richmal was a trainee A. R. P. Warden. She wrote a story, 'William's Unlucky Day', for *ARPeggio: Gasette Extraordinary*, Christmas 1939. The story, which had a local Bromley setting, is a forerunner of 'William Does His Bit' (*William Does His Bit,* 1).

Art and Artists

Generally speaking, William and the Outlaws considered artists (and authors) as 'lunies' (*William – The Bad*, 9). Nevertheless they take a continuing interest in the shifting tide of artistically inclined men and women who take up residence in Honeysuckle Cottage (which must surely be one of the most frequently let properties in England).

Amongst the more notable of these incumbents is young and pretty Miss Pollit; William has a 'kindly indulgence' towards her artistic interpretation of the world around them: 'There wasn't, of course, any purple light, but he knew that all artists suffered from a defect of vision that made them see things differently from other people.' Miss Pollit, however, is more than a mere artist. She appreciates William, and shares several of his outdoor delights: ' "We'll have a fire in the wood . . . and we'll cook sausages and ham and eggs, and we'll make a lock and a backwater in the stream . . . " '

On one occasion when she told him about some of her exciting exploits, such as climbing in Switzerland, travelling half-way round the world in a tramp-steamer, and big-game hunting, 'William listened enthralled. When she finished he asked her breathlessly to marry him.' She had regretfully to decline as she was already engaged. (*William's Happy Days*, 5)

In chapter 10 of the same book, Honeysuckle Cottage has other aesthetic occupants, the Mannister twins, Auriole and Tristram. Both are pale and lean, with light Eton-cropped hair, sporting suits of homespun tweed. The only obvious difference in their appearance is that 'one wore knickerbockers and the other a skirt'; even the worsted stockings and brogues which show below are identical. Auriole's driving ambition (ten years

after Sir Arthur Conan Doyle's publicising of the Cottingley fairy photographs) is to snap a nature spirit; Tristram's is to paint other-worldly, psychically stimulated studies (though his efforts seem nightmarish to William). By those quirks of fate that so often characterise William's relationships, each twin achieves the fulfilment of having a picture published in *Psychic Realms*, thanks almost entirely to William. It is he (smothered illicitly in grass cuttings) who is the subject of Auriole's photograph of what she thinks is a nature spirit, and it is his daubing of 'A Lion' that an art expert has reproduced (in Tristram's name) as 'Vision', 'a splendid example of inspirational painting'.

This is not the Mannisters' only appearance. A character called 'Archie' crops up many times and becomes virtually the saga's resident artist. In *William – The Bold*, 1, his full name is given as Tristram Archibald Mannister, and we are told that his twin sister Auriole has now set up an Arts and Crafts Centre in the Lake District. His elder sister Euphemia is also referred to. In his solo appearances Archie appears younger than in the twelfth book (*William's Happy Days*), more approachable and very different in his looks (he is bearded, and

darker-haired). Archie was to become something of a reluctant ally to the Outlaws in their various plots and fantasies, and a great admirer of Ethel. He appears in the last of all Richmal's William stories ('William's Foggy Morning'), which was completed after her death by her niece Richmal Ashbee and published (out of sequence) as chapter 5 of *William the Lawless* in 1970.

One of William's entanglements with Archie (27.1) was later dramatised by Richmal and published as a one-act play, *William and the Artist's Model*. In this case the model is a tramp. However, on various occasions, notably 1.12 and 34.4, William becomes an artist's model. See also MANNISTER, ARCHIE.

Ashbridge, Duke of

See SWEETS AND SWEETSHOPS.

Atkinson, Lady

This pompous and aristocratic personage erupts into William's life at a critical time. He is in the throes of his 'truthful Christmas' (inspired by the vicar's recent sermon on the importance of abolishing 'all deceit and hypocrisy', and of speaking the truth 'one with another'). William, his mother, Ethel and Robert are spending Christmas with Uncle Frederick and Aunt Emma. (Mr Brown is away, summoned to the sickbed of one of his numerous aunts.) With his usual 'great tenacity of purpose' William casts aside the white lies that make for social harmony and tells his uncle and aunt in perfect truth that he doesn't like their gifts to him (small wonder: these are a book of Church history and a case containing a pen, a pencil and a ruler). He then patiently explains that his presents for them (a pin-cushion and a leather purse) are hand-ons; the first is faded and the second faulty.

When Lady Atkinson sweeps in smugly to bestow her gift (a photograph of herself) on Aunt Emma and Uncle Frederick, the atmosphere is already slightly tense. She soaks up the adults' flannelling remarks about her picture, before asking the 'little boy' what he thinks of it. His 'final offering at the altar of truth' is that the photograph 'isn't as fat as you are . . . an' it's not got as many little lines on its face', and it is prettier than its subject is in the flesh. Mrs Brown, Ethel and Robert are outraged. Aunt Emma collapses into tears because she thinks that Lady Atkinson will never come to her house again. The bright spot is that Uncle Frederick, who actually strongly dislikes Lady Atkinson, is overjoyed that she will not darken his doorstep any more, and he appreciatively slips the truthful William a half-crown. Sadly for Uncle Frederick, Lady Atkinson *does* return – but after William has left. (*Still – William*, 9)

Augustus

A little old gentleman, interested in nature-study, whom William encounters in the woods when he (William), after swapping clothes with Helbert, a gipsy boy, is 'riotously happy' acting out his ragged rôle. Augustus gullibly accepts William's story, lifted from the lurid tale *Stolen by Gipsies* which he has recently read, of having been kidnapped from a noble family. (*William – The Fourth*, 11)

Aunt Emmy (Hubert Lane's)

See CHRISTMAS and FOOD.

Aunts (William's)

See RELATIONS.

Authors

William's surprisingly elastic village always has room for authors who feel the temporary need of rustic surroundings, although these generally turn out to be less peaceful than anticipated. Despite the fact that William finds them worse-tempered than the artists who visit the locality, he takes a strong if sometimes scornful interest in their activities. Possibly this is because he sees himself as a writer, even though for most of his waking hours he appears to be unbookish to the point of philistinism: ' "I've read all the books I want to read," said William tersely' (*William*, 10); 'They went into a large study . . . the walls were lined with books. William looked around him without enthusiasm. "Dull-looking place," he commented' (*William – In Trouble*, 5).

In the rôle of author, William is convinced that

he can give others who live by their pens some helpful tips: ' "I'm goin' to have a picture of a big splash of blood on the back . . . It'd make anyone want to read it . . . " ' (*William*, 1). Certainly his literary creations are all of a sensational nature, revelling in titles like 'Dick of the Bloody Hand', and variations on this. He is deeply affronted when one of his 'epoch-making' tales (written illicitly throughout the whole of afternoon school) is seized, read contemptuously to the form and then burnt by Mr French, a temporary master who profoundly dislikes both William and his linguistic style: ' "With one sweep of his gorry blade three pleecemen's heads roled of into a heap. He shot another through the brane, another fell strangled, an' another, wot had a week hart, fell down dead at the horrible site . . . " ' (*William Again*, 7).

William's literary pride must have been salvaged by the fact that another teacher ('Old Stinks the Science Master') enjoyed exploits like William's 'The Hand of Deth' and 'The Tru Story of an Indian Brave' far more 'than he did many works of better known authors' (*Still – William*, 12).

In *William Again*, two authors tangle with William. The first, in chapter 9, is Mr Monkton Graham, who makes a lot of money by writing in *The Monthly Signal: A Magazine for Mothers*. He writes as 'Peter's Mother' about 'her' supposedly real-life offspring, who is a boy in the Little Lord Fauntleroy mould, greatly appealing to readers. The trouble is that Peter (and his mother) become so popular that Mr Monkton Graham has to ward off would-be visitors from amongst his fans who want to see the winsome wee boy. Unfortunately, Miss Rubina Strange, who lives locally, has inadvertently been given 'Peter's Mother's' address, and when the distraught author realises that she is on her way to his cottage he has to appeal to William (the only boy available at that moment) to play the part of Peter. William has to be heavily bribed with money, a tricycle, and the promise that he can play in the author's garden and private wood every day: he loathes Peter, whose adventures have been inflicted upon him by his Aunt Ellen, who has given him a copy of a book called *Little Peter, the Sunshine of the Home*. William quickly dumped this down a well, but after receiving such generous bribes from Mr Monkton Graham he is prepared to back him up to the hilt. Miss Rubina Strange at first accepts William's explanation that he (as Peter) has had his butter-coloured curls 'clawered off by a monkey, at the Zoo', and that she cannot see his mother because she is upstairs, dying. However, she eventually unmasks both him and the miserable Mr Monkton Graham, on whom she then sets her matrimonial sights because of 'his understanding of a woman's heart'. William enjoys the episode rather more than the wildly despairing and trapped author.

In chapter 13, William's new friend is Vivian Strange (presumably no relation of Rubina), 'the distinguished poet and journalist'. (Strange appeared earlier in chapter 12.) He has come to the village in order to enjoy the quietness that is 'essential to his literary calling'. Unfortunately, instead of this he finds William, who protectively 'adopts' him. Although bitterly aware that his genius cannot flower in the presence of William's playing of the mouth-organ, the siren-like whistle that he has been 'practisin' an' practisin' ' or the interminable tales of blood and thunder which William makes up and, blow by blow, narrates, Vivian is a rabbit to the small boy's snake. He cannot break free, even when William ironically ruins his 'strikingly original essay' on 'Nature the Divine' by spilling a jar of tadpoles and other 'repellent' creatures upon it. Vivian Strange switches from intellectual composition to writing a telegram to a friend: ' "Secure berth on any boat sailing anywhere. Complete nervous prostration. Change and rest urgent." '

In *William's Happy Days*, 7, the Outlaws persuade Miss Victoria Peache, an author who adheres to a rigid timetable of creation and constitutionals, to bend her normally inflexible régime (so that they can secretly dig for treasure in her garden). Unwittingly they play Cupid, thrusting this middle-aged author into the arms of an elderly bird-watcher called Socrates Popplestone. They also prove that they are rather more adept at manipulating the imagery of dreams than Miss Peache, an 'expert' who 'knows all about what a man called Froude' said about them.

In the course of William's saga, he finds himself in relationship with a wide variety of writers. *William the Fourth* is worth mentioning for two memorable encounters. In chapter 10 he skirmishes with MISS EUPHEMIA BARNEY, the 'leader of the intellectual life of the village' who is President of the Society for the Encouragement of Higher Thought. At every meeting she reads from her poems, although none of these has been published. Miss Barney suggests that this is because she likes to set an example of unworldly scorn for money: ' "I think it best . . . that I should not publish." As a matter of fact she had the authority of several publishers for this statement.' She dislikes William – and also his friend Miss Fairlow, ' a real, live, worldly, money-worshipping author' who publishes a book every year and has just come to live in the village. Miss Fairlow refuses invitations to join the Higher Thinkers, and Euphemia tells her cronies that this is in order to mask Miss Fairlow's ignorance. However, when the bestselling author inadvertently gate-crashes a Higher Thought meeting at the Browns' (to give William a tray of butterflies for one of his shows) it is the pretentious Miss Barney who is exposed as the cultural ignoramus, and Miss Fairlow as someone who is knowledgeable. At the root of the duel of words between the two lady authors is, of course, William – or rather, his pet rat, Omshafu.

In chapter 13, the Browns are plagued by the

verbosity and misplaced convictions of Mr Bennison, a bachelor who is staying with them, and who writes books on the training of children. 'He believed that children trailed clouds of glory. He knew very few. He certainly did not know William.' Mr Bennison, who is working on his new book, *Common Mistakes in the Treatment of Children*, begins to fancy Ethel, who can't stand him. William does a deal with her that if Mr Bennison leaves on the following day she will give Ginger and himself two shillings, for the tops they have set their hearts on. Mr Bennison, who fervently believes that a child's 'innocent curiosity should always be promptly satisfied' is fair game for William, who interrupts the earnest author's sleep five or six times that night, apparently thirsting for knowledge about Socrates, compound interest, the position of various constellations, some intelligence tests, the death of Charles I, and wireless. Small wonder that he eventually becomes 'a broken man', driven metaphorically to eat most of his words about children and innocence, and physically to fortify himself with a whisky and soda after his wretched night. He then becomes entangled in Mrs Brown's knitting downstairs and the apple-pie bed which William has thoughtfully provided for him upstairs – and shakes the dust of the Brown household from his feet as rapidly as he possibly can.

Babies

Babies are beneath contempt, in the view of William and the Outlaws, but they furnish several funny episodes in the saga. In *Just – William*, 8, Mrs Brown explains to William that Mrs Butler, who has come to spend the afternoon with her, has succumbed to a bad headache and is worried about her baby not getting out 'this nice afternoon'. When William realises that he is being asked – or, rather, forced – to look after the infant, 'the

Medusa's classic expression of horror was as nothing' to his: ' "*Me*?" he said. "*Me? Me* take a baby out in a pram?" ' Blushing 'for pure shame', he even has to endure the humiliation of Mrs Brown's baby-talk: ' "He's a dear little baby, isn't he? And isn't it a nice Willy-Billy den, to take it out a nice ta-ta, while its mummy goes bye-byes, den?" '

With the help of the Outlaws William makes the best of the ghastly situation. They pretend that they have kidnapped the baby, and take it to the Old Barn, where its face and clothes become covered with paraffin oil, cold cooked potatoes and apple dumplings. Its appearance is not improved when William eventually cleans its face with his (prune-coloured) hanky, liberally moistened with liquorice water. The appearance of the pram, too, has deteriorated considerably because it has been used for wild and muddy rides by the Outlaws.

William's humiliation at baby-minding is echoed by Henry in *William – The Pirate*, 3, when he is forced by his mother to take out his baby sister in her pram. Voicing indignation, he is reproved:

'How *can* you talk like that! There never was such a sweet baby. Hundreds of little boys would give anything to have her for a sister.'

'I wish they could have her then, that's all,' said Henry bitterly.

Once again the other Outlaws rally round. Actually Henry's baby sister suffers a lot at their hands on various occasions. Henry often appropriates her toys and pieces of equipment for some strange project or other, initiated by William. In this instance they lose both her and the pram – and the story revolves riotously on their efforts to find her, and then to return to their rightful parents the three babies they have acquired as pro tem substitutes. To the Outlaws one baby is just as good (or as horrible) as any other. There is a lovely moment when William tries quite sincerely to reassure Henry that his mother won't even notice if they bring back a different infant: ' "I bet she won't see any difference. It looks just the same to me, an' I bet it looks just the same to anyone." ' The realist Henry points out, however, that ' "she'll see its clothes are different" ', and William acknowledges the force of this argument, although he continues to protest: ' "I expect someone took yours by mistake. I expect it's always happening . . . I expect no one ever ends up a single day with the same baby they started out with . . . an' I don't see what you're making all this fuss about . . . " '

It is no wonder that, in chapter 8 of the same book, despite a crusading resolution to rescue anyone who's been kidnapped, William remarks with great depth of feeling: 'I'd rather rescue ten grown-ups than one baby any day. I never seem to have any luck with babies.'

Balham, Mr

'A small, insignificant figure' whom William declares to be an enemy spy (see WARTIME). He

sets out to trap this 'arch-traitor' into surrender or arrest. Actually Mr Balham is 'extremely patriotic': he is an A.R.P. communications worker and the supervisor of Marleigh report centre. This episode includes a classic method of unmasking a suspected criminal or spy – the pulling-off of his bogus moustache. When William applies this technique to Mr Balham, of course, the moustache – being very real – stays put while, yelling in anguish, the normally inoffensive Mr Balham threatens to sue William for assault. (*William Does His Bit*, 1)

Ballater, Mr

Mr Ballater keeps his prize pig, EGLANTINE, in his back garden and has frequently to fall upon William, Ginger, Henry and Douglas with fury and dire threats because, fascinated by Eglantine, they cannot resist feeding her with large (and weight-reducing) titbits of cinders and sawdust. He even catches William riding Eglantine and making her 'scamper'. Mr Ballater, who also fattens marrows and cucumbers for competitions, feels that these, too, are at constant risk. As he confides to a sympathetic female cousin: ' "There's something about pigs and marrows and cucumbers that seems to bring out the worst in people, seems to paralyse their sense of truth." ' (*William*, 10)

Barlow, Jimmy

Small boy associate of the Outlaws who is mentioned in: *William – The Bad*, 5 (advising them against trying for free, squeezing-under-the-tent-flap circus-entry; *William and the Tramp*, 6 (as Boy Blue in MISS MILTON's dramatisation of nursery rhymes for the Festival of Britain); *William's Television Show*, 5 (as audience member), and 8 (bringing his 'dejected looking hen' for treatment in William's Animal Health Service); *William – The Explorer*, 2 (on an organised nature ramble); *William and the Pop Singers*, 4 (participating in a local-history holiday task); and *William the Superman*, 1 (as part of the group organised by the Outlaws to build the foundation of the new civilisation which will have to be developed in the aftermath of a potential nuclear war).

Barlow, Mr and Mrs

The Barlows are mentioned in several of the stories either singly or together. In *William's Television Show*, 4, and *William and the Pop Singers*, 5, it is not clear whether the Barlows are related to Jimmy or Peggy (or both). However, in *William – The Explorer*, 1, the Barlows who are mentioned are clearly the parents of Peggy, while in *William the Superman*, 1, Mr Barlow is definitely Jimmy's father and the president of the local Conservative Association.

Barlow, Peggy

An imperious young lady who, in Robert's eyes, is the current 'beloved' and 'most beautiful girl in the world' in *William – The Bad*, 4 (see ROBERT AND HIS FRIENDS). She is mentioned in seven stories, and finally in *William – The Explorer*, 1.

Barney, Miss Euphemia

A pretentious unpublished poetess, and president of the Society for the Encouragement of Higher Thought (see AUTHORS). Appears in *William – The Fourth*, 10 and in *Still – William*, 7 and 9.

Barron, Sheila

See ROBERT AND HIS FRIENDS.

Barton, Lorna

See FILMS and ROBERT AND HIS FRIENDS.

Barton, Mr

Elderly tenant of a small house called Oaklands, nicknamed 'Scraggy' by the Outlaws, who do not get on well with him, or with his neighbour, the tenant of Beechgrove. When Scraggy seems to disappear, William and Co., under the influence of lurid mystery-stories which they have been reading, are convinced that the man living at Beechgrove has murdered his neighbour – who is simply away on holiday. (*William*, 1)

Barton, Mr and Mrs

Shadowy stalwarts of the village helping with causes, etc., mentioned in *William Does His Bit*, 8 and 7 respectively. 'The Bartons' crop up again in *William's Television Show*, 3, and in *William the Lawless*, 1. Whether they are the parents of Lorna or of Peggy (see ROBERT AND HIS FRIENDS and ETHEL AND HER FRIENDS respectively) or of the Outlaws' small ally Jimmy Barton (*William's Treasure Trove*, 1, and *William and the Witch*, 3) is a matter for conjecture.

Barton, Peggy

One of Robert's and Ethel's crowd. At one time a good friend of Ginger's brother, Hector (in *William's Crowded Hours*, 8), and later of OSWALD FRANKS (*William's Television Show*, 5). She is mentioned in six stories altogether.

Bastow, General

In charge of army manoeuvres centred on William's village. The Outlaws convince themselves that he is at the head of a force of foreign invaders, and harass him and his troops with their Bows and Arrows army. (*William – The Good*, 3)

Beal, Mr

Described as 'the squire of the village' who, after chasing William out of his orchard 'with the help of dogs, sticks and stones', becomes one of the victims of William's Secret Society (*William Again*, 7). Curiously no further reference to him as the squire is made.

Beauchamp, Mrs

William's dancing-class teacher (in *William's Happy Days*, 6). See DOGS.

Beedale, Miss

A tall, thin and sharp-looking Council official whose job seems to be the investigation of environmental complaints. She hopes to tidy away into an old people's home an elderly caravan-dweller, whose neighbours complain that he has disfigured the neighbourhood with a collection of scrap metal. Fortunately, just before Miss Beedale's arrival on the scene, the Outlaws have moved the

junk to prop up a crumbling old underground air-raid shelter which they plan to use for pot-holing. The sympathetic old man, his caravan and his horse are reprieved, and bossy Miss Beedale can only bemoan the waste of her precious time: ' "I have every minute of every day carefully planned, and five minutes lost throws me out for the whole day, if not the week . . ." ' (*William the Superman*, 7)

Beezum, Mr

The keeper of the general store in the village, who refuses to give the Outlaws credit for the few pence worth of marbles that they yearn for from his wide-ranging stock. (*William – The Fourth*, 10)

Bell, Dr

There is no evidence that Dr Bell is related to the Joan and Mary, or the Ronald and George, who share his surname. His first appearance is in *William and A.R.P.*, 8, in which he is described as William's 'old enemy'. This presumably is because he has seen through several previous attempts of William's to evade school by inventing imaginary illnesses, and displayed a 'callous suspicion that had wrecked his most carefully-prepared plans'.

William's current crisis is that he has completely neglected to do some French exercises set for him by Mr Coggan, a schoolmaster 'of the bulldog breed' who refuses to allow William to go his own sweet philistine way and is determined to educate him, even if this involves his pupil in punishments of a painful nature. As William's earlier attempts to sham headaches, rheumatism and lameness have failed ignominiously, he decides this time to try to convince his family and Dr Bell that he has liver trouble. Initially Dr Bell's new assistant, Dr Horace Ashtead, is called in. (He is actually on the spot because, a great admirer of Ethel, he has called to arrange to take her to the badminton club later that day.) Horace is 'pale and pompous . . . with a squeaky voice, a slight lisp, and a distressing habit of missing balls at badminton'. Nevertheless he has temporarily supplanted Jimmie Moore, Ethel's most regular swain (see MOORE, JIMMIE and ETHEL AND HER FRIENDS), because he appears to offer 'a background of dinner parties and titles and first nights and Ascot'. The inept Horace diagnoses William's indisposition as appendicitis, and Mrs Brown rushes him to hospital in an ambulance. Once there the stalwart Dr Bell doesn't take long to reject Horace's diagnosis, as William's allegedly inflamed appendix (or, in William's view, his pretendedly upset liver) seems to move freely from one side of his body to the other. William has to face horrible retribution at home and at school, but the silver lining of this murky episode is that the hideous Horace is discredited, and Ethel falls back on the faithful Jimmie who, realising that his good fortune has in some devious manner been brought about by William, presents him with his current heart's desire – a brand-new badminton racket.

Dr Bell is also mentioned briefly by name in *Just William's Luck*, 10, when his untidy appearance is remarked upon, and in *William and the Pop Singers*, 2, when William and Ginger decide that (like many of the apparently respectable adults in the village) he is in fact 'a crim'nal', with the particular vice of poisoning the unwary.

Bell, George

Plays a very small part in the adventures of William and the Outlaws but is generally favourably disposed towards them. George is mentioned briefly in: *William – The Fourth*, 1; *William – The Showman*, 2 (the most interesting of references to him, as he is then suffering from scarlet fever, with William bemoaning the fact that he hasn't managed to catch it from him); *William and the Evacuees*, 1; *William – The Bold*, 5 and *William the Superman*, 1.

There is also a curious reference to George Bell in *William's Television Show*, 5, but this is plainly a slip of Richmal's pen or typewriter. Ethel, true to type, is playing off two of her admirers, OSWALD FRANKS ·and ARCHIE MANNISTER, against each other, and against an absent boyfriend, whose virtues she is extolling. In this instance she chooses to wax lyrical about George Bell, but it is, of course, George's elder brother Ronald who can be numbered amongst her fans – not George, who is contemporaneous with William. See also BELL, RONALD.

Bell, Joan and Mary

Joan Bell (not to be confused with JOAN CLIVE/CREWE/PARFITT, the little girl next door) is someone whom William admires 'intensely'. 'Occasionally she condescended to notice his existence' but she is, on the whole, rather stuck-up: ' "You're so rough," explained Joan with a little fastidious sniff.' The sweep has left a pile of soot in the Browns' garden after cleaning their chimneys, and William and Ginger, toying absentmindedly with handfuls of it, invite Joan and her small sister Mary, and their companion, Geoffrey Spencer, to come and inspect their precious acquisition. We are told at the outset that Joan, Mary and Geoffrey are dressed in white, so it takes little imagination to guess the outcome of this encounter, especially as Geoffrey is one of those odiously neat boys who mince along in sailor-suits and seem, by their mere existence, to be a challenge to William. Bored with Geoffrey, Joan condescendingly agrees to enter William's garden; Mary in particular is delighted with the soot: ' "Ith lovely . . . Leth – leth danth round it – holding

hanth." ' The jolly dance gets out of hand (or foot) as 'William and Ginger with the male's innate desire of showing off his prowess' begin to 'revolve at lightning speed'. Mary falls into the heap, and a furious soot-slinging battle ensues, with, of course, disastrous effects on the clothing of all concerned – particularly of the white-garbed trio.

Joan and Mary round nastily on William (and possibly his admiration for the former expires at this point). The girls' mother, Mrs Bell, is mentioned only once in the William saga, and that is when Cook calls to Mrs Brown at the end of this episode: ' "Mrs. Bell wants you on the telephone at once, please'm. It's something about Master William." ' (*William – The Conqueror*, 1)

Bell, Mrs

Not to be confused with the mother of Joan and Mary (see BELL, JOAN and MARY), the Mrs Bell who is mentioned briefly in *William and the Evacuees*, 1, is the mother of Robert's friend

Ronald, and his brother George, who is occasionally an ally of William and the Outlaws. Though fond of 'Georgie', Mrs Bell acknowledges sighingly to Mrs Jameson that she only really gets 'a bit of peace' when her younger son is out of the house: ' "Boys *are* like that." '

Bell, Ronald

Ronald, the elder brother of George, is a friend of Robert's and, at various times, an admirer of Ethel's. His part in the plots is small, but he crops up from the early to the fairly late books. He is mentioned in *William – The Fourth*, 1, as a member of Jameson Jameson's Society of Reformed Bolshevists; in *William – The Bad*, 9, partnering Dolly Clavis at Ethel's and Robert's fancy-dress dance; in *William – The Pirate*, 11, when he becomes the secretary of the local football club; in *William and the Brains Trust*, 6, when he is away on war service in Iceland; in *Just William's Luck*, 8, inciting Jimmie Moore's jealousy by inviting Ethel to the tennis club dance and the dramatic society picnic; in *William and the Moon Rocket*, 4, acting in a play; and in *William's Television Show*, 1, taking Ethel out in his car, and in chapter 7.

Again Richmal confuses the Bell brothers – this time in *William and A.R.P.*, 1 – when she lists Ronald Bell amongst the constant friends and supporters of the Outlaws. Of course, she means George Bell.

Bellairs, Julia

See ROBERT AND HIS FRIENDS.

Bellew, Clarinda

See ROBERT AND HIS FRIENDS.

Bellew, Claude

A member of Hubert Lane's gang. (*William – The Bold*, 5)

Bellew, Sydney

See ROBERT AND HIS FRIENDS.

Bennison, Mr

See AUTHORS.

Bergson, Clarence

A young man with 'a tooth-brush moustache, a receding chin, an objectionable high-pitched laugh and a still more objectionable swagger'. He is staying with the young and very pretty Miss Holding who is temporarily renting the Hall. William admires her greatly but has to wreak vengeance on her odious guest because he kicks Jumble (who snaps at Clarence's 'very green and very mauve' plus-fours) and, on another occasion, hands

Douglas and Henry over to Farmer Jenks when they are running away from him after trespassing on his land. (*William – The Good*, 5)

Bert

See ROUNDWAY, MRS.

Bertie

Nephew of William's headmaster who, temporarily staying with his uncle, is in William's form. Charming and deferential to adults, who admire his 'beautiful soul', Bertie also has a 'beautiful conscience' which forces him to tell tales to his uncle about William's plentiful misdoings. Sweet little Bertie becomes the only child in the village to be allowed to take part in a pageant; but, through playing on Bertie's conceit, William ousts him from the rôle of page to Elizabeth I, steps into it himself and is cheered to the echo by his assembled schoolmates who are coerced into watching the pageant. (*William – The Outlaw*, 10)

Bertram, Mrs

A newcomer to the village, living at The Limes, who bears a striking physical resemblance to Elizabeth I and portrays her in a pageant which is somewhat disrupted by William (see BERTIE). (*William – The Outlaw*, 10)

Bicycles

Considering the tremendous importance of bikes in children's lives, particularly during the heyday of the books, it is surprising that they are so rarely featured. They were (and are) of course expensive,

but even boys and girls from working-class homes seemed somehow to beg, borrow or otherwise acquire ridable if somewhat battered specimens.

William tends to rely upon Robert for biking fulfilments. In *Just – William*, 2, he first of all upsets his elder brother by monopolising, when she comes to tea, Miss Cannon – the first recorded embodiment of 'the most beautiful girl' Robert has ever met (see ROBERT AND HIS FRIENDS). Then William, experimenting with Robert's brand-new birthday bicycle, unintentionally disrupts a picnic-party, at which Robert is still trying to impress the

beauteous Miss Cannon. William simply cannot resist the new 'shining and spotless' bicycle, and while the adults of the family are away on the picnic he decides that no harm can be done if he just tries to ride a few yards on it. After falling off a few times William eventually finds himself triumphantly careering through the village on the now slightly less gleaming bike. He has forgotten that he is still garbed in Red Indian gear, with befeathered head-dress, a corked face and the doormat pinned to his shoulders. He also forgets that he doesn't know how to stop, or get off, the bike, and – inevitably – ends up by crashing to a standstill in the midst of Robert's picnic-party, scattering the sandwiches, patties, rolls and cakes. Robert's bitterness about his young brother is not alleviated by Mrs Brown's assurance that William will have no pocket-money until the necessary repairs to the bike are paid for: ' "You'd think," said Robert with a despairing gesture . . . "you'd think four grown-up people in a house could keep a boy of William's age in order . . . You'd think he wouldn't be allowed to go about spoiling people's lives and – and ruining their bicycles . . . " '

In *Just William's Luck*, 3, William learns that because Hector (Ginger's elder brother) is engaged to be married he is clearing out a lot of his things and has given Ginger his bicycle. Naturally William immediately embarks upon a campaign to get Robert married off as soon as possible, so that he (William) might become the legitimate owner of a bike. This theme recurs in several of the stories. (There is an interesting discrepancy here; *Just William's Luck* was published in 1948 and, as we have seen, Hector is then engaged and has given his bike to Ginger. However, some years earlier, in 1930, we are told in *William – The Bad* that Ginger's grown-up brother has got married and given Ginger 'his old push bike, watch and a wireless set, all of which had been replaced by wedding presents'. William decides to get Robert married quickly before his bicycle, watch and wireless

'should be completely worn out'. The chronology is wonky but the idea is amusing enough to stand repetition.)

Birtley, Mr and Mrs Wilfred

An apparently *nouveau riche* couple who acquire The Laurels, whose spacious garden, when the house was unoccupied, had been a wonderful playground for William and Ginger. Their nastiness is immediately apparent: he is a 'bristly little man with a face like a Yorkshire terrier's', while she is stout 'with large pendulous cheeks and a small tight mouth', and they are bullying ARCHIE MANNISTER, the local resident artist. He has been commissioned to paint a picture of The Laurels, and the Birtleys want their home to be portrayed with fine and fancy features which it does not possess. William quickly falls foul of Mr Birtley, which turns out to be a blessing in disguise because in fleeing his wrath he stumbles upon yet another of his brilliant ideas: an 'Annymals nashonal helth servis'. (*William's Television Show*, 8)

Bishops

The clerics with whom William becomes entangled are generally vicars or curates, but on one or two occasions he is concerned with those in the higher echelons of the Church of England. In *Still – William*, 1, the 'fatherly and simple-minded' Bishop comes to the village to open the sale of work and address a temperance meeting. William lusts after a brightly coloured, large silk handkerchief which Ginger has just acquired. Impecunious as ever, he cannot buy a similar one for himself, and is unsuccessful in trying to filch his elder brother's. Robert, who fancies himself as a wit, says ' ". . . you can get the Bishop's handkerchief for me, and then I'll give mine to you" '. The

literal-minded William *does*, more by luck than judgement, and the always honourable Robert sticks to his facetious words and hands over his luridly desirable hanky. The Bishop again honours the village by attending the grand bazaar in aid of the Church schools of the district (*William's Happy Days*, 4), and by supporting (but then felicitously rejecting) an embryonic local branch of Youth on the Prow, a supposedly uplifting but actually repressive movement (see SEDLEY-MORTIMER, MRS.). (*William and the Brains Trust*, 9)

Blake, Miss

See ROBERT AND HIS FRIENDS.

Blake, Miss Amelia,

See CATS. Also appears in *William – The Rebel*, 12.

Blanche

See ETHEL AND HER FRIENDS.

Blank, Mr

The name, obviously assumed, given by a newfound friend of William's who, leaning against the wall of the White Lion, has rather obviously 'not confined his attentions to the exterior' of the public house. His claim to distinction in William's view is that he has no ears. He is one of the few characters in the stories whose army service in the Great War is referred to. Whether or not he is truly 'a pore ole soldier', as he suggests, is unclear, but he *is* a burglar, whom William innocently invites into the Brown household. (*More William*, 3)

Bolton, Nicholas

A friendly young man whom the Outlaws hear referred to as a ghost, which intrigues them enormously. He turns out to be a ghost writer who is tied by a very restrictive contract to work for Mr Raglan, an unscrupulous stealer of other men's words. The intervention of the Outlaws brings about Raglan's discrediting, and Bolton's release from the contract in time for him to take up the offer of going on an Antarctic expedition – something much more to his (and the Outlaws') tastes than writing. (*William and the Pop Singers*, 6)

Books

William's attitude towards books is ambivalent. Generally speaking, he seems the antithesis of the bookish child, intent only on outdoor and extroverted pursuits, with an overall attitude that is pragmatic rather than literary, as shown in *William's Happy Days*, 4: he is recovering from flu, his friends are all at school and he is 'bored and irritable, with no outlets for his energy'. Well-meaning people have given him books to read, but 'unfortunately William was not a reader. Instead he experimented with the hot water system, trying to "lay on" water from the bathroom to his bedroom in rubber tubes and being surprised and aggrieved by the resultant floods.' However, William is also wildly imaginative, a dreamer as well as a doer, and there are many instances when he is fired by a

book or a story to emulate the actions of its hero (with comically disastrous results).

He is, for example, influenced by reading *Robinson Crusoe*: 'His dreams of pirate-king and robber-chief vanished. The desire of his heart now was to be shipwrecked on a desert island.' In trying to achieve this, in the company of Joan, he ends up losing his clothes and facing the ignominy of walking through the village clad only in a table-cloth (*William Again*, 14). In chapter 6 of *William – The Fourth* (the book which most frequently features books and stories), the exploits of Black-Hearted Dick stimulate William to indulge in a spot of kidnapping: 'William heaved a deep sigh and took a long draught of liquorice water. It seemed an easy and wholly delightful way of earning money.' Chapter 12 tells us that 'William didn't read sensational fiction for nothing' when, again inspired by his delvings into sub-literature, he emulates Rupert the Sinister, an international spy in *The Sign of Death*. In chapter 14 William and his friends have been motivated with the idea of digging for hidden treasure: 'From various books they had read (*Ralph the Reckless*, *Hunted to Death*, *The Quest of Captain Terrible*, etc.), they had gathered that the earth is chockful of buried treasure if only one takes the trouble to dig deep enough.' Sometimes even the moral tales which clerics and adult relatives inflict upon William can influence his behaviour, although not perhaps in the way envisaged by the authors and enthusiasts of the stories; an instance of this occurs in *William*, 3, when his hopes of avoiding parental retribution demand the assumption of a false identity: he tells the irate Miss Murgatroyd (whose pond he has been draining of small fish in order to equip his own aquarium) that he is not William Brown but 'Algernon'. This name springs to his mind because the hero of a moral tale recounted at the Vicar's last tea-party was Algernon, a child with a singularly and (to William) maddeningly beautiful disposition. A more obvious negative effect upon William's impressionable mind arises from his reading in *William – The Pirate*, 6. As he explains somewhat laboriously to the Outlaws, a man in the book that he has been reading makes a practice of stealing (and eventually returning) various objects which friends bet he cannot appropriate: ' "You've got to fix on somethin' to bet me I won't steal an' then I'm goin' to steal it an' bring it to show you an' put it back an' it's goin' to be jolly dangerous an' excitin' same as it was in this book. Now you think of somethin' to bet me I won't steal . . ." ' The Outlaws decide on Mrs Bott's Sunday hat, which, large and plentifully trimmed with ostrich feathers, is a conspicuous feature of local life.

We know that as well as reading books William fancies himself as a writer (see AUTHORS). His imagination may outstrip his literary skills, but he is at least persistent: 'He wrote fast in an illegible hand in great sloping lines, his brows frowning, his tongue protruding from his mouth as it always did in moments of mental strain' (*More William*, 11). Even to write a fairly short notice announcing one of their shows or other projects is a difficult and demanding process for William, Ginger, Henry and Douglas: 'They could run and wrestle and climb trees all day without feeling any effects, but one page of writing always had the peculiar effect of exhausting their strength and spirits.'

Unabashed, William considers that he has no superior in the craft of writing: ' "I've written a book," put in William nonchalantly . . . "It was about someone a jolly sight more int'restin' than Shakespeare. It was about a pirate called Dick of the Bloody Hand . . ." ' (*William – The Pirate*, 2).

Boscastle, Guy

William, Ginger, Henry and Douglas yearn to attend the opening night of the Hadley New Theatre, partly because the play is to be a thriller, but particularly because Hubert Lane, their sworn enemy, is taunting them with the fact that he and his parents will be there. The theatre is booked to capacity, so that even if the Outlaws were in funds it would be impossible for them to go. By an extraordinary coincidence they encounter Guy Boscastle, the author of the play. He is supposed to be on his way to the theatre but, daunted by the prospect of seeing his play 'mauled to death', he decides to go straight home to start work on the last chapters of his novel, for which the Outlaws have given him some inspiration. Casually, he enquires if they might care to use the box that has been reserved for him. Thus the Outlaws bask in the glory of the stage box, and the baffled fury of Hubert Lane whose family are occupying less expensive and prestigious seats. (*William and the Masked Ranger*, 6)

Bott, Mr and Mrs

Mr and Mrs Bott and their small daughter VIOLET ELIZABETH come into the stories fairly early (in *Still – William*, 3) and, presumably, from the way in which we are introduced to them, were not necessarily intended to be permanent additions to the village but part of its shifting population:

> The Hall stood empty most of the year, but occasionally tenants re-awoke the passing interest of the village in it. This summer it was taken by a Mr. and Mrs. Bott with their daughter.

It must very soon have been evident to Richmal that with the Bott trio she had produced winners. They didn't recede into the shadows as some of her other promising characters did; neither did they wear thin from over-use. Eventually Mr Bott ('Botty': we never learn his Christian name) was to appear in thirty-two of the stories, his wife Maria in fifty-two, and his daughter Violet Elizabeth in thirty-four. Compositely, as the Botts, they are

mentioned in a further eleven episodes, the last being *William the Lawless*, 1.

Mr Bott had already made a fortune, by the time he came to the village, through manufacturing Bott's Sauce: 'After reading Bott's advertisements one felt convinced that any food without Bott's Sauce was rank poison. One even felt that it would be safer to live on Bott's Sauce alone.' Botty is rubicund and rotund, and Mrs Bott's proportions also suggest that a good table was always kept at the Hall. At their worst, Mr and Mrs Bott can be seen as social-climbing hedonistic *nouveaux riches*; at their best they are enterprising 'self-made' warm-hearted pillars of the community. *William and the Brains Trust*, 2, records that Mrs Bott 'was generous, impulsive, incalculable, short-tempered and irredeemably common – a thorn in the side of her more aristocratic neighbours. What she lacked in refinement, however, she made up for in forcefulness of character' (and, of course, occasional cash contributions to worthy local causes).

Mrs Bott has many weaknesses, but she is not just a gullible fool. Her avid wish to become accepted by the 'County', to discover some aristocratic connections for her family, or to become a Dame in her own right sometimes clouds her judgement of people and events, but ultimately her head is screwed on the right way. We gather that she helped Botty to perfect the recipe for the famous sauce, and she is his partner rather than his pet. Nevertheless he has occasionally to water down her excesses of emotion and ambition. When she feels that she 'can't be a real high-up without ancestors' and wants portraits of some of these characters 'in fancy dress suits of armour and such-like, bustles an' tights an' things', Botty reflects on his wife's various outbreaks of social ambition (*William and the Witch*, 5). She has yearned for write-ups about herself and her family in the local press; in *William and the Brains Trust*, 9, she dreamt so earnestly of becoming a Dame that she even asked a prestigious visitor to the village to come to lunch 'although it meant opening her last remaining tin of Luncheon Meat' (this of course was in Mrs Bott's wartime food-hoarding days).

There are times when Mr Bott recognises that he is basically a simple man who might have been happier if he had never developed the sauce 'that had transformed him from a small back-street grocer to owner of the Hall with its billiard room, library, ten bedrooms, commanding prospect and extensive grounds' (*William and the Witch*, 5). However, in the battle to live up to his sumptuous surroundings he has occasionally to fight his increasing flab (through daily exercises, and even trips to health and massage centres), and, when he drops his aitches, to remember to pick them up. He suffers a little with his liver, is more myopic than his wife (who is short-sighted, too) and, very surprisingly, is president of the local Literary Society (*William and the Tramp*, 1).

Mrs Bott sometimes has twinges of rheumatism, and is very slightly deaf. She dislikes fresh air, though she enjoys living in the country. She is, on the whole, surprisingly friendly towards William, despite the havoc that association with him wreaks on Violet Elizabeth's carefully tended ringlets and carefully laundered clothes. She occasionally, however, displays a childish petulance when dealing with him. In *William and the Evacuees*, 5, for example, she and William try bizarrely to outboast each other. When Mrs Bott talks about how much her 'hartificial lake' costs William says that his father, who is actually a millionaire, is thinking of making 'a nartificial sea one day'. Mrs Bott is unimpressed and, after this acerbic exchange, William refers to her rather nastily as 'ole Mrs. Toad', thus presumably linking her with Kenneth Grahame's rich, arrogant and self-satisfied Toad (who, like Mrs Bott, also lives in a great Hall).

Bott, Violet Elizabeth

The first meeting between Violet Elizabeth and William in *Still – William*, 3, had been presaged to an extent in a story called 'One Crowded Hour', which Richmal wrote for the September 1918 issue of *Home Magazine* (in the name of R. C. Lamburn). This featured Marie Elizabeth, 'the good girl of the neighbourhood', who had short fluffy golden curls, big blue eyes and white gossamery attire, just like Violet Elizabeth, and, at the other end of the scale, Robert Green, 'the bad boy', who was rude, rough and dirty, and very much like William Brown. Marie Elizabeth even had a lisp that was similar to Violet Elizabeth's, and when she persuaded Robert to 'play gameth' they trekked through muddy streams and wild brambles, to the detriment of her gossamer garb, just as Violet Elizabeth was to do with the Outlaws.

When William is forced by his mother to accompany her to tea with Mrs Bott and Violet Elizabeth, his worst fears about girlish ghastliness are realised. In spite of the sauce magnate's daughter's fragile fairy-like appearance she is iron-willed, and determined to dominate him by using tears and sighs and screams, those fearfully feminine weapons against which he has no legitimate defence. The noble savage is about to be tamed by the restrictive forces of civilisation, as embodied by the frill-bedecked six-year-old bundle of precocity that is Violet Elizabeth. Their meeting is a classically comic example of the clash between the sexes. 'William, pirate and Red Indian and desperado, William, woman-hater and girl-despiser' finds no escape from Violet Elizabeth's tear-filled eyes and trembling lips, when she insists that he must play 'little girlth gameth' with her, that he really does like 'all little girlth', and – the most horrific insult of all – ' "You with you wath a little girl, don't you?" '

He is horrified, bewildered and complying:

'Er – yes. Honest I do,' said the unhappy William.
    'Kith me,' she said raising her glowing face.
    William was broken.

And even that notorious kiss is not enough; Violet Elizabeth piles on the ultimate humiliation of ' "Now leth play fairieth. I'll thow you how." ' William then spends most of the afternoon 'in the character of a gnome attending upon Violet Elizabeth in the character of the fairy queen'.

In *Still – William*, 8, Violet Elizabeth asserts herself again with him, insisting that they play the game of being a married couple: ' " 'F you don' play houth with me, I'll thcream n' thcream till I'm thick. I can," she added with pride.' The famous scream is further described in *William – In Trouble*, 4. It would apparently 'have put a factory siren to shame' and 'was guaranteed to reduce anyone within ten yards of it to quite an expensive nervous breakdown'.

Incidentally Violet Elizabeth's lisp, though pretty constant throughout the saga until her last appearance in *William the Superman*, 3, is sometimes variable. In *Still – William*, 6, she has no lisp at all, and in *William – The Rebel*, 7, she pronounces her S's just like anyone else, but cannot sound her R's: ' "I'm a pwincess, William . . . An' you're my subject. You've got to bow when you speak to me." '

William and the Witch, 5, is an intriguing study of power. Violet Elizabeth is to have her portrait painted (see LANE, TARQUIN), and Mrs Bott says that she can choose whether she wants this done by ARCHIE MANNISTER or Tarquin Lane. Archie is the Outlaws' ally; he's hard-up and needs the commission. They try to persuade Violet Elizabeth to choose him. Hubert, however, supports Tarquin, and bribes Violet Elizabeth with whatever sweets she wants: ' "chocolath . . . lolly popth and caramelth and pear dropth and thugar mithe and jelly babieth and candy floth" '. Even more satisfying for her is that for once she can really rule the roost with the Outlaws, and see that they admit her to their games and do not try to avoid her. Drunk with 'the lust for power that lives in every six-year-old breast' she makes horrible demands on them:

'As William's squaw she bossed and bullied and nagged and tormented. There were times when the Outlaws' loyalty to Archie was strained almost to breaking point, but they held on doggedly.'

Botts' Nurse

Unnamed; appears in *Still – William*, 3 and 11. According to Mrs Bott she is far from being a paragon: ' "Always reading these here novelettes, the girl is . . ." ' Violet Elizabeth slips through her fingers in the first-mentioned chapter to embark upon a particularly mucky outdoor adventure with the Outlaws (see BOTT, VIOLET ELIZABETH); while she is missing from home the nurse becomes the second in a chain of hysterics and petty vengeance which, starting with the distraught Mrs Bott, swishes through the domestic staff in order of descending seniority, down to the kitchen maid (who, with no time for hysterics, takes it out on the cat). The nurse's only function in chapter 11 is to attend Violet Elizabeth at a fancy-dress dance (' "Look at me. I'm a thtar!" ') and to sew on again to her charge's costume the sequin stars which she sheds at every excited leap.

Bretherton, Mrs

A rival to MRS ROUNDWAY – the Outlaws' friend – who always beats her into second place in the prize cucumber competition, but is discovered by William & Co. to be cheating, aided and abetted by her nurseryman nephew from a village five miles away. (*William – The Bad*, 8)

Brown

Unrelated to William; one of his school classmates who, encountering the Outlaws when they are off to play truant on Ringers' Hill, is rendered temporarily inarticulate by the twopenny bull's-eye of giant proportions which he is sucking. (*William – The Outlaw*, 1)

Brown Family

William's immediate family is not particularly close-knit:

It happened that, on that particular day, the whole Brown family was assembled for lunch. William made spasmodic efforts to work his way into the conversation but was firmly ejected at each attempt. Robert, who was off with the last girl-friend and not quite on with the next, sang praises of his motor-cycle, Mr. Brown recounted his morning's triumphs on the golf course, Ethel gave a slightly catty description of Dolly Clavis's new hair-do, and Mrs. Brown expressed a dark suspicion that the man who delivered the laundry had been drinking. But the steak and kidney pie was delicious, the treacle tart had the right quality of sweetness and stickiness . . .

(*William and the Witch*, 4)

Except for William, who is a compulsive communicator both of events and his thought processes, members of the Brown family seem to function for longish periods within the parallel lines of their separate interests and purposes. Except when his actions impinge on them directly, they give William short shrift: only Mrs Brown – so often chained to her chair by her knitting and mending – finds the time to listen to his relentless questions and interesting preoccupations. Even then it is generally at the yes-dear-but-how-do-you-manage-to-make-such-very-large-holes-in-your-socks level:

'I'm goin' out, mother,' he said in a voice which expressed stern sorrow rather than anger.

'All right, dear,' said Mrs. Brown sweetly.

'I may not be coming back – never,' he added darkly.

'All right, dear,' said William's mother.

(*William Again*, 3)

Despite this kind of dismissiveness, Mrs Brown does have finer feelings about William: ' "I've always thought that William must be better at his work than they make out. I've *never* believed those awful reports he gets" ' (*William's Happy Days*, 8). And when a Sunday-school carol-singing expedition is planned: ' "I think it would be a very beautiful experience for you. I told Mr. Solomon so. He seemed afraid that you might go in the wrong spirit, but I told him that I was sure you wouldn't." Mrs. Brown's faith in her younger son was one of the most beautiful and touching things the world has ever known.' It appears to be unquenchable. Surely William must have inherited his truly splendid optimism from her; it certainly doesn't come from his father. See also CHRISTMAS. (*William – In Trouble*, 9)

Mr Brown's attitude towards William seems basically that of hoping that he will go away. When there is no alternative but the acknowledgement of his existence through conversation, Mr Brown leans heavily on sarcasm, which, fortunately for William's ego, often goes over his head:

William's father lowered his newspaper.

'William', he said, 'the effect upon the nerves of the continued sound of your voice is something that beggars description. I would take it as a personal favour if it could kindly cease for a short time.'

(*William Again*, 11)

Mr Brown, one suspects, slightly resembles Mr Bennet in Jane Austen's *Pride and Prejudice* in feeling superior to his various offspring because of their superficiality. (In fact William is the least lightweight of the three children, and the one who most resembles his father.) On the whole Mr Brown is tolerant towards the flighty Ethel, probably recognising the fact that the patterns of her life and personality are immovably set. Robert, however, is occasionally on the receiving end of his father's caustic comments. When William is summoned to Ireland by the supposedly dying Great-Aunt Jane, and someone has to accompany him, there is little enthusiasm on the part of his family. Ethel baldly states that she ' "simply couldn't face the crossing alone – much less with William" '. Robert says ' "I've got my finals coming off next year . . . I'm working rather hard these vacs." "No one," said his father politely, "would have noticed it." '

Ethel can be quite malicious towards William, who constantly punctures her own image of herself, and embarrasses her by his scruffy appearance and inelegant manners, on which she frequently and nastily comments. William, of course, gives back as good as he gets. He is genuinely at a loss to understand what all her male admirers see in her. In his view she is 'interfering and bad-tempered and stingy, and everything that an ideal sister should not be'. He does, however, have moments of genuine rapport with Robert, who, in spite of his irritation with his younger brother on numberless occasions, seems – being basically a more kindly person than Ethel – to have some fondness for him. For example, when William brings about some wonderful debunking of a rival for his latest inamorata's affections, Robert will show his gratitude with a fairly significant treat, gift or tip (such as the tin hat that William lusts after in *William and the Evacuees*, 7). When he does some service for Ethel, he is lucky to get even a gracious 'thank you' and more than a few pennies.

The short-lived moments of deep empathy between the brothers often occur when both have been disillusioned by 'unreasonable females':

> 'Bossy,' said William. 'Whatever they start like they always end up bossy.'
>
> For a moment a bond of sympathy seemed to unite them, then Robert hastened to resume his elder brother dignity.
>
> 'You look as if you'd been dragged through a hedge backwards,' he said severely. 'Don't you ever brush your hair?'
>
> William gave his ironic snort.
>
> (*William's Treasure Trove*, 5)

Although Mr and Mrs Brown and Ethel and Robert appear altogether in several hundred of the stories, it is surprising how few facts we know about them. Mr Brown's rarely used Christian name is John (first mentioned in *William – The Fourth*, 4); Mrs Brown is called Margaret in *William Again*, 2, but Mary in *Just William's Luck*, 17, and *William – The Explorer*, 5, and *William's Treasure Trove*, 5. Mr Brown enjoys fishing, has occasional touches of 'liver', is – surprisingly – 'mad on' curios and antiques (*William – In Trouble*, 3), likes playing golf, and eating Stilton cheese, and was nicknamed 'Podger' during his schooldays (*William's Television Show*, 7). Mrs Brown has brought to the family the red hair (from which Ethel's Titian locks and William's carroty spikes have sprung), is slightly short-sighted, a great needlewoman but hardly an avid reader, and her main interests, apart from her family, are the less outlandish village groups, fêtes, sales of work, and so on. See also DARNING, MENDING, KNITTING AND SEWING.

Ethel sings, acts, plays golf and tennis, swims and dances; she is a good runner, and she can ride. Robert is the perpetual student, who dabbles in poetry and politics when prompted by his more intellectual friends; he is interested in football, tennis and badminton, in his motorbike and, later, his car. See also ETHEL AND HER FRIENDS and ROBERT AND HIS FRIENDS.

Bryant, Major

A military gentleman, now resident in William's village, who was a heavyweight boxing champion in his younger days. He makes a habit of running down the road to the station every morning 'to catch his train', so presumably is no longer on active service but has a desk-job. (*William – The Pirate*, 5)

Bryant, Mr

An official of the local football club (presumably not connected with Major Bryant) who seems to be responsible for deciding who should become the club's secretary. (*William – The Pirate*, 11)

Buck, Mr

Secretary of the local Temperance Society, who is impersonated by Douglas when the Outlaws, at Joan's suggestion as a change from pirates and Red Indians, play at pretending to be the various inhabitants of Jasmine Villas. Their games are watched and savoured by Henri, a French youth with a limited understanding of English who is staying in the village. In an excited and garbled manner he describes to various people riotously outrageous events involving Mr Buck, Mr Burwash, Mr Luton and Miss Milton (as portrayed by the Outlaws). Not unnaturally, the teetotal Mr Buck is furious when Henri's description of his being ' ". . . oh, ze crumbs . . . 'ow say you? . . . tight . . . boozed . . . derrunk " ' is taken as gospel by various influential residents (*Still – William*, 2). Mr Buck is mentioned again in *William – The Bad*, 8, as one of the judges in the prize cucumber competition (see BRETHERTON, MRS).

Bullamore, Miss

'On the strength of possessing a handbook on palmistry' this lady is generally supposed to be the village psychic, and is much in demand for fortune-telling at local fêtes. (*William – The Showman*, 4)

Bumbleby, Mr

A fellow of the Royal Geographical Society and an author 'who has travelled all over the world', Mr Bumbleby is another of those unfortunate lecturers who come to speak in William's village and are waylaid and diverted before reaching their expectant audience. On this occasion the Literary Society is assembled in Mrs Bott's new 'garden room' unaware that the Outlaws and Violet Elizabeth have substituted a tramp for the real speaker. When Mr Bumbleby turns up he is shep-

herded through the unlit garden and locked into the coal-shed by Ginger, Douglas and Violet Elizabeth. Even when he eventually breaks out his troubles are not over because, in his grimy and gasping state, *he* is mistaken for the tramp (whom Mr Monks, the Vicar, has spotted earlier in the day lurking about the village). Mr Bumbleby is saved from arrest only by the fact that the tramp takes himself (together with Mrs Bott's diamond brooch, and the watches of General Moult and Mr Monks) off the scene while everybody's attention is drawn to the dishevelled and expostulating Bumbleby. (*William and the Tramp*, 1)

Bunker, Mr

A history teacher at William's school, presumably employed on a temporary basis as he is mentioned only once by name. (*William – In Trouble*, 1)

Burford, Sadie

An 'astonishingly beautiful' young woman, to whose sapphire-blue-eyed charm William succumbs; she is a zestful portrayal of the stereotypical American tourist who is rapidly 'doing' Britain: ' "Say, kid, what's the name of this lil' old town?" ' She is lost, and sobbingly searching for

' "Stratford-on-Avon, that Shakespeare guy's place" '. Not wanting to disappoint her, William pretends that his village is Stratford and takes her on a conducted tour of pseudo-Shakespearian properties, etc. Suitably impressed by these, and 'The Avon' (the sluggish stream that idles through the village), she asks wistfully if any of Shakespeare's 'folks' are still around, so William promptly claims to be one of the Bard's descendants. She insists on accompanying him to his home, to inspect any 'relics' which might be there. Mrs Brown is astonished, but, fortunately for William, neither understands Sadie's Shakespeare-slanted prattle nor disillusions her about William's identity. The young American is so delighted with her visit to Stratford that she gives William a ten-shilling tip. Mr Burford, Sadie's 'Pop' and travelling companion, wisely sleeps in the car throughout the whole episode. (*William – The Conqueror*, 5)

Burwash, Mr

See BUCK, MR.

Bute, Mrs

Helping at his mother's 'white elephant' stall at the fête, William inadvertently sells (for a shilling) the Vicar's wife's coat which has been deposited for just a moment or two at the corner of the stall. Mrs Bute is the lady whom William (wrongly, as it turns out) suspects of having bought and taken to her home the coat in question. The Outlaws 'rescue' (steal, according to Mrs Bute) two of her black coats hoping that one of these will be the missing garment. Neither is, of course. (*William – The Outlaw*, 5)

Butler, Mrs

See BABIES.

Buttermere, Mr Sebastian

In William's view, a literary 'luny', temporarily resident at Honeysuckle Cottage. Mr Buttermere needs stimuli for his prose: he uses a writing-desk which is a replica of Charles Dickens's and, on hearing that 'it was Balzac's custom to wear a monk's habit when he wrote', orders one for himself. William 'borrows' this for a fancy-dress dance, but it is Robert who wears it. Just as he is sitting out in the garden with someone whom he has just discovered to be 'the most beautiful girl in

the world', Robert is called away by the irate Mr Buttermere, who, forcing him to strip down to pants and vest so that the costume might be retrieved, then locks him in a shed. (*William – The Bad*, 9)

Cannon, Miss

See BICYCLES and ROBERT AND HIS FRIENDS.

Carew, Miss

Another of William's dancing-class teachers (*William Again*, 11). See also BEAUCHAMP, MRS.

Carrol, Miss

See CHRISTMAS.

Carroway, Mr and Mrs

A blameless couple (with their companion, Miss Seed!) who probably regret giving dinner on one occasion to the Great Man (the visiting lecturer-cousin of William's headmaster). William's pursuit of the Great Man to the Carroways' house is designed to persuade him not to abandon his usual request that the school be given a half-holiday in honour of his visit to speak there. (Regrettably William has inadvertently catapulted the Great Man earlier in the day, and he rightly fears that the headmaster's cousin will 'take it out on' the whole school.) The evening is a hectic one, with rumours of an escaped lion near by driving Mrs Carroway into frequent hysterics and the Great Man into cravenly seeking refuge in a rug-box. William not only discovers him there but, when he raises the lid, also hears his high-pitched scream of terror.

Needless to say, after that, to save his reputation, the Great Man promises as the price of William's silence to obtain two half-holidays for the school instead of the usual one. (*William – The Good*, 8)

Carruthers, Cyprian

A writer and non-stop talker, with an obsession about breaking the Force of Habit, who takes up temporary residence at Corner Cottage in Marleigh. Inspired by the concepts, if not by the man, William tries (unsuccessfully) to revolutionise his parents' routines. (*William – The Explorer*, 8)

Carruthers, Miss

A middle-aged newcomer to the village, who acts as a go-between when Mrs Bott decides to find a child companion for Violet Elizabeth (who seems unhappy then at Rose Mount School). Miss Carruthers has not lived within William's orbit for

long enough to know that it is never entirely wise to entrust a note or an errand to him. (*William the Superman*, 3)

Cars

For many years the Browns were carless. In fact, Mr Brown vowed in *William – The Outlaw*, 8, never to have one. However, Robert's car is mentioned in *William – The Pirate*, 11, and *William – The Gangster*, 11. Mr Brown's car is not mentioned until *William and A.R.P.*, 8. William takes surprisingly little interest in his brother's or his father's car.

Carter, Miss

One of William's teachers who arranges a 'Pageant of Ancient Britain'. (*William – The Fourth*, 14)

Carter, Molly

Described as 'Little Molly Carter', she is one of the cast of the play (*The Bloody Hand*) written and produced by William. She is neither impressed by, nor impressive in, the rôle of Lady Elsabina, despite the enhancement of being garbed in Ethel's purloined silk petticoat, a lace curtain and a toilet-cover. (*William Again*, 1)

Catchpole, Mr

A ventriloquist whose dummy gets damaged. He is entertaining at a birthday party just before Guy Fawkes day, so improvises with a lifelike guy belonging to the Parsons family which has involved William and Archie Mannister in some curious exploits. (*William's Treasure Trove*, 6)

Cats

In *William – The Fourth*, 9, we are told that 'William treated all cats with supreme contempt' and considered that 'their only use in the world was to give exercise and pleasure to his beloved mongrel, Jumble'. He expands on his dislike of the feline species in *William Again*, 6: ' "Cats! Who'd call cats an animal? They aren't int'restin'. . . They don't follow you like dogs, do they? They haven't int'restin' habits like insecks . . ." '

His dismissiveness about cats seems frequently to be reflected in the narrative voice of the stories; there seems some vagueness, for example, about the Browns' family cats, and, even allowing for the fact that turnover in this type of pet is generally higher over a period than in family dogs, the coming and going of their felines is somewhat puzzling. (Ginger's cat, too, changes from Rameses to Dasher, and back again to Rameses.) In *Just – William*, 5, 'a cat, belonging to William's sister' is mentioned. His name is Smuts. Short-tempered and cherishing 'a bitter hatred of William', he is forced to take a reluctant part in one of the Outlaws' fund-raising shows. The following book, *More William*, 2, finds William shut up in the larder (to purloin some cream blancmange for the small girl next door) and realising that 'the cat' is there, too. This time the animal is nameless, and recognising his 'inveterate enemy' (William) he sets up a vindictive wail which nearly 'gives the show away'. In the next book, *William Again*, 6, Ethel seems to have forgotten both Smuts and the nameless cat, and is pleasurably anticipating the white Persian cat which her latest admirer, Mr Romford, plans to give her for Christmas. (William, forced to act as cat-carrier, inadvertently switches the pedigree puss for a ferret, thus not only keeping down the cat population in his home but also breaking Ethel's relationship with a suitor whom William dislikes.)

William – The Fourth, 9, quite definitely states

that 'Bunker, the old black cat, had been an inhabitant of William's home ever since he could remember'. He officially belongs to Ethel, who has long ago lost interest in this 'very old and very mangy animal', who has developed a sustained, horrible and ear-splitting yell which forces the family to take self-protective action: 'Mr. Brown remarked many times that that cat and that boy would drive him to drink between them, but at least that boy slept at night.' It falls to William to gather up the unfortunate Bunker, and take him to the petshop to be destroyed (surely a strange task to entrust to any eleven-year-old boy, and, of course, particularly to one with William's notorious capacity for causing mayhem). That evening, when a 'familiar hair-raising, ear-splitting sound' shatters the peace of the Browns' house and garden, William realises that he has not taken the mangy Bunker for destruction but Luky, the petted puss belonging to Miss Amelia Blake, who was at that time their next-door neighbour. Happily, Mr Gorton the petshop owner has too keen an eye for profit to destroy Luky: instead he has sold him to a Miss Cliff. Meanwhile Nemesis overtakes the

unlamented Bunker, and William, relieved that he has not actually been responsible for the murder of Luky, finds the animal, renamed Twinkie by Miss Cliff, living at the other end of the village.

Pricked by conscience and the anguish of Miss Blake who fears that Luky has been killed or abducted, William embarks upon the awkward and wearisome procedure of transferring Luky/Twinkie at weekends from the residence of one of his owners to that of the other. Neither lady can understand where her cat goes during his long absences, but each at least is partially satisfied. William is not. He begins to think that if he has 'to spend every Saturday of his life stalking Twinkie-Luky and conveying him secretly from one end of the village to the other, he might just as well not have been born'. (In *William – The Gangster*, 4, while staying with his Aunt Florence, William is again responsible for some cat-switching. He loses his aunt's pampered Siamese, Smut, when attempting to teach him ratting, and 'borrows' Smu, another Siamese who is Smut's deadly rival in all the local cat competitions, to take his place. Even though Aunt Florence has constantly commented earlier to William that her beloved Smut is infinitely more handsome and impressive than Mrs Hedley-Smith's Smu, she fails to realise that a substitution has been made.)

In *Still – William*, 12, the cat on the Browns' domestic hearth is called Terence. Like his predecessors, he 'dislikes William intensely'. Apparently Terence, too, is soon supplanted, for *William – The Bad*, 5, refers to yet another nameless 'mangy and undersized creature who represented the sole feline staff of his household'. (This 'worst-looking cat of the village' has to be taken by William to a competition. Brushed and groomed until it was in 'a state bordering on madness' it escapes his clutches, but William finds a magnificent 'wild cat' in the woods to take its place. This wins the coveted first prize from under the nose of Hubert Lane, who has expected that his family's fine big cat will walk off with the prize. To console himself, Hubert jeers, ' "Who can't afford to go to the circus?" ' but, fortunately for the impecunious William and Ginger, the wild cat turns out to be a lion-cub escapee from the sawdust ring; when the truant is returned, William and Ginger are allowed not only to watch the circus without paying, but also to help with moving apparatus between turns, to the stupefied amazement of the Hubert Laneites who are sitting in the front row.)

Yet another puss, Trouncer, adorns the Brown home in *William – The Detective*, 4. In William's eyes this animal is a 'savidge', but his mother patiently points out that it only scratches William because he teases it.

The lack of empathy between William and cats is probably best illustrated in *William – The Gangster*, 6. The Outlaws wish to experiment with William's aunt's sleeping draught, hoping that they might use it at school on certain people, and thus get out of doing lessons. They test it first on some of William's rats, and a mangy bony stray cat 'ragged of ear and fierce of eye'. All the animals die from being over-dosed, but no regrets are expressed. (William kills another cat in *William – The Bold*, 4.)

As well as William's, there are many other cats in the saga; all are spoilt or savage or both, with perhaps the exception of the cat next door to William – not Luky, whom he so nearly had destroyed, but another unnamed pet who is presented with a measure of sympathy. William uses him for pebble-throwing target practice from time to time, and sometimes as an audience for the expostulation of his ideas and grievances, all of which the friendly feline takes in good part, purring loudly in response.

Cedric

See PROTEST MARCHERS.

Chambers, Susie

A little girl from the village who is, presumably, well behaved as she is one of the children whom Mrs Brown suggests (and William rejects) as a potential guest at his birthday party. (*William's Happy Days*, 6)

Chance, John

See ANTHONY.

Charles

See ETHEL AND HER FRIENDS.

Chesterfield, Miss

A bird-lover who organises a bird-week, and fusses so much about our little feathered friends that she disgusts the Outlaws – and indirectly inspires William to set up a rat-week. (*William – The Detective*, 4)

Cheytor, Mr

A Conservative parliamentary candidate who lives in the village. During one of his campaigns William, too, has entered politics, in support of the Liberal candidate, Mr Morrisse. He is influenced in his choice of party by his politically aware uncle; we are informed that William's father takes no interest in politics. William is at first rather belligerent to Mr Cheytor, even entering his house and charging him wildly 'in the region of the abdomen'. However, Mr Cheytor proves himself a sport, providing William with roasted chestnuts. He seems rather more sympathetic than the Liberal candidate, which perhaps is why William decides to give up politics (at least for the time being) because it is so confusing. See also POLITICS AND POWER. (*William – The Fourth*, 12)

Chris

The intellectual of the pop group called the Argonauts (who dreamt up their name). The four performers, who punctuate their lyrics with 'Yeah! Yeah! Yeah!', are presumably to an extent influenced by the Beatles. Their encounter with the Outlaws is a rather bizarre affair, the most positive aspect of which is that they give the boys one of the advertising spin-offs which are showered upon them. It seems a curious gift to eleven-year-olds,

for it is an electric razor. However, as Douglas has just ruined the one belonging to his brother (he used it for planing wood to make a model boat) and has to provide him with a new one (costing £2.15*s.*), the electric razor from Chris and the Argonauts is much appreciated. (*William and the Pop Singers*, 1)

Christmas

Christmas played an important part in the earlier books, although it faded from prominence in those which were written after the mid-1940s. Perhaps Richmal felt by then that she had said almost all she could about William's constant battles to ensure that his immediate family and numerous aunts and uncles provided him with decent presents rather than the soppy or stuffy ones they were inclined to choose for him. Also she had frequently reiterated the rather touching theme of William, ever impecunious, struggling to find ways and means of buying a really nice present for his mother (he didn't bother much about anyone else).

The first Christmas stories occur in *More William*: this book contains two chapters about the festive season, one at the beginning and the other at the end. Curiously they have been published here in reverse order, with the 1920 Christmas story from *Home Magazine* appearing to precede its December 1919 story, 'William's Christmas Eve'. The latter is the only sentimental Christmas exploit in the William canon. It starts, however, in customary facetious and iconoclastic style: 'William, whose old-time faith in notes to Father Christmas sent up the chimney had died a natural death as the result of bitter experience, had thoughtfully presented each of his friends and relations with a list of his immediate requirements.'

William is also very robust about the arrangements for his Christmas party; as well as inviting Ginger, Douglas, Henry and Joan, he wants to ask the milkman, and the butcher's boy, Fisty Green, who 'can whistle with his fingers in his mouth'. His mother, of course, makes it clear that no such riff-raff can attend. In her view parties are opportunities for reciprocating invitations from people of the same social class. William promptly loses interest in his party. He is more preoccupied with thoughts of a small auburn-haired girl whom he has encountered on the doorstep of a poverty-stricken house in the village, who fervently believes that 'there's a chap called Father Christmas wot comes down chimneys Christmas Eve and leaves presents in people's houses'. Pathos is piled on: her mother is bedridden, and her father is expected home from prison; all she wants is for Father Christmas to bring 'a nice supper for Dad when he comes out'.

William realises that he has to play God (or, rather, Father Christmas) to make the little girl's dream come true, and he does so by absconding, with Joan, from his own party and taking all its comestibles in a handcart to the young hopeful's home. William, in an old red dressing-gown and white scarf, makes a quaint Father Christmas; Joan, all in white, wearing a muslin dress and a swansdown-edged satin cloak, is more convincing as a Christmas fairy. The small girl, her sick mother and her ex-convict father are all delighted, and, maintaining the mellow mood, the story stresses that the erring daddy has reformed; he turns down William's 'wistful' request to accompany him when he goes 'stealin' some day' with the assurance that he now has a 'real steady job – brick-layin' ' which he intends to stick to (*More William*, 14).

Chapter 1 treats Christmas without a glimmer of mawkishness: 'It was a jolly day, of course – presents and turkey and crackers and staying up late. On the other hand there were generally too many relations about . . .' Three aunts (Jane, Evangeline and Lucy) are assembled at the Browns' for the holiday, as well as two small cousins, Jimmy and Barbara. Jimmy turns out to be a kindred spirit: he and William disrupt the household, with the best of intentions, with snails, worms, centipedes and water. Also, stimulated by dipping into William's only worthwhile Christmas present, *Things a Boy Can Do*, they dismantle the drawing-room clock (' "Well, the cog-wheels was wrong" said William doggedly . . . "we've got to take it all to pieces to get it right . . ." ') and thus ruin Aunt Lucy's day because, without the chimes of the clock, she misses morning church and the Vicar's Christmas sermon. This early Christmas story clearly outlines William's attitude towards presents. Most of those which he receives are boring; to make up for this he buys things he likes (lurid-looking sweets for his father, a copy of *The Pirate of the Bloody Hand* for Robert, and some coloured chalks for Ethel) in the hope that the recipients will either hand these quickly back to him or make no fuss when he retrieves them a little later on. Significantly, however, he buys his mother a small cream-jug which, of course, he intends her to keep.

Still – William, 9, describes William's funniest (his truthful) Christmas (see ATKINSON, LADY). In *William – The Conqueror*, 12, he is encouraged by his mother not to worry about the lack of money to spend on presents, but to use his imagination and make things instead. He exercises his ingenuity on Ethel's nearly new white straw hat, which, to her horror, he paints green and fills with earth and a cyclamen appropriated from the greenhouse. In chapter 11, his perpetual enemy, HUBERT LANE, and his followers sabotage William's party (amongst other things they substitute a dead cat for the live white rabbit which the conjuror is supposed to produce). So, in chapter 13, the Outlaws avenge themselves on the day of Hubert's party by locking him out on his roof and his gang in an attic during a game of hide-and-seek. They then convince Hubert's short-sighted and ineffectual Aunt Emmy that they (William & Co.) are the genuine guests, and scoff the gargantuan tea!

William plays Santa Claus again in *William – The Outlaw*, 4. He stands in for Mr Solomon, the Sunday-school superintendent (who is so entranced by chatting over tea with Ethel that he can't tear himself away from her), and unfortunately mixes up the two sacks of presents. At *their* party, the irate Old Folks receive what they consider to be useless toys, puzzles, etc., instead of the anticipated tea and baccy. Those attending the Mixed Infants party, however, are better served. William, now in Pied Piper garb, marches the whole group off to a garage where, urged on by the Outlaws, they engage in an exciting battle using the Old Folks' tea-leaves and tobacco as ammunition.

Poor Mr Solomon suffers again at the hands of the Outlaws in *William – In Trouble*, 9, when he allows them to join his carol-singing party. They take over, and use the group of loudly bawling boys to ·intimidate local relatives of William, Ginger and Douglas who are planning to give them dreadfully dreary Christmas presents.

In *William*, 8, because most of the village's juvenile population have succumbed to mumps, the Vicar's wife 'not without misgiving' commissions the Outlaws to gather holly from the woods to decorate the church at Christmas. Equipped with the vicarage wheelbarrow they have a day of glorious adventures in the woods, with William, blacked up, being mistaken for a Martian at one point. Only when they have returned, and the Vicar's wife finds them using the wheelbarrow, upside down, as a platform for clog-dancing, do they remember in horror that they have completely forgotten the holly.

The Outlaws' running feud with the Hubert

Laneites again provides a Christmas theme in *William's Happy Days*, 3. The doting Mrs Lane, who can't understand how anyone can quarrel with her '*awfully* sweet' Hubie, persuades Mrs Brown that the two gangs must arrange a truce and attend each other's Christmas parties. At William's, the Laneites are as slimy as ever, needling William but ingratiating themselves with his mother. When the Outlaws are due to go to Hubert's party William rightly suspects foul play; he takes the precaution beforehand of surreptitiously switching the labels on the parcels which 'Father Christmas' (the Lanes' long-suffering gardener, Bates) 'is to hand out at the party. Mrs Lane has entrusted Hubert with the buying and wrapping of the presents, and he and his henchmen are dumbstruck when they become the recipients of penny and twopenny pencils and rubbers, while William, Ginger, Henry and Douglas gleefully acquire splendid gifts (respectively a mouth-organ, an electric torch, a fountain-pen and a penknife).

William's Crowded Hours, 10, sees the beginning of the Christmas holidays, and the Outlaws building a snowman which William dresses in the outdoor clothes of Robert (who is temporarily bed-bound with a feverish chill). By a series of coincidences and misunderstandings (in which William is deeply involved) the snowman becomes the means of reconciling Robert with fierce old Colonel Fortescue, who has hitherto resented his interest in his niece, Eleanor, who is Robert's latest 'goddess'.

It is not Robert but William who is infatuated in the Christmas episode from *William – The Pirate*, 7. William is taken to the pantomime by the reluctant Robert who, in the throes of a highbrow phase, ostentatiously reads from Chekhov during the intervals. William's bliss, however, is total; he laughs so much at the comedians that he fears he has broken a rib: 'he cheered the hero, he hissed the villain, he clapped and shouted applause long after everyone had stopped'. Most of all, 'he fell in love with Princess Goldilocks, the heroine'. Afterwards he indulges in wild fantasies about her until, eventually meeting her in the flesh, he discovers that she is 'much older and much less sweet' than she appeared on the stage. He quickly returns her 'in imagination to the brigands and pirates and wild beasts' from which he has in so many fantasies rescued her!

In *William – The Rebel*, 6, Robert is being given a new watch for Christmas, and William is lusting after his old watch and chain. But in the run-up to the festive season William is the unwitting instrument of humiliating Robert in the eyes of his latest inamorata, Honoria Mercer, who can only admire men of great and proven courage. William's visions of owning his elder brother's soon-to-be-cast-off watch and chain seem to be receding but, happily for all concerned, at the Christmas fair Robert mistakes a real lion for William dressed up, and thrills Honoria with his aggressive and courageous approach to the potentially ferocious beast. So William gets what he wants for Christmas!

The Christmas fair is again visiting Hadley in *William – The Gangster*, 3, and Laurence Redwood wants to spend his time there instead of with his godmother (who hasn't seen him since he was little). William, tempted by Laurence's promise of the wonderful tea which his godmother is likely to provide, agrees to pretend to be Laurence for the afternoon, with, as always, complicated – if un-Christmassy – results.

The Outlaws are bemoaning 'having so many relations round' for Christmas in *William – The Detective*, 11, and also the perpetually unsatisfactory situation concerning presents. They are fed up with receiving 'only ties an' books an' pencil boxes an' things like that', and irritated at once again not having enough money to buy presents for those who are their nearest and dearest. Only their mothers come into this category: ' "I'd like to be able to give my mother somethin' nice," said Ginger wistfully. The others agreed . . .' In this episode one other female relative also appeals to them: Miss Carrol, who is Ginger's mother's second cousin (see AMBITIONS). Miss Carrol is hard up, but William puts this right after Jumble has badly damaged her only legacy (a stuffed cat) from a horrible old uncle to whom she was housekeeper. In trying to restuff the gruesome relic, William is instrumental in finding Miss Carrol's real legacy, a wad of hundred-pound notes hidden inside it. She tips the Outlaws gratefully and generously, and, as a result, William's mother receives a silk scarf, Ginger's a travelling-clock, Henry's a cut-glass scent-spray and Douglas's a leather handbag. The Outlaws really do turn out to be surprisingly devoted to their maternal relatives.

They remain, however, unenthusiastic about aunts, and William expects to have one foisted upon him and the rest of his family in *William and A.R.P.*, 6, when Mrs Brown announces that her sister, 'Aunt Lucy', will be coming for Christmas. As 'she's never been able to come till now', one imagines that she cannot be the same Aunt Lucy who was constantly grumbling (in *More William*) about missing the Vicar's sermon because of William's clock-'mending'. *This* Aunt Lucy is Ethel's godmother, and the threat of her visit stirs Ethel into bribing William with the promise of sixpence to retrieve the 'indescribably hideous' vase which was Aunt Lucy's last birthday present to her. Ethel has passed this on to Dolly Clavis, who has passed it on to someone else, and so on. William eventually brings home the wrong vase and indirectly heaps wrath on his mother, who is suspected by its owner of theft. Fortunately Aunt Lucy develops flu and after all fails to come for Christmas.

William and the Brains Trust, 8, deals with a Christmas of wartime shortages, with William still wanting to buy an attractive gift for his mother. He tries to sell his tin soldiers to raise the necessary cash; things go wrong, but by the usual series of misunderstandings he manages to give her some rare commodities that she very much appreciates,

especially a Christmas cake, a few paper table-napkins and a pan-cleaner: ' ". . . a pan cleaner! I've been trying to get one for months!" ' Charged with the Christmas spirit, and 'wearing an expression of complacent magnanimity', William actually allows himself to be embraced.

Church and Religion

Despite the fact that regular church-going and Sunday-school attendance have always been part of William's life, religion on the whole leaves him cold. Apart from experimenting with St Francis of Assisi's approach to the religious life (in *William – The Conqueror*, 4) and various iconoclastic entanglements with bishops (see BISHOPS), vicars and vicars' wives (see MONKS, MR AND MRS), William and his followers find little stimulation in spiritual enquiry or in the conscious application of Christian principles to the many challenges which beset them: 'Mr. Solomon was the superintendent of the Sunday School, on which the Outlaws reluctantly shed the light of their presence every Sunday afternoon. Mr. Solomon was very young and earnest and well-meaning, and the Outlaws found it generally quite easy to ignore him' (*William – In Trouble*, 9).

There are, however, one or two occasions when William *is* inspired by some gem or other from the Vicar's sermons, notably when he decides to tell the truth at all costs (see ATKINSON, LADY and CHRISTMAS) and when he feels called upon to prevent others from treading the tricky path of evil: 'He had been so frequently urged to reform himself that the appeal had lost its freshness. But to reform someone else. There was much more sense in that; he wouldn't mind doing that . . . He'd rather like to try reforming someone else' (*William Again*, 4).

This episode also tells us that William's 'Pegasean imagination soared aloft on daring wings' in the invention of excuses to get out of church-going; and that, these having failed to achieve their purpose, he would spend most of his enforced time in church in face-pulling contests with one of the choirboys. Other pleasing occupations were staring out the Curate during the Vicar's sermon, and ear-splitting delivery of hymns: 'Any stone-deaf person could have told when William was singing . . . by the expressions of pain on those around him. William's singing was loud and discordant. It completely drowned the organ and the choir. Miss Barney . . . said that it always gave her a headache for the rest of the week . . .' (*Still – William*, 9). A further frequently mentioned time-passing standby was the training of William's various insects, which, conveyed to church in a matchbox or a pocket, often managed to escape from their receptacle and their trainer's attentions, and to cause havoc elsewhere. There was also, of course, the occasion when one of William's rats distracted the attention of the congregation from

spiritual to earthier matters (see ANIMALS) in *Just – William*, 11.

Apart from what William saw as the time-wasting rituals that took place inside the church, there were those that preceded it, including the fearful scrubbing and polishing of his person that his parents deemed essential, the family's Sunday-best dressing-up (with Ethel in gorgeous garb and his father 'tophatted and gloved'), William's passionately reiterated protests that he'd rather stay at home and his family's unsympathetic response to these.

Circuses

Circuses of the professional variety as distinct from those organised by William and the Outlaws are mentioned enthusiastically, if sometimes only

briefly, in the following books: *William Again*, 11; *William – The Good*, 8; *William – The Bad*, 5; *William – The Detective*, 2; and *William and the Pop Singers*, 5. An equestrian act, known as the Wonder Cossacks and performing amazing feats, also visits the village (Five Acre Meadow) in *William and the Moon Rocket*, 8.

The most detailed circus adventure is the one conveyed in *William Again*, in which we learn that William has 'lived the eleven years of his life and never seen a circus'. He is rapturous at what he sees from a distance of the animals and clowns: 'A ragged man leading one of the horses looked curiously at him – a small boy leaning against a lamppost with all his soul in his eyes.' Despite a parental ban, William is determined to see the circus. Creeping out to do so one night he stumbles upon Grandfather Moore who, fearfully ancient and frail, is visiting the Browns. He has wickedly stayed up when he should have gone to bed, and, sharing William's enthusiasm for the circus, decides to accompany him, braving retribution on the following day from Aunt Lilian who devotes her life to cosseting him. The conspiratorial bond between youth and age is here delightfully expressed (and echoed in the next book, *William – the Fourth*, when William and Great-Aunt Jane go to the fair: see FUNFAIRS and FÊTES). Both boy and elderly man are transported with joy by the magnificence of the ringmaster, the cavortings of the clowns, the exploits of the animals and the golden-haired bareback rider (whom William immediately decides to marry when he grows up; he also makes up his mind that he will become a clown).

In *William*, 3, William's rather unfruitful attempts to make his own circus are mentioned. In *William – In Trouble*, 5, to celebrate the fact that Joan has come back to the village after being away, the Outlaws create a circus for her entertainment. It consists of Douglas's aunt's parrot, William's 'trained' insects and pet rat Whitey, Ginger's all-spitting, scratching and swearing cat Rameses, and the clockwork monkey which Henry abstracts from his little sister's toybox. 'Oh, *William*, isn't it all lovely!' says the adoring Joan.

Claribel

See HOLIDAYS

Clarke, Doris

See ETHEL AND HER FRIENDS.

Classics

Richmal's abiding love for the classics is often exuberantly expressed in William's adventures. Most memorably, it inspires episodes in *William – In Trouble*, 1, when the Archaeological Society is excavating near by. William is dismissive about the whole business: ' "I always knew there was something fishy about those Romans. Their langwidge is enough to put you off to start with – hic haec hoc an' stuff like that . . . an' then we're supposed to

think 'em great an' all they did was to bury broken bits of pots . . . I've *never* liked 'em. I'd rather have pirates or Red Indians any day." '

The story's comic climax occurs when the eminent archaeologist Professor Porson gives a lecture at the village hall. Unfortunately, a bag of William's has accidentally been substituted for his. The Professor's comments on the 'exquisite grace and beauty' of certain artefacts which he has excavated are made ludicrous by the fact that his uninformed and inexperienced assistant displays, for example, Henry's sister's grimy toy goose instead of a perfect Greek statuette, and an old sardine-tin in place of 'a dainty piece of Castor pottery'.

Claude

See CYNTHIA.

Clavis, Dolly

See ROBERT AND HIS FRIENDS.

Clayton, Mr and Mrs

A serene couple who, as well as having children of their own, are happy to have others (who are apparently lost) foisted on to them. However, the lost baby, Peter, whom the Outlaws are supposedly looking after, turns out to be their own; the other lost child, Billy, is also one of their offspring, who, after prematurely leaving a fancy-dress party disguised as a gryphon, is thought by the Outlaws to be a Space Animal (Billy cannot explain things too well as the gryphon head becomes stuck, and seems temporarily to muffle not only his speech but also his intelligence) (*William and the Space Animal*, 1). Peter Clayton is also mentioned in *William and the Pop Singers*, 4, as the finder of a

Roman coin; by this time he appears to be the Outlaws' contemporary, ageing ten years or so, while for William & Co. time has stood still!

Cliff, Miss

Distinct from the feline-loving lady of the same name (see CATS), Miss Cliff of Lilac Cottage is one of William's none too numerous adult friends. He is particularly helpful to her when she temporarily swaps houses with Mrs Nichol of The Elms, so that she has room to give an aged aunt a much needed holiday. He indirectly helps her to find some silver spoons which Mrs Nichol (who feels rivalry towards Miss Cliff) almost accuses her of stealing. Also, to save disappointing Miss Cliff when he intercepts a message that Hassan, a Persian boy, is unable after all to come to tea with her, William takes on the rôle, heavily disguised and liberally draped in some embroidered shawls and crêpe de Chine scarves belonging to Ethel. So understanding is Miss Cliff that even when she later discovers the true identity of her 'Persian' visitor she is 'very sweet and forgiving'. Of course, Mrs Nichol has seen 'Hassan' arriving at Miss Cliff's and she feels that her rival has scored. (*William – The Detective*, 9)

Miss Cliff also appears in *William Carries On*, 2.

Clive, Joan

See 'JOAN'.

Clive, Mr

See 'JOAN'.

Clive, Mrs

See 'JOAN'.

Clothes and Appearance

William's disregard for his appearance, and his family's efforts to tidy him into respectability, is a frequently recurring theme. We gather that even when William is fresh from his mother's ministrations, with sleeked-back hair, clean collar, firmly gartered socks and shining shoes, he is still hardly prepossessing. Generally, of course, his clothes are dishevelled and dirty, his carroty hair is spiky and upstanding, and his socks are crumpled round his ankles because he has used his garters as catapults. His liberally freckled face is often screwed into a scowl or allowed to sag into a vacuous look which William thinks conveys innocence, though it is more suggestive of imbecility. Worst of all, perhaps, is his often assumed expression of

'inscrutability'. His terrible appearance is a constant embarrassment to his elegant sister and conformist brother. This is especially well conveyed in *William – In Trouble*, 8, when at a garden-party he has a wonderful time which results in him getting scruffier and stickier by the minute. Ethel and Robert, each engaged in trying to impress a stunner of the opposite sex, wince visibly as 'the horrible rock-licking, ice-cream-sucking', chocolate-smeared, muddy-kneed figure of William follows them around. That their disgust is somewhat coloured by snobbery is shown in *William – The Fourth*, 3, when 'Robert and Ethel, glasses of fashion and moulds of form' are shocked 'at the sight of William with torn coat and jersey, dirty scratched face, no cap and tousled hair, consuming ice-cream horns among a crowd of his social inferiors'.

Coggan, Mr

See BELL, DR.

'Corky'

A Royal Air Force flying officer hero admired by the Outlaws. See also WARTIME. (*William and the Brains Trust*, 11)

Cornish, Mr

See DOGS.

Cotton, Molly

See ROBERT AND HIS FRIENDS.

Courtnay, Mr Evelyn and Miss Felicia

Once again William has to resort to psychological blackmail with one of the temporary masters who so frequently have to hold the fort at his school. Old Stinks, the regular science master, is absent recuperating from scarlet fever, and his temporary successor, Mr Evelyn Courtnay, takes a dislike to William and unfairly punishes him with an excessive number of lines. William learns (from servants' prattle) that Mr Courtnay's Aunt Felicia is to dine with him: she has an obsessive fear of mice; Mr Courtnay can't stand cats. For William it is

the work of a moment to put a mouse, and Terence, the Browns' current cat, through the window of Mr Courtnay's dining-room during dinner. Both Courtnays are reduced to chaotically screaming cowards, when William enters 'like a *deus ex machina*' to remove both cat and mouse. Miss Felicia is deeply grateful, and Evelyn, afraid that his funkish behaviour might be reported round the school and the village, tells William 'with elaborate nonchalance' that there is no need to talk of the evening's happenings; also there is 'no need to do those lines'. (*Still – William*, 12)

Craig

An archetypal, fanatically boy-hating gardener. (*William and the Masked Ranger*, 2)

Cramps, Mr

The school caretaker, who hates the Outlaws because he knows that the nut-shells and ink-soaked blotting-paper pellets that make his life 'a perpetual burden' can generally be traced to them. (*William*, 4 and 6)

Crane, Miss

See ROBERT AND HIS FRIENDS.

Crane, Mrs Adolphus

This lady is William's mother's second cousin and William's godmother. Her connection with William is hardly close, and generally speaking their past encounters have been unfortunate, so, to make amends (Mrs Adolphus Crane is, after all, rich), Mrs Brown has a studio photograph taken of

Cranthorpe-Cranborough, Mr

We are told that Mr Cranthorpe-Cranborough is a very distant cousin of Mr Brown ('so many times removed as to be almost out of sight'). He comes on a self-initiated visit, an over-bright character, with an over-packed mouthful of teeth, some of which seem to threaten to fall out when he gives his broad insincere smile. His interest in the Browns is basically pecuniary; he is starting a new boarding-school and hopes for William as a potential pupil (though, meeting him, he realises that the high fees he intends to charge Mr Brown for William's attendance will be well earned). Inwardly William is horrified at the suggestion: he

William which, rather surprisingly, appeals so much to his godmother that she invites him to her birthday tea-party. Until the other guests arrive he is alone with Mrs Adolphus Crane, who suggests that he passes this time in looking at her album of family photographs. William, scrubbed and polished to the point of great discomfort, feels trapped, 'trapped in a huge and horrible drawing-room by a huge and horrible woman', while his friends are probably out bird-nesting! He relieves his feelings by pencilling embellishments to Mrs Crane's photographs which change them from dignified portraits to grotesque cartoons: this is much appreciated by the other guests, all of whom have the photograph-album inflicted on them. William's godmother, whose parties tend usually to be funereal, cannot quite understand why her guests are so animated and full of laughter. She does not bother to look into the album, which she knows so well, but feels sure that it is William who in some strange way has managed to make her party so successful. (*William – The Fourth*, 2)

'could not even contemplate a life divorced from the beloved fields and woods of his native village, his beloved Outlaws and Jumble his mongrel'. He plays his cards close to his chest, however, remaining outwardly inscrutable and apparently calm. He doesn't take long to discover Mr Cranthorpe-Cranborough's weakness, which is a fear of the supernatural, and to concoct a ghostly incident that sends Mr Cranthorpe-Cranborough scuttling for the next train home, and determined to keep William, who will apparently bring him bad luck, as far away from himself as possible. Mr Brown guesses that William has cooked up some scheme to put him off, but confides to his wife that, although it would have been nice and quiet at home, with William at boarding-school, 'it would also have been extremely dull'. (*William – The Outlaw*, 6)

Cremer, Mr

William's form-master at one time. In *William Again*, 7, he is described as being ill, with his place taken by the tougher Mr French (see FRENCH, MR and ALBERT 1). Mr Cremer is long-suffering, apparently 'a pacifist' who wants 'peace at any price'. His policy therefore is to avoid conflict with William as far as possible: 'If he saw William quietly engaged in drawing beetles during his lesson, he did not expostulate. He thanked Heaven for it. He was not a proud man.' (see SCHOOLS.)

Crewe, Joan

See 'JOAN'.

Crewe, Mrs

See 'JOAN'.

Crisp, Mr

Known as 'Crispie', he is yet another temporary master at William's school. In *William – The Explorer*, 2, he takes the boys for a nature ramble, on which surprisingly the Outlaws win a prize of ten shillings for finding the most unusual flower. Crispie cannot make up his mind 'whether to establish himself as poet or novelist (in both of which capacities he considered that he already outstripped most of his contemporaries)'. He regards teaching very much as a stop-gap.

Croft, Miss Tabitha

An inoffensive woman who 'didn't look the sort of person to write letters of protest to William's parents'. William likes and feels protective towards her (see FUNFAIRS AND FÊTES). (*William – The Fourth*, 3)

Crompton, Richmal

When children first come across the William books many of them think that the author is a man, because her unusual Christian name suggests this. In fact it has been in her family for generations, and is given to girls rather than to boys. Richmal's full name was Richmal Crompton Lamburn; she wrote several of her early stories – but not the William ones – as R. C. Lamburn.

She was born on 15 November 1890 in Bury, Lancashire, the second child of the Reverend Edward John Sewell Lamburn and his wife Clara (whose maiden name was Crompton). Edward and Clara had another daughter, Mary Gwendolen (Gwen), who was seventeen months older than Richmal. When Richmal was in her third year, her brother John Battersby Crompton (Jack) was born. Richmal (or Ray, as the family dubbed her) and

Gwen always remained close. Their father was a clerk in holy orders and licensed curate who had decided to become a schoolmaster instead of taking a parish. He was soon able to infuse both his daughters with his own passion for learning, but was less successful in this respect with his son.

Jack – unlike his sisters – had little relish for school-work or private study. He was the typical active outdoor boy, and it was from some of his most colourful exploits that Richmal eventually drew the inspiration for William. From childhood she was an avid reader and story-spinner. She 'scribbled' in an attic, which was her secret refuge, and before going away to boarding-school used to edit her own magazine, *The Rainbow*: 'Its circulation was confined to two. I used to read it to my small brother and my beloved rag doll (she was called Lena) sitting on two doll-sized chairs in the attic.'

During the first decade of her life, Richmal was treated as an invalid. Slighter and quieter than the outgoing Gwen and Jack, she was forced to lie for long periods on a backboard, because her parents were afraid that she showed signs of developing a spinal curvature. Although Richmal would have liked to be running around the fields near their home with her brother and sister, with characteristic lack of self-pity she made the most of those times of enforced rest by reading and dreaming up stories and poems of her own. Possibly some of the seeds of William were sown then.

Following in Gwen's footsteps in 1901, when she was in her eleventh year, Richmal went to St Elphin's, the clergy daughters' school in Warrington. It moved to Darley Dale in Derbyshire, and she remained there until 1911. The hated backboard had long since been abandoned; she was able to savour to the full the social, sporting and scholastic opportunities offered by St Elphin's. She proved an excellent scholar, and was awarded an open entrance scholarship to London University's Royal Holloway College.

She enjoyed college life and in 1914 obtained her B.A. degree in classics, 'being the best candidate of her year' according to a testimonial from the college's senior staff tutor in classics. This same lady, like other tutors of Richmal, was impressed by her 'mastery of language' (which no one ever then dreamt might be lavished on such literature as the William stories!).

Even when she was still a schoolgirl, Richmal had decided on teaching as a profession. It offered more security than writing, which she would continue to pursue part-time, and the opportunity to combine her love of classics and her interest in young people. She went back to her old school, teaching there from 1914 to 1917. By that time her mother Clara had been widowed and was living in south-east London with Gwen, who in 1914 had married Thomas Rhodes Disher, a successful entrepreneurial businessman. (The Dishers' son, Thomas Edward Lamburn, was born in 1915; his mischievous boyhood was to provide Richmal with further ideas for William's exploits. Family inspiration for her fictional character continued into the next generation, through the childhood activities of her great-nephew Edward Gordon Crompton Ashbee.)

Richmal decided to move south to be near her mother and her sister, and she took up the post of classics mistress at Bromley (Kent) High School for Girls in 1917. There is no doubt that she was a dedicated and charismatic teacher, who is still warmly remembered by several of her pupils. 'She was most inspiring and enthusiastic – laughter and fun were the essential ingredients of the lessons . . .' 'Miss Lamburn was always tolerant and patient, and her keen sense of humour was a great help; amusing stories, atrocious puns, silly jokes, impressed rules and vocabulary on our minds . . .' "'. . . of course, we girls had "crushes" on her. One girl used to bring a single rose, and place it on her desk before she came in.' At this time Richmal was a handsome young woman, who wore her plentiful light-brown hair in buns, plaits or the 'headphones' which were then fashionable.

Her first story to be professionally published appeared in the *Girl's Own Paper* in 1918. Called 'Thomas', it was doubtless inspired by Gwen's small son. Despite the demands of teaching, Richmal's writing went from strength to strength, and her stories began to appear regularly in various magazines (see HOME MAGAZINE and HAPPY MAG). Once William had been created in 1919, it soon became clear that he would be taking up great chunks of her time for the foreseeable future. Her editors began to urge her to stop being a school-marm and to concentrate on writing, while her headmistress was pressing her to abandon author-ship and give all her energies to teaching.

In the event the decision was taken out of her hands. An attack of poliomyelitis in 1923 left Richmal with the permanent disability of a 'dead' stiff leg. Concerned about her pupils who were half-way through the university scholarship year, she continued to teach them, showing, in their view, 'wonderful courage' as she dragged herself on crutches into the classroom, teaching them 'more than Latin by her courage and cheerfulness'.

However, after some months of struggling to make the three-and-a-half-mile cycle-journey to school and back (with the dead leg sticking out at a perilous angle), she was urged by her doctor to give up teaching, which he felt was putting far too great a strain upon her. Teaching's loss, of course, was literature's gain. Richmal produced not only the William stories but also a steady stream of adult novels (starting with *The Innermost Room*, 1923, and ending with *The Inheritor*, 1960).

Her mother, Clara, had come to live with Richmal soon after she moved south. Gwen had two daughters, Margaret and Richmal, as well as Tommy; her marriage eventually broke up, and she and her children remained very close to Richmal throughout her life. Richmal seems to have been the ideal and universal 'aunty', always having an empathy with children, and a rich fund of ideas from which to stimulate and entertain them. She never married or had children of her own. Her writing provided her with a very good income, a large house – The Glebe – at Bromley Common, which was specially designed and built for her (and later, Beechworth at Chislehurst), and the where-withal to travel and pursue her artistic and literary interests.

Her brother Jack had eschewed the Church career which his father had envisaged for him. He found the adventure that he craved when he joined the Rhodesian Mounted Police; later he worked and travelled a great deal in China, as the employee of a merchant and shipping company. There was always a room available at The Glebe for him dur-ing his leaves, when Richmal enjoyed his vivid tales about his exploits (which apparently included capture by bandits). It is interesting that Jack, the original inspiration for William, should have embraced a career of action of which William would have heartily approved. He would have also applauded Jack's interest in natural history which prompted him to write a series of wildlife books (as 'John Crompton'). Jack also produced several suc-cessful adventure-novels with African back-grounds, writing as 'John Lambourne'.

Richmal wrote an article called 'Puppet Pulls the Strings' for the December 1957 issue of *Books and Bookmen*. She explained how William, who began as a pot-boiler, had flourished into extraordinary resilience:

> . . . for many years I looked on William as 'my character'. He was my puppet. I pulled the strings. But gradually the tables have been turned. I am his puppet. He pulls the strings. For he is resolute, indomitable and inclined to be tyrannical. Like all characters who have been over-indulged by their authors, he insists on hav-ing his own way. He refuses to co-operate in some plots. He makes fantastic demands on

others. He pushes his way unceremoniously into situations in which he has really very little concern.

Richmal continued to write zestfully about William until she died in January 1969. Her last book, *William the Lawless*, was published posthumously in 1970, with one uncompleted story, 'William's Foggy Morning', finished (from notes which she had left) by her niece and literary executor, Richmal Ashbee.

Croombe, Mr and Mrs

See VICTIMS.

Cummins, Miss

See 'JOAN'.

Curates

See ETHEL AND HER FRIENDS.

Cuthbert

William dislikes the idea of sharing Joan's 'adoration and homage' with anyone else, and has pangs of apprehension when he hears that her cousin Cuthbert is coming on a visit. He turns out to be a cissy – the same age and height as William, but dressed 'in an embroidered tunic, very short knickers, and white socks'. He has appealing blue eyes, and curls which are brushed into a 'golden halo'. Needless to say, the boys hate each other on sight: Cuthbert doesn't like William's 'rough gameth', and suggests that they should 'thit down' and tell 'fairy thtorieth' instead. Anxious to see William

get into trouble, Cuthbert eggs him on in his defiance of authority; the more dirty and dishevelled William gets, the brighter and more radiant Cuthbert seems to become, to the delight of the local ladies, who think he is a darling, adorable, a picture, a sweetheart! Worse: Joan also seems to like this prissy paragon. In the climax of the story – a production of *Red Riding Hood* in which William, as the Wolf, apparently goes berserk and savages Cuthbert in public – William sinks low in almost everyone's estimation. Joan, however, slips her arms around his neck and tells him she's glad that 'softie' Cuthbert is going home the next day: ' "Oh, William, I do *love* you, you do such 'citing things!" ' (*More William*, 6)

Cynthia

Cynthia, who is staying with her aunt, Mrs Stacey, appeals to William because she resembles Joan (who, we are told, is away at boarding-school). Unfortunately, he finds himself competing for her affections with Claude, a tall, languorous, well-travelled and sophisticated youth who is also staying at Mrs Stacey's. Neither William's eloquence nor his rigged 'heroic' rescue of Ginger (from what turns out to be a very shallow pond) impresses Cynthia, who prefers to listen to Claude's lectures on civilisation, or to practise dance-steps with him. However, when William inadvertently strikes up an acquaintance with an escaped lunatic and holds him in conversation until his keeper arrives, Cynthia begins to admire him no end. (William at the time is under the misapprehension that the

escaped inmate from the asylum is the keeper, and that the keeper is the madman, so little courage on his part was actually required!) Ironically when Cynthia is overcome with admiration for William he suddenly realises that her charms for him have utterly vanished: 'It was her disdain of him that had made her so desirable in his eyes.' (*William – The Bad*, 2)

Dalrymple

A schoolmate of William's who, though he has 'adenoids' and a slight lisp, is, to William's jealous indignation, given the part of Hamlet because of his excellent memory. (*William – The Pirate*, 2)

Dalrymple, Miss Felicia

A rather formidable lady who claims as part of her garden, and fences off, the tadpole-pond which has long been a favourite haunt of the juvenile population. William gets it back for them when, cunningly hiding a message in the pond, he falls in, and Miss Dalrymple thinks the green slimy object (William, of course) rising from the pond is a ghost. (*William – The Bad*, 3)

Dancing Classes

Dancing classes, forced upon him by his mother, are the bane of William's life, and how he spends (or tries to avoid) this 'longest hour' of his week makes stimulating reading in *William Again*, 11 and *William's Happy Days*, 6. William's terpsichorean efforts seem as distressing to his partners as they are irritating to himself. Small girls sidle up to their dancing teachers (see BEAUCHAMP, MRS and CAREW, MISS) or stamp their impeccably shod feet and whine: '*Need* I have William . . . He's so

Brown is socially ambitious here; but, fortunately for her younger brother, the ever-realistic Ethel succinctly points out that it might put the d'Arceys 'a good deal more' against them if William *did* attend! See also D'ARCEY, LADY BARBARA, and KIDNAPPINGS.

d'Arcey, Lady Barbara

This pretty but imperious seven-year-old appears in *William – The Fourth*, chapter 6, and seems a fore-runner of Violet Elizabeth, the spoiled darling who emerges in the following book, *Still – William*, chapter 3 (see BOTT, VIOLET ELIZABETH). We know that Barbara is another example of the type of fluffy female that affronts William, but with her as with Violet Elizabeth he gets tougher responses than he bargains for. 'That soft-looking kid' (Barbara) utters a threat that presages Violet Elizabeth's later attempts at emotional blackmail; the difference is that Violet Elizabeth warns that she will 'thcream and thcream' till she's 'thick', while Barbara threatens unlispingly 'I'll scream an' scream till I burst' (see DANCING CLASSES and KIDNAPPINGS).

Dare, Harry

A skilled poacher, though under-sized and timorous. (*William and the Evacuees*, 7)

Darlington, Mrs

William has the idea of establishing a boy sanctuary at Gorse View, an unoccupied house. Mrs Darlington, who has just bought it, arrives when William, Ginger, Henry and Douglas have finished hanging buns, tarts, etc., on the trees in the spinney (for the sanctuary). Mrs Darlington's daughter

awful.' His dancing-class ignominy is, of course, compounded by his having to be ruthlessly spruced up for this (as he sees it) utterly abortive and time-wasting ritual. One dancing class which he seems successfully to avoid is that planned by Lady d'Arcey, a newcomer to the village in *William – The Fourth*, 6. To teach her 'frilly, fascinating' seven-year-old daughter, Barbara, she engages a dancing master to come from London once a week, and invites several of the village children to join in these lessons. William is 'horrified to the depths of his soul' at the prospect; Mrs Brown, almost weeping, explains to Ethel that if William refuses to participate it puts the family 'at a sort of disadvantage'. One feels that the generally placid Mrs

Sally and her friends delightedly eat some of this food as 'a fairy feast', and Mrs Darlington, convinced that William has kindly arranged this imaginative treat for the girls, congratulates him on his 'pretty' ideas: 'I shall always think of you as the Little Boy who Believes in Fairies'. See also FAIRIES, MAGIC AND THE SUPERNATURAL. (*William – The Dictator*, 2)

Darning, Mending, Knitting and Sewing

Mrs Brown's pivotal rôle as mother and homemaker is symbolically expressed by the darning of her menfolk's socks. This, augmented by other forms of needlework from time to time, is without doubt her principal function. In *Still – William*, for example, there are no fewer than seven references to her sock-making or -mending; thirty-seven years later, in *William's Treasure Trove*, 2, we are

told that she is still darning socks. As by this time nylon and other synthetics were thankfully established as integral elements of masculine hosiery, there seems a certain perversity about her persistence in this occupation. When, occasionally, readers are told that Mrs Brown has stopped darning for some reason or other, it is pointed out that she only did so 'in moments of deep emotion'. Even when she is approached by some member of her family who is in the throes of real or imagined crisis, the darning rituals remain sacrosanct: 'Mrs. Brown calmly cut off her darning wool as she spoke, and took another sock from the pile by her chair. William sighed' (*Still – William*, 1). National or global calamities are similarly not allowed to disrupt the darning process:

'I tell you he's bleeding the country to death . . .' snorted Mr. Brown . . . 'He ought to be hung for murder. That man's policy, I tell you, is wicked – *criminal*. Leave him alone and in ten years time he'll have wiped out half the population of

England by slow starvation. He's killing trade. He's *ruining* the country.'

'Yes, dear,' murmured Mrs. Brown, 'I'm sure you're right . . . I think these blue socks of yours are almost done, don't you?'

(*Still – William*, 11)

There are occasions when Mrs Brown is roused by the grisly state of William's socks to protest about his mistreatment of them: ' "I simply can't think, William," said Mrs. Brown feelingly, "how you get such dreadful holes in your heels." ' William's answer to this (in *William – The Fourth*, 11) is that it's the fault of the hard road on the way to school and that he would be happy 'not goin' jus' to save you trouble. I wun't mind growin' up ign'rant like wot you say I would if I didn't go to school . . .' On other occasions he advances the theory that the learning of Latin is not only tough on the brain but also hard on his hosiery.

One presumes that after all Mrs Brown's years of mending and sewing she must be something of an expert in the field. However, the stories also refer to the embarrassments inflicted upon others by over-enthusiastic but inept needlewomen. In *William and the Evacuees*, 1, Miss Milton's shapeless knitted-for-charity garments are mentioned. In *William and the Brains Trust*, 10, we read about William's Aunt Florence who is a catastrophic but keen knitter; luckily William is around niftily to exploit the situation in one of his shows: 'WOT IS SHE NITTING NOW? PENNY A GESS. PRIZE FOR WINNER.'

Dayford, Claude

The over-fed, spoiled and spiteful son of Mrs Dayford, a self-styled expert on Child Psychology whose System is one of No Discipline but Suitable Mixing. She is constantly trying to find for Claude a suitable companion whose gentleness will nicely

counter-balance his 'manliness'; in fact Claude simply bullies the succession of mild children whom his mother recruits. William is invited to stay with Claude because when Mrs Dayford meets him at one of Violet Elizabeth's parties he is abstemious and quiet (she doesn't realise that William is suffering the drastic after-effects of having consumed large quantities of 'toffee' which the Outlaws have made by mixing cocoa, syrup, coconut, lemon curd and sardines). Of course, William soon cuts the odious Claude down to size. (*William Does His Bit*, 10)

Deborah

An earnest fellow-attender of William's Sunday school who tries (unsuccessfully) to get him to follow their teacher's passionate injunction to 'turn', i.e., reform. (*More William*, 12)

Dewar, Mr

See DOGS and ETHEL AND HER FRIENDS.

Dewhurst, Miss

A teacher at the mixed-sex school at first attended by William, who is not so important to him as Miss Drew. She makes William 'a swain' in the school's May Day celebrations, but William rearranges events so that he is the May King, and Bettine Franklin, whom he likes, the Queen (instead of Miss Dewhurst's choice, Evangeline Fish, whom he dislikes). (*More William*, 8)

Dexter, Marion

See Robert And His Friends.

Dimtritch

Dimtritch is the villain of a book called *Hunted by the Reds*, which has enthralled the Outlaws. Their excitement mounts when they encounter in the village a broken-nosed and cross-eyed character who, they feel sure, is the real-life Dimtritch. He isn't, of course; he is Mr Finchley, a 'very distinguished' author, but the Outlaws remain convinced that he is a murderous Bolshevik, who holds a princess captive at his temporary residence, The Limes. They shut him up in a disused pigsty while a sympathetic young man whom they have recently met ostensibly creeps into The Limes to rescue the princess. Actually he steals the spoons! (*William – The Conqueror*, 7)

Discrepancies

Given the large body of material, the number of discrepancies which defy even the most imaginative of explanations is quite remarkably small. Confusion of Christian names (e.g., George and Ronald Bell: 21.1, 31.5; Victor and Jameson Jameson: 18.3) or of surnames (e.g., Roundway for Radbury: 37.2; Mrs Marks for Mrs Monks: 7.5) or of house-names (e.g., Beechcroft, 10.10, for Beechgrove: 10.1) are trivial slips of the tongue which can befall any storyteller. The occasional reference to Ginger's family as Flowerdew instead of Merridew (6.2, 7.3) is a more serious lapse. However, the Mrs Flowerdew in 24.4 is not *stated* to be Ginger's mother, even if this was the author's intention. One may consequently suggest that the presence of separate Merridew and Flowerdew families in the village led to occasional confusion. As for Mr Marsh, may he not have chosen to move his junkshop from the village into Hadley town, possibly after the death of his aged mother (6.9, 28.3)? The number of awkward hyphenated surnames in the village suggests a reasonable solution to the Marks/Markson problem. That the feud between the Outlaws and Hubert Lane can be described as 'from time immemorial' yet Hubert's companionship tolerated by them at his first textual appearance (5.8) is explicable if one considers their differing pre-grammar-school background (see Schools). If Mr Brown is a teetotaller who likes a glass of wine 'to his dinner', a political apathetic who chairs political meetings and a regular churchgoer who 'seldom goes to church', perhaps we are witnessing habits changing with the years.

When the pretentious OSWALD FRANKS was disconcerted by Dorita Merton who 'was going through a high-brow phase and wanted to talk about William Empson and T. S. Eliot . . . when Oswald wanted to talk about himself' we may be observing a pseudo-intellectual caught (not for the first time) on the wrong foot (31.5). The relocation in the text of the 'church room' (a free-standing building, not a room attached to the church) or the Vicarage or Miss Milton's house suggests a rebuilding or a removal. (See WILLIAM'S VILLAGE for further information on discrepancies involving location and distance.) The windowless Old Barn of 24.5 may have been boarded up. That the proletarian Mrs Bott should have a godmother who goes annually to Paris to 'get the cobwebs blown away' and declares that '*noblesse oblige*' (34.2), or that a little boy of about four wearing an uncomfortable gryphon costume should walk four or five miles (over hilly country) without complaint, although surprising revelations, are not necessarily discrepant with life as one knows it.

When, however, in 5.1 William shares a branch with a caterpillar while collecting acorns at the time of year when the days are drawing out 'so pleasantly', one's sense of actuality is disturbed. But such slips are exceedingly rare. More frequent are slips of the type found in 5.14. Miss Lomas's Bible class is stated repeatedly to be on a *Saturday* afternoon. 'Next morning' William attends school until lunch-time, then enjoys an afternoon's half-holiday. Incidentally, 6.8 asserts that Miss Lomas's class had been held on Sundays, which fits the facts much more happily. There is likewise confusion in 33.4 where careful reading reveals that a Wednesday morning is followed directly after lunch by Thursday afternoon.

It is in relationship to the process of ageing and the question of the 'twice-told tales' that the time-discrepancies present problems which are positively metaphysical. Although William asserts that

he will be twelve next birthday, he never reaches that age despite the passing of many a Christmas, summer holiday, Guy Fawkes day – and even birthday. But time exists for those around him. GENERAL MOULT, eighty in 33.4, reaches ninety in 37.2. 'Ole Mr. Gregson', says William (35.2), 'died las' week.' Within William's immediate family time moves erratically. Ethel's age is somewhat variable. Robert is eighteen when we first meet him, then randomly seventeen, nineteen, even twenty-one, while still allegedly having a constant eight-year superiority over William. A brief examination of the text is sufficient to show that one cannot support the view that when Robert is seventeen the family still lives in the old house and William attends the primary school, nor that when William joins the grammar school Robert is still a sixth-former. One must simply admit that Robert's age moves backwards as well as forwards.

Just William's Luck poses unique problems. As a numbered book in the series (26) it cannot be dismissed as pseudepigraphic as can the unnumbered *Just William – The Book of the Film* (1939), which, although loosely based on six canonical stories, presents us with a strangely unfamiliar Mr Brown standing as a candidate in a local election and Mrs 'as sure as my name's Maria' Bott signing herself 'Amanda Bott'. This latter book, together with a large quantity of material outside the numbered volumes, forms part of a William apocrypha, which would be a study of its own, were the material all extant. There is a sense of *déjà vu* in *Just William's Luck*. To cite but three examples, the Knights of the Square Table (first heard of in 11.1) are re-created, William again tries to beg two shillings from his family in order to pay for his admission to the tramp fraternity (see also 13.8), and again attempts to goad Robert into proposing marriage (see also 11.4 where Robert is two years younger). Setting aside prosaic explanations, may one not suggest that we have here two differing versions of the same events recalled by two informants? One is after all inclined to wonder how our narrator has access to so much information unless someone – say, Henry – reminisced for her benefit in later years. *Just William's Luck* shows more than the customary interest in Ethel's affairs and is perhaps drawn from *her* reminiscences of events, reminiscences which are characterised by a tendency to dramatise at the expense of precise accuracy – which would be alien to the literal-minded Henry. Yet how can reminiscences in later years at the same time be published accounts of roughly contemporary events, as the books purport to be? To explain these Mysteries of Time, perhaps we should turn to *William and the Brains Trust*, 1: ' "Can you explain the Infinite Regress Theory of Time, Professor?" said one of the women earnestly. "Sure, sister," said the pseudo professor easily. "There's not much old Knowall can't explain, but let's give the thing a break for a bit. We've all had about enough of it . . ." ' (K.C.W.)

Dobson, Miss Doreen

The pretty, golden-haired, blue-eyed cousin of Miss Lomas, who runs a weekly Bible class for the Sons and Daughters of Gentlefolk (the 'beautiful atmosphere' of which William has recently destroyed). William, smitten with Miss Dobson's charm and pulchritude, makes her an enormous (and very sticky) Valentine but finds that he has a rival for her attentions: his brother, Robert. To pick up some tips on the courting process, he sits in on a romantic *tête-à-tête* between his sister Ethel and 'her latest admirer', Laurence Hinlock, and rehashes for Miss Dobson garbled versions of Laurence's amorous epithets: ' "Has anyone ever told you that you're like a bottled cherry?" said William doggedly . . .' (*Still – William*, 14)

Dogs

In addition to Jumble's many adventures, there are well over forty stories in the William books which feature dogs. One feels that Richmal considered boyhood incomplete without the presence of a canine chum, but she showed dogs in unfavourable as well as positive rôles. Some of the regular inmates of the village owned spoiled and spiteful dogs, generally Pekes or Poms, about whom William was as dismissive as he was of cats. Not surprisingly, Mrs Lane – the complacent mother of horrible Hubert, William's enemy – has a Pom (*William*, 2); tubby Mrs Bott has a 'sweet little fellow' with 'a weak digestion' called Chin Chin – presumably a Peke, who is as rounded and over-fed as his mistress (*William – The Pirate*, 9); the fussy Miss Milton has 'an obese and cherished Pom' which Jumble, egged on by William, is in the habit of chasing (*William – The Detective*, 9); while

another of William's traditional enemies, Farmer Jenks, has at different times a variety of dogs, including Rover (*Still – William*, 6), whose antagonism towards the Outlaws ('Kill 'em, Rover! Eat 'em, Rover!') is fervent, and a more engaging, scatterbrained collie called Victoria (*William – The Showman*, 4).

A sympathetic dog who might well have become a regular adornment to the books is Henry's fox terrier, Chips, who appears in *Just – William*, 7, 'rabbiting' in the woods with Jumble and the Outlaws, and in chapter 5 of the same book, when, ignominiously painted blue, he has to make an appearance on one of William & Co.'s money-making shows. Chips seems to have faded out of the saga after this first book; possibly Richmal considered that in looks, character and likeableness he too closely resembled Jumble to justify the retention of both dogs in the stories.

William's Happy Days includes two rather bizarre doggy episodes. In chapter 6, when Jumble is staying temporarily at the vet's where his damaged foot is being treated (see JUMBLE), William truculently demands not one but two new dogs as a birthday present. His family point out the unreasonableness of this, especially as Jumble will soon be returning; and, in William's eyes, they then add insult to injury by insisting that, even though it is his birthday, he must attend his hated dancing class. He will also have to tolerate the presence at tea afterwards of Mr Dewar, Ethel's current admirer, who is always nastily facetious towards William. His spirits soon lift when, a little later on, he finds two splendid collie pups tied to a tree in the drive of his house. Naturally he thinks that, after all, his family have come up trumps. 'How terribly he'd misjudged them!' William's heart swells with love and gratitude, and he decides to attend the loathsome dancing class out of respect for his family's wishes (earlier he had decided to play truant). The magnificent dogs accompany him. One plays havoc with the stockings, gaiters

and navy-blue knickers left in the little girls' dressing-room while, garbed in 'fairy-like frills and furbelows', they perform their dainty antics, somewhat impeded by William, in another room. The second dog is equally busy. True to his collie instincts, he has managed to round up 'a sea of sheep' and to bring them to 'his master' (Mr Dewar), who is at that moment smugly sitting in the Browns' drawing-room (with his back to the window) and playing the rôle of the male provider to Ethel (who had told him previously that she 'adored' collies): ' "Oh! By the way, I forgot to mention it but I just bought a little present – or rather presents – for you this afternoon. They're in the drive . . . Have a look at them and see if you like them," he said.' Ethel does, and, on seeing 'hundreds and thousands of sheep' filling the drive, the lawn, the steps and the road outside, she not surprisingly collapses in hysterics. William arrives home to find that Mr Dewar has been sent packing. A further celebratory happening is that his dancing teacher, Mrs Beauchamp, has complained so rudely to Mrs Brown about the damage done by the dog taken by William to the dancing class that his mother decides he should not go there again.

In chapter 9, William becomes involved with a dead dog, Pongo, who, football-shaped and over-fed, had nevertheless been the pride of his mistress's (Mrs Porker's) life. A temporary resident at the Hall, she longs to communicate with Pongo's spirit, and William (through a ventriloquially gifted acquaintance) appears to arrange this, to the advantage of his friend Miss Rossiter, whom Mrs Porker sees as a rival organiser of the fancy-goods stall at the bazaar.

There are more dead dogs in *William – The Pirate*. In chapter 5, Miss Morall, 'an unoffensive maiden lady' who lives next door but one to William, tearfully confides to him that her dog, Prince, has been poisoned by 'the gorilla' (her and William's new and nasty neighbour). Needless to say, for this and other ruthless acts William inflicts

an appropriate revenge upon the monstrous new-comer whom he forces to leave the district. In the preceding chapter William has arrived at his Aunt Jane's house. He has accepted her invitation to stay because things have become rather hot for him at home. Aunt Jane is the dull kind of aunt who asks him history dates and is obsessively house-proud and tidy. The ever optimistic William tries to look on the bright side; he remembers that a fat Pekinese lives near by 'into whose ordered life considerable excitement might be introduced'. He quickly learns, however, that the unfortunate animal 'died of overeating the month before'.

One of the most obnoxious of the spoilt dogs to cross William's path is a Pom called Sweetikins in *William – The Gangster*, 2. He belongs to an aunt who is staying with Ginger and, hopeful of helping Ginger to receive an end-of-visit tip, William, Henry and Douglas agree that he should bring Sweetikins on an exploration of the woods with

them. Ginger's aunt lumbers them with loads of instructions before they set off, including an admonition not to let 'that great rough mongrel' (Jumble) go near him – an unnecessary warning, as it turns out, because Jumble gives 'one look of disgust at Sweetikins' and walks off disdainfully. Sweetikins so horribly impedes the Outlaws' progress that they dump him at the bottom of a disused quarry whilst they pursue their customary exuberant adventures. Going to collect him afterwards they find that he has disappeared. (In fact BERTIE FRANKS has 'rescued' him, so that he might receive the medal which the Kindness to Animals League, a cranky organisation founded by the Vicar's wife, awards each month.) Fortunately William saves the day by substituting Henry's baby sister's toy dog for Sweetikins who is, so to speak, waiting in the wings while the Vicar's wife dilates long and ramblingly on the presumed sufferings of the abandoned dog and the bravery of Bertie. Ginger's aunt is happy at the safe return of her pet – 'Well, duckums, did 'ums have a nice walkums, den?' – and gives Ginger the hoped-for generous tip. Meanwhile Sweetikins snarls eloquently, trying to tell his mistress of the humiliations which have been inflicted upon him that afternoon. 'William had often wished that human beings could understand the language of animals, but now suddenly he felt glad that they could not.'

His encounters with canines get most out of hand in *William – The Showman*, 4. Things first go awry when he gives what he thinks is a mushroom to Nero, 'the elderly, cantankerous, short-sighted Yorkshire terrier' belonging to Miss Tressider, who is also elderly, cantankerous and short-sighted. He hears later that day that Nero has died and, convinced that he has 'murdered' the dog by giving him a toadstool in mistake, is overcome with remorse. To put things right he tries to buy a replacement brown Yorkshire terrier for Miss Tressider, but is unsuccessful because he has only sixpence halfpenny and the cheapest Yorkie in the petshop costs £10. Nothing daunted, William decides to find an unwanted dog instead. A genial mongrel called Hitler ('Itler to his owners) seems at first to fill the bill but slips through his grasp. His next choice is Hereward, who looks exactly like the late lamented Nero and is one of three dogs owned by Miss Mortimer of Marleigh. When chained by William to Nero's kennel Hereward howls so mournfully that Miss Tressider is convinced that her pet has returned to her in spirit. She goes to fetch Miss Bullamore, an amateur psychic, for an interpretation of the supposed ghost-dog's messages, but meanwhile William, ever conscientious over a problem for which he feels responsible, removes the howling Hereward in favour of Mr Cornish's bull terrier, Oberon. But he is the wrong colour, so William decides to put Farmer Jenks's young collie, Victoria, in his place. The climax is reached when Miss Tressider, Miss Bullamore, all the irate owners and their dogs come together in Miss Tressider's garden. Jumble turns up, too, and helps to trigger off the frantic four-cornered dog-fight which flares into 'a mass of growling, snarling, biting fur', with owners as well as animals being bitten. It is at this moment that Miss Tressider's housemaid, calmly watching the fray, informs William that Nero has not died from toadstool poisoning, but from being run over: 'A great big van, it was. Flattened 'im out, pore ole thing! . . . Blew 'is 'orn like mad, but Nero, 'e was that deaf . . ." '

Suddenly and wonderfully freed from qualms of conscience, William, exulting that after all he didn't waste his sixpence halfpenny on a replacement dog for Miss Tressider, washes his hands of the whole thing and walks cheerfully away. 'It was no use calling Jumble. Jumble never left a fight till there was no one left to fight with . . .' See also ANIMALS and JUMBLE.

Donber, Betty

See ROBERT AND HIS FRIENDS.

Douglas

See OUTLAWS, THE.

Dramatics

Amateur dramatics are featured in many of the stories, both at the adult level (with Ethel frequently in the heroine's rôle) and amongst the juvenile population, with plays and other entertainments written and produced by, and generally starring, William. These shows are a wonderful amalgam of comedy, melodrama and chaos. Similarly over-the-top elements dog William's efforts to assist in adult productions. A fairly early and interesting example occurs in *William – The Good*, 2, when he is co-opted by the local 'entirely feminine' Literary Society to help backstage, with sound and other effects. (It is hearing his fearful whistle – evocative of howling winds – which first suggests to the literary ladies that he might be useful in this function.) True to Miss Featherstone's nervous prediction that 'as soon as you begin to have men in a thing, it complicates it at once', William starts to impose upon the group his interpretation of how the play should be presented. Although his

tain-manipulator and scene-shifter for an R.A.F. production in Marleigh village hall. There is an unusual degree of mutual liking between him and the adult cast, and when some of these airmen actors are posted elsewhere at the last minute, William is determined to help out by providing a celebrity attraction for their show.

Professor Knowle bears a strong resemblance to the real-life C. E. M. Joad, a long-standing leading light in the popular B.B.C. 'Brains Trust' programme. The fictional professor (Knowle) is due to take part in a local version. William diverts him to the R.A.F. show where the audience (thinking that he is 'Professor Knowall', a comic impersonator of the real-life professor) is full of lively appreciation. Professor Knowle is gratified by this warm response but cannot understand why his comments on the Theory of Relativity are *quite* so well received, or why these stimulate questions from the audience such as 'Where do flies go in the winter time?' and 'What makes the fizz in champagne?' (each of which he tries conscientiously to answer).

Once again, William has saved the day!

Dressing Up

William, Ginger, Henry and Douglas sometimes dress up for their rôles in shows and so on, sometimes in order to disguise themselves in real life (for example, William as a spoof pensioner trying to obtain an official handout in *Sweet William*, 9) and sometimes simply to add conviction to their various games and fantasies. Whatever the purpose, their approach to dressing up and disguise is deadly earnest and never frivolous. In *William and the Evacuees*, 2, for instance, William, hoping to pursue a lucrative film career, plasters his face with lurid light-green house-paint because Ginger tells him that film make-up is yellow; and when investigating the activities of a supposed witch 'William

over-enthusiastic efforts are quenched by the producer at rehearsals, on the opening night he gives full rein to his sense of the dramatic, creating a truly deafening and what at first seems a never-ending storm and, although the action does not demand this, throwing a few squibs around during passages of dialogue to suggest that the war between the Cavaliers and the Roundheads is still being waged. The climax of the production comes when William (through ignorance rather than through intent) hurls the contents of a bucket of water over the heroine's head (instead of the torn-up pieces of paper which, reposing in another bucket, are supposed to represent falling snow).

References to plays and wide-ranging shows in which William has a hand are scattered plentifully through the saga. One of his most amusing contributions to the amateur stage occurs in *William and the Brains Trust*, 1, a story with a Second World War background. William has been appointed cur-

ultimate dressing-up irony occurs when, through one of the several mishaps in which he temporarily loses his own clothes, William stands 'revealed as the Fairy Queen in the middle of the Workhouse courtyard' in *William – The Fourth*, 11. See also Gipsies.

Drew, Miss

An attractive and long-suffering teacher of William, who appears in *Just – William*, 4; *More William*, 4; and *William – The Fourth*, 3. In her first recorded encounter with William she rather

wore a moustache that he had got out of a cracker at Christmas, Ginger wore a thick woollen scarf, covering his nose and mouth, Henry a tweed fishing hat of his father's and Douglas an old nylon stocking of his mother's drawn over his face' (*William and the Witch*, 4). Their costume improvisation is ingenious, with everything from formal table-linen to Ethel's lacy underwear being pressed into action. The only kind of dressing-up despised by the Outlaws is that inflicted on them by their mothers – in preparation for parties, or visits to and from relatives – which involves the wearing of Etons or other Sunday-best suits (and, of course, meticulous washing). Similarly William looks loftily down upon the garb of little girls who attend parties and his hated dancing classes 'dressed in fairy-like frills and furbelows with white socks and dancing-shoes' (*William's Happy Days*, 6). The despairingly keeps him in after school so that she can drum into him the arithmetical problems which have reduced him to boredom and bafflement in class. She doesn't really succeed, but William earnestly assures her that he now 'unnerstands'. He suddenly wants desperately to please her because 'William the devil-may-care pirate and robber-chief, the stern despiser of all things effeminate, felt the first dart of the malicious blind god. He blushed and simpered.'

Drink

The demon drink plays only a small part in the stories. Its most liberal partakers tend to be characters from the lower classes with unsocial habits and occupations (tramps, burglars and so on). There are few alcoholics amongst the village's middle-class adults, though frequently one of its impeccably sober citizens will accuse another of heavy drinking because of some uncharacteristically outrageous or irrational behaviour (which has almost certainly been triggered off, directly or indirectly, by William). Popular hostelries in and around the village include the Black Bull, the Blue Boar, the Blue Cow, the Blue Lion, the Green Dragon, the Red Lion, the Staff of Life, the White Lion and the Yellow Lizard, together with an unnamed village inn and village pub.

An early instance of supposed drunkenness affecting the story-line is seen in *William Again*, 3. Feeling, as he does so frequently, that his family do not appreciate or understand him, William takes temporary solace in a charabanc ride. An elderly lady with a pince-nez takes pity on him when they stop for tea, for which William has no money, and provides him with copious refreshments. The speed and relish with which he consumes these make her suspect that he is badly treated at home, and when she asks if his father drinks William nods 'sadly' and adds for good measure that his mother

drinks as well: 'William wondered whether to make Robert and Ethel drink, too, then decided not to. As an artist he knew the value of restraint.' The kindly lady buys William chocolates, sweets, bananas and a top as, carried away by his fantasies, he maintains the rôle of ill-treated innocent. Even when his benefactor insists on accompanying him to tackle his pitiless parents, and a flabbergasted Mrs Brown protests 'But we're both tee-totallers', the visitor is not wholly convinced that William is properly cherished. (Incidentally the Browns' abstinence from strong liquor is not maintained; there are instances of pre- and post-prandial tipples elsewhere in the stories which suggest that their younger son's anarchic exploits have occasionally driven them to drink.)

There is a fairly active Temperance Society in the village (see *Still – William*, 2, and *William – The Gangster*, 6) and one promoting Total Abstinence (see *William – The Good*, 9), but despite their persuasiveness there are fears that Ethel has embraced the bottle when William mistakenly thinks that his sister's temporarily reddened nose (the result of a cold) is alcohol-induced. He quite casually mentions to Dolly Morton's mother that Ethel drinks (and in the same episode draws Blanche Jones's mother's attention to her daughter's supposed kleptomaniacal tendencies). Ethel's response to this tarnishing of her reputation is not recorded (*William – The Good*, 1).

Dulcie (Mr Bagshott's niece)

See Robert and His Friends.

Durrant, Inspector

An officer in Hadley Police Force. (*William and the Witch*, 3)

Edwards, Miss

Serves in the post office. (*William the Lawless*, 5)

Egerton

A studious, bespectacled, conscientious boy, the
cousin of Robert's current girlfriend, Roxana. He
is staying with her family while his parents are
abroad. A birthday party is given for him during
his visit to which both the Outlaws and the Hubert
Laneites are invited; the uneasy atmosphere is
made more tense by the fact that Roxana coerces
Robert into performing conjuring tricks at which
he feels inept (though he is rescued by a MR
JONES), and Hubert's over-confident uncle is to
entertain the young guests for half an hour with 'a
little talk on his experiences abroad'. Egerton
behaves like the 'perfect little gentleman' throughout all the vicissitudes of his party. (*William – The
Explorer*, 3)

Egerton, Sir Julius

See FUNFAIRS AND FÊTES

Eglantine (1)

'Heglantine' – according to her own pronunciation
– is the leading light in a group of slum children
who are having a country day out in William's village. She is sufficiently spirited to appeal greatly to
William; she is also determined to enjoy her day
out, which is more than can be said for some others
in the party. City-bred urchins in the saga often
fail to appreciate the charms of country life.
The comments of one of Eglantine's associates,
Elbert 'Olmes, are typical: ' "Gimes! . . . Running
rices an' suchlike. An' lookin' at cows an' pickin'

flowers. Thanks! *Not much!*" ' In this episode
William succumbs to inverted snobbery, when he
learns that Elbert's 'farver . . . goes rahnd wiv a
barrer sellin' things' while Eglantine's 'sweeps
chimeneys' (sic). Bowing his head in shame,
William cannot bring himself to confess that his
father merely 'catches a train to London and his
office every morning', and so disowns him, in imi-
tation cockney language: ' "Ain't got no father," he
said doggedly.' (*William Again*, 5)

Eglantine (2)

A prize pig whose owner 'worshipped' her 'as a
savage might worship the totem of his tribe'. (See
BALLATER, MR). (*William*, 10)

Eleanor

See ROBERT AND HIS FRIENDS.

Ellen

See SERVANTS.

Emily

See SERVANTS.

Emma

See SERVANTS.

Emmeline (1)

See ROBERT AND HIS FRIENDS.

Emmeline (2)

A little girl who goes to the same (early co-educational) school as William. He detests her. (*Still – William*, 13)

Emmett

A fairly tough character who runs the local pet-shop, and appears in *William Carries On*, 8; *William – The Bold*, 8; and *William and the Space Animal*, 1. (In *William – The Fourth*, 9, the petshop owner was Mr Gorton: see CATS.)

'Erb

The leader of a street-gang with which William links up when the Browns are staying briefly in London: 'They had brought William with them chiefly because it was not safe to leave William behind.' 'Erb is a character after William's own heart, and so is each member of his gang. William finds life in London bleak and stale; he pines for his native fields and lanes, for the Outlaws and even for the 'irate farmers who helped to supply that spice of danger and excitement without which life to William and his friends was unendurable'. The only thing that intrigues him in the capital is the occasional glimpse of the 'world of street urchins, who fought and wrestled, and gave vent to piercing whistles, and hung on to the backs of carts, and paddled in the gutter, and rang front-door bells and fled from policemen'. Of course, such boys are not in his social milieu, but when he is invited to a party on his last evening in London by his mother's cousin in Kensington William spots and seizes his chance to get to grips with some exuberant juveniles. (Incidentally this episode from *William – The Fourth*, 7, illustrates

the callousness his family sometimes displays. None of them will escort him to this evening party. Ethel is going to the theatre, Robert thinks he deserves 'a bit of a rest' from William, Mrs Brown's rheumatism has come on again, and Mr Brown wants to read the evening paper. So they send an eleven-year-old boy, who is used only to the country, out alone into the great wicked city at night! Needless to say, William rejoices in his uncluttered-by-genteel-company state; even though he has been 'brushed and encased in his Eton suit', he is determined to seek out the urchins whom he has admired from afar – and, of course, to skip the party he should be attending.)

William, after linking up with 'Erb & Co., quickly sheds his pristine appearance, growing grimier by the minute, and 'happy at last . . . He was no longer a little gentleman staying at a select hotel with his family. He was a boy among boys – an outlaw among outlaws once more.' The climax

of his evening comes when 'Erb invites him ('Wot you doin' to-night, maite?') to join him in helping his 'o'd woman [mother] with the "corfee-stall" '. Delightedly William accepts the invitation, but Nemesis soon overtakes him in the shape of his family approaching the stall: hearing that William hasn't arrived at the party, their none too tender consciences are roused, and they have formed themselves into a search-party. While 'Erb's mother is reminding him that 'hevery thin' ' is double price for 'toffs', Mr Brown begins the process of penetrating his son's cockney disguise, and welcoming him back into the family with caustic and 'deadly' politeness; Robert snatches 'Erb's cap from his brother's head and says, 'You young devil!'; Ethel sneers, 'Goodness, just *look* at his clothes'; and Mrs Brown – who at least has some finer feelings – says, 'Oh, my darling little William, and I thought I'd lost you.'

Ethel and Her Friends

Ethel's age seems established (unlike Robert's, which fluctuates) at around nineteen. She is without doubt one of the best-looking girls in the village, a queen with a small but shifting group of courtiers and adherents. She thrives on admiration from the opposite sex, although her relationships with women seem unsatisfactory and in the realms of rivalry rather than of friendship. Catty comments on the new hat or hair-do of Dolly Clavis or some other village belle occasionally punctuate the text; 'friends' of her own sex, such as Blanche, Daphne, Gladys Barker, Peggy Barlow or Doris Clarke, are shadowy figures and, like Ethel, apparently short on intellectual, political or philosophical interests. It is significant that Ethel manages to avoid involvement in the more serious activities of the Under Thirty Club of which Robert is the conscientious president: she attends its fortnightly dances, but not its regular lectures (*William – The*

Explorer, 1). She is in essence a fatuous and work-shy 'flapper', whose red-gold hair and wonderfully blue eyes ensnare at one time or another almost every eligible unmarried male resident of the village as well as every eligible bachelor who visits it. William, of course, frequently if unintentionally throws a mucky spanner into her seductively perfumed works, especially when he is motivated by a wish to marry her off, as in *Still – William*, 8. He fixes on a stumpy, bald, short-sighted, arch and conceited young man who is 'gone' on Ethel. This admirer, Mr March by name, has also 'gotter lot of money an' a nice garden an' a big house'. William thinks that he is doing Ethel a favour in cooking up (with Joan) an elaborate and – for Ethel – acutely embarrassing match-making scheme. Her threat when all is revealed – ' "You *hateful* boy . . . I'm going straight home to tell father" ' – and her subsequent passionate plea to her mother – ' ". . . can't we do anything about William? Can't we send him to an orphanage or anything?" ' – are, with variations, repeated throughout the saga. It is not surprising that she frequently feels her life would be happier without

The 1930s (by Thomas Henry)

The 1920s (by Thomas Henry)

The 1960s (by Henry Ford)

him, and that he heartily reciprocates: ' "I've took a lot of trouble trying to get her married . . . and this is how she pays me . . . She's turnin' out to be an ole maid . . . Seems to me she's goin' to go on livin' in our house all her life till she dies, an' that's a nice look out for me, isn't it?" '

The shallowness of Ethel's friendships with girls of her own age is indicated by the fact that her most selfless action for any of them is to help Peggy Barlow with a home perm when requested: the lack of depth and the edge of rivalry in such relationships is neatly conveyed, too, in *William – The Showman*, 10, when Doris Clarke, 'her girl friend of the moment', is discussing with her a 'love test' which Ethel is setting up as a gauge of the true feelings of two rivals for her affections: Richard and Charles.

Doris first suggested that Ethel should shave her eyebrows completely and cut off her hair close to her head and see which of the two suitors still loved her thus disfigured. Ethel received this suggestion coldly. Next, Doris suggested that Ethel should go to the tennis tournament wearing clothes selected from the 'jumble' that was stored in Mrs. Brown's attic in readiness for the rummage-sale and see which of them would then wish to be her escort. This suggestion, too, Ethel received coldly. Nothing daunted, Doris next suggested that Ethel should pretend to be drunk at the tennis tournament and see which of them continued to love her thus publicly disgraced. Ethel's coldness deepened in intensity.

Even if Ethel's girlfriends are not always fully appreciative of her charms, there is no doubt that her boyfriends are. Even before she starts to flutter her long eyelashes alluringly, they respond to her appearance and general charisma:

Suddenly someone appeared in the doorway. To the young man it was as if a radiant goddess had stepped down from Olympus. The barn was full of heavenly light. He went purple to the roots of his ears.

To William it was as if a sister whom he considered to be elderly and disagreeable and entirely devoid of all personal charm had appeared. He groaned . . .

A fairly comprehensive list of Ethel's admirers, and some of her girlfriends, and the books in which they are first mentioned, is given below. It should be noted, however, that Jack Morgan is only a friend (despite William embarrassingly mistaking him for a suitor and acting accordingly), and that JIMMIE MOORE has a special claim on Ethel, as he seems to be the only boyfriend with whom she has been genuinely in love. See also BROWN FAMILY.

Book	Character
27.8	Archie
21.8	Ashtead, Dr Horace
5.8	Barker, Gladys
26.8	Bell, Ronald
4.2	Blanche
4.11	Brooke, Mr
19.10	Charles
19.10	Clarke, Doris
6.8	Curate, The
9.6	Daphne
12.6	Dewar, Mr
3.6	Drew, Mr
29.4	Fenchurch, Lionel
9.6	Foxe, Lucy
26.8	Franklin, Gordon
26.8	Franks, Oswald
1.11	French, James
3.6	French, Mr
9.6	George (Douglas's brother)
22.3	Glover, Wing Commander
7.6	Greene, Moyna

9.6	Hector (Ginger's brother)
5.14	Hinlock, Laurence
13.8	Jameson Jameson
26.8	John (Henry's brother)
2.11	Jones, Mr Percival
3.6	Loughton, Mr
27.2	Maidstone, Colonel
5.8	March, Mr George
8.3	Markson, Mr (Markie)
26.8	Monkton, Bruce
13.8	Moore, Jimmie
13.8	Morency, Marmaduke
1.1	Morgan, Jack
26.8	Peter
19.10	Richard
3.6	Romford, Mr
7.4	Solomon, Mr
7.4	Vernon, Rudolph
6.8	a young curly-haired man
8.8	an elegant man
9.4	a youth (projecting teeth)
9.6	an artist
13.1	a youth (immaculate)
15.1	a young man

Evacuees

See WARTIME.

Everton-Massinger, The Honourable Mrs

The Secretary of the Women's Guild. (*William and the Space Animal*, 4)

Evesham, Miss

William – The Bold, 4, begins with William receiving a letter from Joan asking him to succeed where smart solicitors have failed, in evicting Miss Evesham, the 'unfurnished' tenant of their home in the village. William's campaign starts inauspiciously: he accidentally kills Miss Evesham's cat, Hector, with his air-gun. He manages, however, to find her a substitute feline, without her realising that this is not her beloved Hector, and he discovers her weak spot: a very emotional belief in witchcraft. Exploiting this, with 'catty' props and the help of Miss Perrott (the current writer-in-residence at Honeysuckle Cottage, who looks like a witch although she is firmly down-to-earth), William is soon able to frighten Miss Evesham into shaking his village's dust from her heels for ever. The chapter ends with a terse but fulfilling letter:

'Deer Joan,
   It's orl rite, you can cum bak now.
   luv from
    WILLIAM.'

See also 'JOAN'.

Fairies, Magic and the Supernatural

There is an undeniably down-to-earth quality about the William books, but Richmal Crompton nevertheless allows her flair for fantasy and the supernatural to flourish occasionally, even though the context tends to remain firmly humorous. We are told in *William's Happy Days*, 7, that although the Outlaws 'treated the idea of fairies with incredulous scorn' they had 'a wholesome respect for witches'. Spooks, too, although William is not above mocking up a ghost when the occasion demands (see *More William*, 7, in which, in repayment of her generous gifts of sweets, etc., he provides his elderly would-be-esoteric Cousin Mildred with the 'psychic revelation' she longs for so much). Psychic (or pseudo-psychic) moments in the stories make invigorating reading; William accidentally smothered in soot, mud or pond-slime can strike terror into the heart of many a hysterical domestic servant or householder. In fact he is probably more convincing when he is unconsciously ghostly than when he deliberately sets out to 'haunt' someone: ' "It'd be more *fun* being a ghost than *anythin'* – even a pirate." "I dunno," said Douglas, "they can't *eat . . ."* '

One occasion on which he and the Outlaws are mistaken for ghostly visitants is described in *Still – William*, 7. He tangles again with the Society for the Encouragement of Higher Thought (see also AUTHORS) when, under the guidance of the redoubtable Miss Hatherly, the high-minded ladies decide to explore potential psychic phenomena in the empty house of the recently demised Colonel Henks: 'The Society for the Encouragement of Higher Thought had exhausted' nearly every relevant subject and 'had almost been driven to begin again at Sublimity or Relativity. (They didn't want to because . . . they were all still doubtful as to what they meant.)' Unfortunately the late Colonel's residence is not only a 'haunted house', but also a secret refuge of the Outlaws – the smugglers' den, Indian camp or castle where they can reasonably expect to function undisturbed by irritatingly inquisitive adults. They arrive there for a midnight feast of fruit, cheesecakes, chocolate creams, pickled onions and liquorice water on a night when Miss Hatherly and her cronies are installed, awaiting psychic messages. Fleeing guiltily from Miss Hatherly's approaching footsteps, they leave behind Robert's overnight bag, 'borrowed' by William for the purpose of transporting the provisions. Miss Hatherly finds the bag and excitedly reveals its supposed esoteric contents at a meeting of the Society on the following day. Sadly, its contents are only too ordinary and physical: Robert's heavily darned socks and other garments, and a romantic poem addressed to Miss

Hatherly's niece, Marion (Robert's current inamorata), which unfortunately is also a hymn of hate against her dragonish guardian aunt.

Higher Thinkers are not the only gullible characters encountered by William. Hubert Lane believes in fairies and magic generally, and William has occasion to exploit his naïveté several times. In *William Carries On*, 3, it is the period of the Second World War, and the Outlaws and the Laneites are building up rival collections of shrapnel and other air-raid memorabilia. The Laneites are greatly helped by the fact that Hubert's mother offers money to her acquaintances in bombed areas for trophies such as pieces of incendiary bombs, nose-caps, copper driving-bands, and so on. The Outlaws, however, have a wonderful ally in Katie, Farmer Jenks's land-girl, who provides them with whatever trophies she can find, including a German bomb-stick, which becomes the pride of their collection and the envy of the Laneites who then vengefully steal Katie's (or, rather, Farmer

Jenks's) fork. William is determined to retrieve it for her before Jenks docks from her wages the cost of replacing it. He tells Hubert that on Midsummer Eve (fortunately fast approaching) Jenks's scarecrow will come to life, visit ' "anyone what's stole anythin' out of their fields . . . and get it back off them" '. When, for good measure, he adds that the scarecrow knocks about its victims with the strength of ten men the cowardly Hubert is suitably ready to capitulate. When at 10.30 on Midsummer Eve he spies from his bedroom window the familiar figure of Jenks's scarecrow (it is, of course, actually William in the scarecrow's clothes) stomping up his garden path, he flings the stolen fork down from his window in bleating terror.

The Outlaws, however, are similarly gullible about the power of supposed witches. They decide in *William and the Witch*, 4, that Miss Tyrral, who lives in an isolated house and makes clay models, is a witch, and that her models are for the purpose of putting spells on people. They terrify themselves into believing that she is sticking pins in a model which resembles Mrs Brown, in order to murder her. (Mrs Brown *does* develop a very bad cold.) Similarly, in *William – The Outlaw*, 2, prompted by Joan whose 'soppy fairy-tale stuff' they eventually believe, they feel sure that Mr Galileo Simpkins, 'a very simple and inoffensive and well-meaning little man' and a newcomer to the village, is a magician because they spot a skeleton in his house, and note that he is pottering with 'test tubes and pestles and mortars and crucibles' (he is, of course, a scientist). Their gullibility leads them eventually to believe, when they get the chance to dabble with his equipment, that they can put a spell on Mr Simpkins and turn him into a donkey. It transpires that they see him peacefully reading a novel in a field; minutes later he is, unknown to the Outlaws, called away suddenly. Farmer Jenks brings his donkey, Maria, into the field, and she settles down in a position which sug-

gests that she is reading the book which Simpkins has forgetfully left behind. William & Co. come along and, convinced that Maria is Galileo transmogrified, are appalled by what their experimentation with 'magic' has achieved.

In *William – In Trouble*, 2, William has more prosaic dealings with the fairies. Susceptible to the 'dimples and dark curls' of a little girl who wants to get out of performing in her school play, he offers to take on her part. It is, however, the rôle of 'Fairy Daffodil', and the little girl protests that he doesn't really resemble a fairy. He presses into action what he considers to be his histrionic ability, and rearranges his rugged features into a simper that is 'a mixture of coyness and imbecility'. Dressed like a daffodil, but distinctly un-flower-or-fairy-like, he *does* play the part, with comically disastrous results.

Fairlow, Miss

See Authors.

Fairman, Miss

Yet another temporary resident of Honeysuckle Cottage (*William – The Detective*, 8). Miss Fairman is a charitably minded lady who is collecting waste paper to sell in aid of a home for deaf and dumb children. William is collecting scrap paper for a paper chase and he takes some old hand-written 'exam papers' from Robert's bedroom; it transpires that these have been left there by Robert's 'brilliant' friend Ward Hadlow. Robert is frantic when they disappear, telling his family that they represent the manuscript of his friend's great historical novel! Meanwhile William has handed the papers to Ginger, who has passed half of them to Miss Fairman. The latter has made a house-to-house appeal for scrap paper, and Ginger, surrendering 'abjectedly' to the charms of Miss Fairman's niece who accompanies her, has been moved to respond. (The niece has 'golden curls and blue eyes and dark sweeping lashes'; having 'flickered her blue eyes at Ginger' she serves no further purpose in the plot and does not reappear. Ginger's temporary moment of mild infatuation is, however, worthy of note.)

In an effort to retrieve Robert's friend's manuscript, William is presented by Ginger to Miss Fairman as a deaf and dumb boy, for whom the papers, rather than the proceeds obtainable from their eventual sale, are important. Miss Fairman, of course, is too conscientious to leave the matter there; she visits William's house. (Ginger has claimed that William is the son of the charwoman there, because the charity supported by Miss Fairman can only help *poor* deaf and dumb children.) It is her intention to get William into a special school which will enable him to make the best of his handicap. She gets short shrift from the Browns' charwoman, Mrs Hobbins, who resents being called a char anyway: ' "I obliges here occasional, if that's what you mean," she said with great dignity.' Mrs Hobbins is convinced that the well-meaning Miss Fairman is simply ' "comin' insultin' of decent hard-workin' folks an' tryin' to kidnap their children" '.

Miss Fairman realises that Mrs Hobbins is not William's mother, and then addresses herself to Mrs Brown, whom she tactfully calls a 'lady help', as the term 'charwoman' has obviously upset the belligerent Mrs Hobbins. In the middle of the ensuing conversation, in which Mrs Brown is, as so often, rendered speechless with astonishment, Robert joyfully interrupts with the news that Ward Hadlow's manuscript has turned up in his own home after all, and that the papers abstracted by William are merely a rough draft which Ward was going to destroy anyway.

Falkner, Mr

An ex-schoolmate of Mr Brown who, in *William – The Conqueror*, 3, has been staying in the Browns' home 'for a very long time'. A bore and a thundering egoist, 'Mr. Falkner talked perpetually, and the subject of all his conversation was Mr. Falkner. Mr. Falkner was a never-ending source of interest to Mr. Falkner.' The Browns' guest is short and stout, with a round face and 'a small blighted moustache'. Apart from diligently practising his imitations of Mr Falkner's squeaky voice and glassy stare, William leaves him well alone, though he rather welcomes Falkner's accounts of his supposed exploits of 'dauntless bravery and dazzling cleverness' which reduce the adults to 'a certain apathy of hopelessness' at mealtimes. Mr Falkner is impervious to hints about terminating his lengthy and open-ended visit, untouched by the glorious gems of sarcasm which occasionally fall from Mr Brown's lips.

However, the time comes when William has to take things in hand. Aghast at the low levels of attainment suggested by William's school report (see REPORTS), Mr Falkner takes it upon himself to make William's holidays hideous by imparting regular instruction each morning; he also commits the unforgivable sin of referring to him as 'Willy'.

One evening William announces (quite erroneously) that a leopard has escaped from a visiting circus. Falkner, who on previously noticing the Browns' leopard-skin rug has boasted about his skill in shooting leopards (' "No leopard would dream of attacking me . . . Big game shooting is like knocking down skittles to me . . ." '), is made by Mr Brown to go out with his host's gun to stalk and shoot (or subdue by sheer force of personality) the escaped leopard. The boastfully tough but inwardly soft-centred Falkner finds himself in the darkened garden, with strange, stealthy and then aggressive animal noises all around him. In terror he clambers on to the roof of the summer-house, while William (half-hidden by the bushes and the leopard-skin rug) prowls noisily below. After a night of craven anguish, Mr Falkner learns from an apparently innocent William that he had taken the leopard-skin rug into the garden for some 'spring-cleaning' fresh air, and that as he couldn't sleep he had been playing in the garden 'mos'ly round the summer house'. Like so many visitors to the Brown household, Mr Falkner gratifyingly rushes to take the next train home, knowing that even though his skin has been saved his face, with William's knowledge of the facts of his night outdoors, will certainly not be!   There is a rare moment of rapport between William and his father who, with Falkner's departure, seems to have discovered 'the elixir of perpetual youth'. A half-crown discreetly changes hands.

Farqueson, Augustus

One of those unfortunate people who come to William's village or a nearby location to lecture on some innocuous subject (in this instance, Central Asia) but are diverted by William to suit his own purposes to another venue, which generally involves long and arduous tramping over stiles and through muddy fields. (*William – In Trouble*, 7)

Faversham, Lord

See V.I.P.s.

Fawshaw, Miss Rubina Thomasina

A speaker who is giving 'a lucid account of the effect of alcohol upon the liver' to a Total Abstinence meeting, and whose flow is interrupted by rude and rumbustious comments from Ginger's aunt's escaped parrot who – with William – has gate-crashed the meeting. (*William – The Good*, 9)

Fellowes, Maisie

William and the Evacuees, 1, tells us that Maisie is 'a roly poly of a girl, who bore a striking resemblance to Queen Victoria in her old age'. She is not a particular ally of William and the Outlaws but is often one of the group of juveniles which comes to support (or to sneer at) their shows and other ventures. She is also mentioned in *William and the Tramp*, 6; *William and the Space Animal*, 1; *William's Television Show*, 5 and 8; *William and the Witch*, 3; and *William the Superman*, 1 and 4.

Fenchurch, Lionel

See ETHEL AND HER FRIENDS.

Ferris, Mr

Temporary head of William's school in *William's Happy Days*, 8, when the regular headmaster is 'away with a nervous breakdown' (something fairly common among William's teachers). Mr Ferris is the regular sixth-form master, 'a muscular young man with a keen eye, upon whose notice William has always modestly shrunk from obtruding himself'. He has the saving grace of a sense of humour. See also ANGELA (2) and SCHOOLS.

Films

Although William and the Outlaws are hardly regular cinema-goers, there is no doubt that films have influenced their actions and ideas fairly frequently. In the first book of the series, *Just – William*, the opening chapter is called 'William Goes to the Pictures'. As has been pointed out elsewhere, the order of the stories in the books certainly does not always correspond with the order in which they were originally published in the magazines (see Appendix 2), nor with the order in which Richmal Crompton wrote them. However, there *are* indications that 'William Goes to the Pictures' is indeed the first William story ever written; Richmal confirmed this to Eric Fayne (then the editor of the *Collectors' Digest*) during the 1950s and in conversations with others.

This chapter is one of the most amusing of the William stories. Given a shilling by an aunt (for posting a letter and carrying her parcels from the grocer's) the unusually affluent William lashes out on 'sixpennoth' of Gooseberry Eyes, and spends his remaining sixpence on a visit (the second of his life) to the cinema. He sees a very full programme of four films, each thrilling in its own way. Still under the influence of these cinematic delights, he alienates his father by knocking him into a rhododendron-bush (William is at the time escaping from imaginary pursuers), and moves Joan, the little girl next door, to pity by suggesting that he will die young like the juvenile hero of one of the films, and, like another small boy cinematic character, tries to sort out his sister's romantic entanglements (with disastrous results for Ethel). Lastly he emulates one of the workmen in the funniest of the four

films which he has seen by attacking the paint on his bedroom door 'with a lighted taper in one hand and penknife in the other'. It is no wonder, perhaps, that at the end of the day the infuriated Mr Brown declares that his younger son is 'stark, raving insane', or that William, in response to his father's extraordinarily vituperative behaviour, wonders if Mr Brown, like the renegade in one of the afternoon's films, is a drunkard!

The cinematic influences conveyed in *Just – William* are very much those of the early pre-talkies films. *William – The Rebel*, 12, is concerned with the effects that Hollywood in its 1930s heyday had on the smart young things (rather than those of William's generation) in the village:

> The root of Robert's trouble, of course, was that he frequented the 'pictures' and fell in love regularly with the star who took the principal part in every film he saw. He had fallen in love with Cornelia Gerrard because she reminded him of Greta Garbo, but a few weeks later he went to see a film featuring Marlene Dietrich, with the result that he had decided that Cornelia was not his type, after all, but that Lorna Barton, whose profile really had a distinct look of Marlene Dietrich, was his true soul's mate.

(Similarly Cornelia has tired of Robert and wonders how she ever considered that he resembled Ronald Colman. She has now become engaged to Peter Greenham – mainly, one gathers, because he reminds her of Maurice Chevalier.)

Film influences in the full-length novel *Just William's Luck* have moved on from the high drama and heady romances of Hollywood to the more obvious home-grown glamour of the postwar Rank-starlet type of world (see ABBOT, ROSALYN).

It is intriguing that after so often seeking satisfaction and stimulus from watching films William should himself inspire the making of real films (see WILLIAM IN PERFORMANCE).

Finch, James

William – The Conqueror, 9, refers to Finch as 'the village reprobate'. He seems to make only one appearance in the saga (see ANGELA (1)), and it suggests he has a penchant for alcoholic liquor.

Finch, Miss(es)

Two separate ladies called Miss Finch are featured in *William's Crowded Hours*, 2. The Outlaws hear with foreboding that their headmaster (here referred to as Mr Marks, rather than as the more usual Markson) is going to marry a Miss Finch. They are determined to blight his romance

because, though stern in school, he remains deliberately unaware of his pupils' possibly questionable activities outside, whereas (in the Outlaws' view) any potential headmaster's wife will be monitoring (and complaining about) their out-of-school exploits. They hit upon the scheme of displaying William (bandaged because he has exploded the family geyser) and suggesting to Miss Finch that her fiancé is a violent drunk who at times assaults his pupils. It turns out that this Miss Finch, who is angular, bespectacled and humourless, is *not* the headmaster's fiancée, but is engaged to Augustine Potter, a 'gloomy-looking man' who is one of the school governors. Later they encounter the other Miss Finch, who *is* to marry the head; she is 'extremely pretty . . . with dark eyes, dimples, and dark curling hair' and a sympathetic lively nature. When they tell her the whole story she promises to put things right both with the other Miss Finch and with Mr Potter, as well as with her fiancé, 'Ole Markie'. See also MARKS/MARKSON, MR and SCHOOLS.

Finchley, Mr

See DIMTRITCH.

Fireworks

William rather despairingly points out to his father in *William and the Space Animal*, 3, that 'it's a sort of *juty* to have fireworks on Guy Fawkes day', to celebrate the fact that he tried to save the country 'from havin' a Parliament'. With his shaky knowledge of history he equates Guy Fawkes with national heroes such as Nelson. His pleas, however, do not move Mr Brown, who has just received a 'smouldering, sputtering rocket' (used by William hopefully to enable one of his arrows to reach the moon!) full in the stomach. Not surprisingly, perhaps, William's bow and arrows are confiscated, and he is forbidden to have any fireworks on 5 November, or even to go to a public display of them. This kind of parental ban is not uncommon, and William generally manages to circumvent it. Other reasons than misbehaviour, however, put adults off the idea of providing fireworks for their child relatives or friends. In *William's Treasure Trove*, 6, Frankie Parsons – one of William's friends – is bemoaning the fact that the aunt who used to send him money for fireworks has joined a society which is against blood sports and, by some connected but convoluted reasoning, she has decided to cut off his usual Guy Fawkes subsidy. (This, published in 1962, is probably a reflection of society's increasing fears about the dangers and misuses of fireworks. It is in marked contrast with another episode (*William*, 7) in which the Outlaws' rather stern fathers are carried away with enthusiasm one Guy Fawkes day and have a whale of a time letting off their sons' fireworks.)

Fish, Evangeline

See FOOD.

Fisher, Thomas Henry

See HENRY, THOMAS.

Flower, Miss

See ROBERT AND HIS FRIENDS.

Food

Food is used in the William stories as a symbol of both acute enjoyment and power.

William and the Outlaws have the normally healthy appetite of boyhood, and details of their repasts are often recounted lovingly in the stories. In *Sweet William*, for example, chapter 1 shows William dulling 'the keen edge of his appetite' with some thick slices of bread and jam, and on another occasion being diverted from the tricky business of bringing a criminal to justice by demolishing at one of Mrs Bott's afternoon teas the best part of a large chocolate iced cake. In chapter 3, although he is preoccupied in working out another of his great schemes and therefore getting through his tea as soon as possible, William still manages 'three helpings of jelly'. His presence, in chapter 5, at Sir Gerald and Lady Markham's Christmas party embarrasses fellow-guests Ethel and Robert, but undeterred by their disapproval he does full justice to an excellent supper and continues 'to eat for quite five minutes' after everyone else has finished. In chapter 6, mistaken for the thatcher's boy, he erroneously thinks he is being offered refreshments, and devours a jelly, a trifle, a plate of biscuits and half an iced cake before he realises that the feast which he is tackling single-handed has not been laid out for his delectation but for someone's party. Chapter 9 highlights the Outlaws' problems in obtaining provisions without the knowledge of their families; in this instance they are preparing to tramp to London as part of their campaign to secure 'penshuns' for boys:

> Ginger had been put in charge of the provisions. He had brought a broken and discarded attaché-case of his brother's to carry them in and each of the four had contributed what they could. William had brought some apples, Henry some bulls'-eyes and a packet of ants' eggs (which, he said, must contain nourishment or goldfish could not live on them), Douglas some rock cakes into which the cook had forgotten to put baking powder, and which she had given to a

beggar who had tasted one and left the others on the front doorstep, Ginger a tin of sardines, opened and half full.

William has a very good understanding of certain people's psychological dependence on food, and he harnesses this to good effect when tangling with Evangeline Fish, the fair-haired, blue-eyed and self-conscious beauty of his class at school. She is elected by the other pupils to be the May Queen (but not supported by William who, despite accepting from Evangeline a bribe of six bulls'-eyes, deliberately spoils his voting paper). William, cast in the rôle of swain, is horrified when he realises that he is expected to hold Queen Evangeline's train. He makes up his mind radically to alter the May Day plans: he will be the May King, and quiet, dark-haired, unassuming Bettine Franklin will be the May Queen. At a schoolmate's party he becomes aware that, despite Evangeline's ethereal appearance, she has a gargantuan appetite: 'William accorded her a certain grudging admiration. Not once did she falter or faint. Iced cakes, cream cakes, pastries melted away before her . . .' On May Day he expends a conveniently acquired five-shilling tip on sweet and sticky comestibles and, waylaying Evangeline on her way to her coronation rituals, shows her into the Browns' wood-shed where she sees rows of 'pastries, and sugar cakes, and iced cakes, and currant cakes'. He

leaves her rapturously gobbling, and goes on to become the triumphant May King (garbed in his bus-conductor's cap and a corked moustache), supported by Bettine as his consort (with an old fairy-dress of Ethel's slipped over her workaday print frock) (*More William*, 8).

On several occasions William & Co. worst their principal enemies, the fat and greedy Laneites, by seizing and devouring the cream buns, jellies and ice-creams which Hubert's besotted mother has provided for her darling boy and his cronies. This is a comparatively easy manoeuvre when Hubert's Aunt Emmy is put in charge of the party. She is kindly, well meaning, vague and extremely short-sighted, being unable apparently to differentiate between one boy and another (with the exception, of course, of 'darling Hubie'). Examples of William's taking over a party of Hubert's whole-sale occur in *William – The Conqueror*, 13 (see CHRISTMAS) and in *William Carries On*, 10, when his triumph has a special edge because it is wartime when food, particularly of the sugary fancy variety, is in short supply.

Another wartime party worthy of mention is one of Violet Elizabeth's (there was never a real food-shortage at the Botts'; the implication is that they were discreet dabblers in the black market). The party is attended by the 'self-styled expert in child psychology', Mrs Dayford (see DAYFORD, CLAUDE), who urges the village children to eat as little as possible of the wonderful spread which has been put before them, so that generous leftovers might be given to 'the strangers we have welcomed into our midst, the evacuees'. Ignoring her appeal to their 'honour', and 'self-sacrifice', 'as one man the little guests fell upon the feast . . . The thought that the residue was to go to the evacuees had whetted their appetites.' They all, apparently, had suffered at the hands of the 'tough young guys from the East End of London whose methods of warfare were novel and unpleasant', and the knowledge that 'their tormentors' might profit from their abstinence 'urged them on to yet greater feats of gastronomy' with jellies, trifles, blancmange, biscuits, and cakes disappearing 'as if at the wave of a magician's wand' (*William Does His Bit*, 10).

Violet Elizabeth remembers that food, especially during wartime shortages, represents power. In *William and the Brains Trust*, 2, she invites William to tea and, seeing a refusal about to be uttered, hastens to add: ' "There'th chocolate bithcuith." "All right, I'll come," he said . . .' See also LIQUORICE WATER and SWEETS AND SWEETSHOPS.

Football

See SPORTS.

Forrester, Dolores

See ROBERT AND HIS FRIENDS.

Fortescue, Captain (nicknamed 'Capting-Fusspot')

See GROWN-UP FRIENDS.

Fortescue, Colonel

See CHRISTMAS.

Fountain, Mrs Priscilla

See GROWN-UP FRIENDS.

Frame, Mrs

See NEIGHBOURS.

Francis

William's cousin of the same age as himself. Francis is fat and a cissy, and in *William Again*, 2, is, like William, summoned to the supposed deathbed of Great-Aunt Jane. (She lives in Ireland and has never seen William, which seems to be the only possible reason why she should invite him to

darken her doorstep and deathbed.) One feels that Francis's parents, who are also in attendance, hope that their son's white suit, golden hair and winsome manner will ensure for them rich pickings from Great-Aunt Jane's estate. However, while Great-Aunt Jane is asleep, Francis and William, who are in the sickroom, pass the time by exchanging deadly insults and then starting to fight. The excitement of this seems to resuscitate their dying relative, who makes no bones about her partiality for William: ' "Go it, William . . . Get one in on his nose," ' she exhorts, sitting up in bed, bright-eyed and full of interest in life once again. Her great-nephews (or more probably her great-great-nephews), the cissy and the desperado, have effected a cure.

Franklin, Bettine

See Food and Insects.

Franklin, Gordon

See Ethel and Her Friends.

Franklin, Major

An elderly man of military appearance whom the Outlaws encounter when they are wandering in the wood. He is *very* fast asleep in a Bath chair; and, fascinated by the spectacle, William, Ginger, Henry and Douglas take over both the chair and its occupant as apparatus for their various games. When they tire of their new 'toy' they sell it as a package to Victor Jameson and some of his friends for threepence. They in turn pass on the sleeping Major, and when eventually William tries to track down his whereabouts it is a complicated process. However, it leads to William's receiving a half-crown tip from desperate relatives (who fear a kidnapping), although neither they nor the Major are particularly pleased to find that he has ended up in a pigsty! The military gentleman hasn't been in command of his own destiny on that day, because his relatives, fed up with his 'absolutely foul' temper and having to dance attendance on him, have popped a sleeping draught into his wine. (William's Crowded Hours, 9)

Franks, Bertie

The second-in-command of Hubert Lane's gang, and a sworn enemy of the Outlaws, Bertie appears in twenty-two stories, beginning with William – The Conqueror, 13, and ending with William and the Witch, 3. The first reference describes him as 'the most odious of the Hubert Laneites next to Hubert himself', and he is said to be – like all Hubert's followers – pale and fat. However, in

Thomas Henry's illustrations Bertie doesn't look particularly overweight, but possibly the artist kept him leanish to distinguish him from his podgy leader. In *William – The Gangster*, 1, we learn that Bertie has started his own gang, but his independence from the horrid Hubert is short-lived, and by chapter 9 of the same book he has 'long since tired of having a gang of his own' and rejoined the Laneites. Hubert is 'making him pay for his defection by detailing him off to do all the unpleasant work connected with the gang'.

Franks, Oswald

Oswald, the elder brother of Bertie, is about the same age as Robert (or Ethel); one of Robert's associates rather than chums, he plays a part in eight episodes, beginning with *William – In Trouble*, 7, and ending with the last of all the books, *William the Lawless*, 5. An admirer of Ethel, he very nearly achieves the distinction of being her finally favoured boyfriend, but is ousted almost in the last moments of the saga by ARCHIE MANNISTER, the ever faithful artist-devotee of William's fearfully fetching sister. Oswald has a sophistication which Robert would dearly love to emulate and, being the brother of the nasty little Bertie, it is not surprising that he is insecure, pretentious and unscrupulous.

All these characteristics are well illustrated in Oswald's first appearance, when he takes over the poetry circle which is made up of Robert, his friend Jameson Jameson, Ginger's brother Hector and Douglas's brother George. Oswald loftily names the group the Society of Twentieth Century Poets; he rules the roost, both administratively and poetically, easily winning each week the badge which is presented to the member who produces the best original poem. (Oswald's poems aren't originals but cribs from the classics and elsewhere; fortunately for him, the other would-be poets are

too ignorant of the subject to realise this.) Robert and his friends become more and more depressed by their ineptitude and Oswald's brilliance. William and the Outlaws (who secretly but determinedly observe their elder brothers' literary flounderings) also become more and more infuriated by Oswald's triumphs, which are constantly rubbed in by Bertie. Happily Oswald's over-confidence brings about his downfall. At Hector's suggestion, the members of the Society of Twentieth Century Poets all enter a poetry competition organised by a newspaper called the *Young Crusader*. Intent upon winning, Oswald arrogantly submits a 'fairly well-known sonnet of Shakespeare's'; he is disqualified ignominiously, with the editor writing a long article pointing out Oswald's immorality to all his readers. Rather astoundingly, Robert wins – and on his own merits, though William thinks that he has ensured his brother's success by nobbling the adjudicator (he has actually tackled the wrong man). Robert and his friends – despite their pseudo-sophistication – are cock-a-hoop at his achievement and at the fact that the uppity but unmasked Oswald has to retire temporarily into a very private life until his 'unenviable notoriety' fades. William and the

Outlaws probably feel even more triumphant than their brothers as they have the double joy of seeing both Oswald and Bertie well and truly worsted.

This episode, incidentally, provides plenty of (un)poetic gems, including 'He bashed him dead/ An' blood came pourin' out of his head' from William.

French, James

One of Ethel's earliest admirers, who enlists William's help in the initial stages of the courting process. He bribes him with the gift of two white rats. See also ETHEL AND HER FRIENDS. (*Just – William*, 11)

French, Mr

Often referred to as Frenchie, he is one of William's teachers (see SCHOOLS), appearing (or mentioned) in some fifteen stories from *William Again*, 7, to *William the Lawless*, 3, by which time he has become engaged and is sufficiently popular with the Outlaws for them to want to buy him a wedding present. See also ALBERT (1) and ETHEL AND HER FRIENDS.

Funfairs and Fêtes

The zest with which funfairs are described in the saga is well demonstrated in the first mention of them (*Just – William*, 11). William is receiving generous handouts from James French, a young man who has succumbed to Ethel's charms, and who hopefully but erroneously thinks that William's assistance will aid the courting process. William spends one of his half-crown tips at the fair; after eleven rides on the merry-go-round, and the consumption of a large bag of popcorn, two sticks of nougat, two bottles of ginger beer and some red sticky mixture called Canadian Delight even the aggressively healthy William feels groggy. (He has also done justice to several side-shows.)

William's Great-Aunt Jane comes to stay in *William – The Fourth*, 5. She is a puritanical old dear, who garbs herself in floor-length late-Victorian coats and dresses, a prim little hat adorned with black ears of wheat, and elastic-sided boots. (Her father had been a member of the Plymouth Brethren, and 'Great-Aunt Jane had been brought up to disbelieve in pleasure except as a potent aid of the devil'.) She plans to give William a 'quiet and orderly' treat; he inveigles her into taking him to the fair. Once there she shies coconuts, flings hoops, rides on roundabouts, helter-skelters, switchbacks, fairy-boats and Wild Sea Waves as frequently and addictively as gamblers are drawn to the gaming-tables. Even William has grudgingly to admit that 'she must have gotter inside of *iron*'!

'There's something rejuvenating about it all, William,' she murmurs, and indeed it seems that all these new fairground experiences really do temporarily transform Great-Aunt Jane from prissiness to sensuality. The roundabout in particular is a revelation: 'She paid for William and Douglas, and Henry, and Ginger, and herself, and mounted a giant cock. It began. She clung on for dear life. It went faster and faster. There came a gleam into her eyes, a smile of rapture to her lips . . ." It's – it's quite a pleasant motion, isn't it? It seems a pity to get off," ' she is reported as saying innocently. She and William round off the evening by devouring quantities of 'soft pull-out candy', and afterwards, safely and quietly back at the Browns' home, Great-Aunt Jane cannot believe she could have enjoyed that wild mixture of sensations. Surely she must have walked round with William and watched him indulging himself. 'Of course . . . The other was unthinkable . . .'

In *William*, 4, the Outlaws are savouring in anticipation the delights of a fair which is coming for one evening only to the village. William, Ginger, Henry and Douglas look forward to the Aunt Sally, hoop-la and the 'glaring, blaring', diabolically noisy roundabouts. Previous fairs have brought attractions such as fat women, india-rubber men, and 'Pictures of Two Hundred Forms of Tortures (the Outlaws had much enjoyed that)', but this one offers something new: waxworks. Horror strikes when, trapped into schoolroom horseplay by the obnoxious Hubert Lane, William is kept in by Ole Markie (Mr Markson, his headmaster). Without him the Outlaws find the fair rather flat, until Ginger has an idea, worthy of William's flights of fancy, about how to release his leader from detention. They carry a life-size waxwork of one of the princes in the Tower (black velvet lace-collared suit, befeathered hat and all) to the school, dress it in William's clothes, and prop it up in his desk. He goes with them to the fair, but has of course to don the princely waxwork's ticklish attire. In no time at all he finds himself taking part in the waxwork show, standing next to the effigy of his 'brother', and resenting the audience's comments on the fact that one prince is handsome whilst the other (William) is ugly: 'No wonder they murdered 'im if 'e looked like that.' Worse is to come: the Laneites notice the waxwork's likeness to William, and tauntingly dub it 'Little Lord Fauntleroy', which brings it to enraged and pugnacious life. Meanwhile back at the school the headmaster has discovered the substitution in detention of the waxwork for William. All in all, this is one fair which William does not wholeheartedly enjoy.

In *William and the Tramp*, 7, the Outlaws are gloomily commenting that the fair has not come, as promised, to Hadley that year, but happily they are soon 'whooping with joy' as the familiar train of caravans turns up. Their enthusiasm is still sizzling in *William – The Explorer*, 6, even though

William is without financial resources, and denied even a loan by his family until the new glass put into the garden frame (after he broke it) has been paid for. William remarks darkly and pathetically that this might be the last fair he ever gets the chance of visiting. (His prediction is almost accurate, for fairs only come into the stories after this on two more occasions.) How William eventually gets his fairing makes hilarious reading: he helps a friendly old man, whose garden is near an archaeological site, with some digging, and the broken brooches and pottery pieces which they unearth and dismissively toss aside turn out to be much-valued Roman remains. William's fairing is showered upon him by a group of excavators (which includes Robert whose archaeological interest has been awakened by Hermione Monson, the latest 'beautiful, intelligent and charming and cultured' object of his affections). For once William has not disgraced his elder brother: he has succeeded where the erudite archaeologists on the adjacent site have failed. Even more important, he goes to the fair with pockets full of money.

In *William and the Pop Singers*, 2, the Hadley fair is only briefly mentioned as something which temporarily diverts the Outlaws from their current occupation of rounding up local – and unsuspected – criminals. Similarly, the last reference in the stories to funfairs occurs as a joyous postscript to one of the Outlaws' adventures:

'There's an octopus.'
  'An' dodgems.'
  'An' a Buz Bump.'
  'An' monkeys doin' wrestlin' matches.'
  'An' we've got ten an' six to spend.'
         (*William the Lawless*, 3)

The visits of fairs to William's village and its environs were indeed high days and holidays, but fêtes were a different matter as they lacked rarity value. By the time the William books had been running for over four decades, Richmal acknowledged that their frequency might well have put a strain on the village:

The 'summer season' of the village was at its height. Fête succeeded fête, sale of work succeeded sale of work, flower show succeeded flower show . . . Each Saturday was a battle-field strewn with nerve-racked openers, stall-holders, treasurers, rummage collectors, competition organisers, miniature train-runners, programme sellers, tea helpers and refreshment providers. And the number of Saturdays the summer afforded proved always insufficient for their needs . . . Conservatives, Liberals, Labour, Church, Baptists, Scouts, Guides, Old People's Homes, Young People's Clubs, scrambled to snatch a Saturday from the fast diminishing pile. Openers rushed frantically from one stately home to another, every household was scoured for the last lonely white elephant, the last infinitesimal shred of rummage.
        (*William and the Witch*, 3)

William and the Outlaws take sometimes a lively and sometimes a bored attitude towards these proceedings. From their point of view the organisers are often unsympathetic and obsessional: 'The Vicar's wife was afflicted with the Sale of Work mania. It is a disease to which Vicars' wives are notoriously susceptible. She was always thinking of the next but one Sale of Work . . . She was always praised in the local press and she felt herself to be a very happy woman . . .' (*William – The Fourth*, 3). Nevertheless they often lend their energies to sales and fêtes and shows and pageants organised in favour of various causes; and William plays a starring rôle in the King of Fêtes, which is the name given by the Vicar's wife to the enterprise which follows one of her particularly successful sales of work. The unassuming Miss Tabitha Croft (who can be numbered in that very select group of adults who are friends of William) is telling fortunes at half a crown a time. As 'the Woman of Mystery' she wears a voluminously enveloping gown which covers not only her body but also, except for her eyes, her whole head. When she is called away suddenly William helps out by donning the gown and assuming her psychic rôle. His clients include his teacher Miss Drew, Ethel and Robert, each of whom is currently bearing a grudge against him, and is sufficiently gullible to be taken in by the anonymous Woman of Mystery. 'She' tells them that a certain Boy (obviously William) 'is not strong and may die soon'; he rapidly reaps the results of his subterfuge, with Ethel and Robert guiltily bestowing sweets, chocolates and treats upon him, and Miss Drew, too, providing goodies and 'doing most of his work for him at school'. His intervention at fêtes and sales of work is not always so successful. On one occasion he accidentally sells the Vicar's wife's good coat. On another (*William's Crowded Hours*, 8) he offers a selection of photographs for sale (on the understanding that part of the proceeds goes to the cause but the rest can be kept by the

Outlaws, who are desperate to find the two shillings each that an unscrupulous but engaging tramp is demanding from them as fees for entry into his profession). The display of these photographs causes high drama amongst the local bright young things, for they are portraits of themselves given to Ethel at one time or another by various admirers; the pictures are of course suitably and passionately inscribed and, as every one of Ethel's ex-boyfriends seems to be attending this particular sale with his current lady-love, business is brisk. Distraught young men pay the asking price many times over in order to grab and quickly tear to shreds the offending pictures. 'Very thoughtfully William took his notice and altered "1d" to "1s". Evidently the market value of old photographs was higher than he had supposed.'

In *William and the Witch*, 3, the Outlaws' efforts again go slightly awry. They are helping out their artist friend, Archie Mannister, who has been press-ganged by Mrs Monks, the Vicar's wife, into organising the hoop-la stall at the church fête. Unfortunately William & Co. use as prizes the contents of a suitcase belonging to Sir Julius Egerton, the local celebrity who comes along to open the fête. In the same book (chapter 5) Mrs Bott arranges a garden-party and tries to upstage every event of a similar nature. In a looking-for-ancestors mood, her pretentiousness nearly gets out of hand: 'Mrs. Bott had decided to strain every nerve to make the affair unique in the annals of the village . . . it took all Mr. Bott's firmness to restrain her from transforming the front of the Hall into a *son et lumière* effect by flood-lighting and gramophone records.'

Another unusual event was the 'War-time Hollydays at Home Fun Fair Entrunce one Hapenny' which William and his followers held in and around the Old Barn in the 1940s (*William and the Brains Trust*, 4). Echoing the real-life 'holidays at home' situations of the Second World War, this *divertissement* for the children of the village is a cross between a funfair and a fête. Violet Elizabeth Bott insists on helping and, like her mother, she goes her own way. The day's most exciting event is the rout of the Hubert Laneites at the end (they have been running a rival funfair).

Games and Toys, Fantasy and Imagination

Crazes in children's games and toys are reflected in the William books, and particularly the seasonal nature of many such activities: 'Ginger . . . had seen the tops in the shop window and realised suddenly that the top season was upon them once more. The next day, almost the whole school was equipped with tops . . .' (*William – The Fourth*, 13). The same book reports in chapter 10 that William and his friends are desperate for 'a few dozen of ordinary glass marbles which could be bought for a few pence'. They are in their usual impecunious state, however, and not considered a good credit risk by Mr Beezum, the shopkeeper. Their only resource is to raise the cash by putting on one of their famous shows.

Certain toys (or weapons) such as catapults, water-pistols, pea-shooters and bows and arrows are, for the Outlaws, fairly permanent pieces of apparatus, except when they are confiscated by interfering grown-ups. The same applies to small musical instruments like mouth-organs and trumpets. Conkers, acorns, tops, marbles and cigarette-cards are amongst their more ephemeral equipment.

Some of the games which they play are recognisably linked to those which are universally popular in streets and school playgrounds; others are very much their own invention. Thus every reader identifies, if only tenuously, with the Outlaws' pirate or Red Indian games, though William's favourite (and Mrs Brown's much-abhorred) game of Lions and Tamers (*Just – William*, 7), with its

variations – Tigers and Tamers, Tamers and Crocodiles, Lunatics and Keepers – seems open to much development and different levels of rumbustiousness.

William's wonderful imagination gives him the capacity to live out his fantasies rather than to play 'let's pretend'. For example, when ambling along a lane and finding himself followed by a solitary cow, he immediately casts himself in the rôle of 'the greatest cattle farmer in the world . . . driving a huge herd . . . from one pasturage to another somewhere in the heart of Africa or India' – presumably somewhere on the American continent, too, as he sees the woods around him 'thick with' potential Red Indian rustlers (*William's Happy Days*, 5).

A stray horse causes his imagination to flare just as quickly as does the stray cow. As the Outlaws' leader (and after several falls before he manages to seat himself) William claims the first ride, and the horse lumberingly traverses the field:

William's feelings were beyond description. No medieval knight in gleaming armour ever bestrode a gaily caparisoned horse with feelings of greater pride and arrogance. To William, in fact, both knight and horse would have seemed shabby in comparison with his mental picture of himself. A grubby little boy, perched on a saddle from which the stuffing was oozing at all points, on a large, clumsy, untended horse of one of the less distinguished breeds, with three other little boys trotting at its heels . . . Not so did William see himself. He was a king, surrounded by his bodyguard. His thoroughbred pranced beneath him. The gold and jewels of his crown, the scarlet ermine of his cloak, made a noble splash of colour. Massed crowds cheered him on all sides as he rode along . . . He was a general at the head of his army. His war horse pawed the air, snorted, neighed. His armour gleamed in the sun. The enemy fled in confusion before him.

(*Sweet William*, 2)

Even a simple train journey is an exhilarating exercise in fantasy. Travelling to a seaside resort, William sees himself by turns as a spy passing through enemy country, a general on his way to war and 'a circus man travelling with his show (the large man with the long nose was an elephant and the woman in the black satin coat was a performing seal)' (*Sweet William*, 10). However, a colourful imagination *does* have limitations as well as positive aspects; it is the work of a moment for William's imagination to leap from seeing the notice 'To stop the train, pull down the chain' to wondering what would happen if he pulled it 'a tiny bit', and then to force his fingers to pull hard on it. (Even this actually has felicitous results as the train's emergency stop prevents a passenger in another carriage from being assaulted and robbed: William – temporarily – is a hero.) There are moments when his fancies cannot fly quite high enough, when he recognises that his imitations of certain stirring adult activities are 'puny', that he hasn't actually captured 'all those thieves and brigands', and that real life doesn't offer the broad sweep of adventure that his nature demands; but, just as he begins to feel dispirited by these sober reflections, some trivial incident or conversation will once again send his imagination soaring.

Gaye, Gloria

See ABBOT, ROSALYN.

George (1)

Suitor for Mrs Roundway's widowed sister in *William*, 9. See ROUNDWAY, MRS.

George (2)

A shadowy friend from William's school who heads his list of boys he would like to ask to a party, if he could have one, coming even before 'Ginger and Henry and Douglas'. George attends the illicit tea-party which William arranges in his parents' absence in *Just – William*, 6. He 'banged the drawing-room door with such violence that the handle came off in his hand' and 'with great gusto drank a whole jar of cream'. After that, oblivion!

George (3)

A baker's man, who gives William a ride in his cart, yodels, blows smoke-rings and lets him help unharness his horse. 'In William's eyes George was a demi-god', so he supports his suit of Molly (William's Aunt Jane's attractive maid) rather than that of his rival JAMES, a chauffeur-coachman. (*William – The Pirate*, 4)

Gerrard, Angela

Small sister of Cornelia, a one-time girlfriend of Robert. (*William – The Rebel*, 12)

Gerrard, Cornelia

See FILMS and ROBERT AND HIS FRIENDS.

Ginger

See OUTLAWS, THE.

Gipsies

In *William – The Fourth*, 11, William remarks ' "I've always wanted to be a gipsy – next to a Red Indian and a pirate . . ." ' However, considering that he is an outdoor country-child, he generally shows surprisingly little interest in gipsies. A memorable exception crops up in the above-mentioned book when he swaps his clothes with Helbert; a gipsy boy who goes off in William's waistcoat and suit while William proudly sports Helbert's 'ragged jersey and knickers'. Sometimes, like Jane in the *Daily Mirror*, William loses his clothes more than once in the same episode. Here his unsavoury gipsy garb is taken away by a well-meaning lady to be fumigated. Meanwhile he has to cover his nakedness in a fairy dress made originally for the lady's niece (see DRESSING UP).

Gladhill, Frances Mary

One of those 'perfect' children who, after spending a short time with William, are turned into lively, natural – and scruffy – characters. (*Sweet William*, 2)

Gladhill, Mrs

The mother of Frances Mary, who addresses the Women's Guild on the Upbringing of Children, and is immensely proud of her 'dainty, docile, beautifully mannered' seven-year-old daughter who is 'quite a cult among childless elderly ladies'. She explains patiently to her audience that it is all a question of the right method, and that she could trust her little girl 'among any children'. It is of course at this moment that Frances Mary erupts on to the scene, crumpled, torn, dirty, noisy and happy after an encounter with William and the Outlaws. (*Sweet William*, 2)

Glover, Wing Commander

See ETHEL AND HER FRIENDS.

Godwin, Graham

A businessman, staying with his aunt, Miss Godwin, at her home (Marleigh Court) and hoping for some quiet fishing. William confuses him with his cousin of the same name who is a film-producer. Seeking a career in films (which he thinks will bring him £200 a week), William visits Marleigh Court in order to impress Mr Godwin with his acting prowess. Meanwhile Miss Tomlinson, the pageant mistress, is also at the house (where Queen Elizabeth I once stayed), which she thinks will make a wonderful venue for her pageant. However, after catching some shadowy glimpses of William (who has painted his face green, in lieu of putting on proper screen make-up) Miss Tomlinson feels that Marleigh Court is haunted by a 'dreadfully malevolent' manifestation, and shifts the scene of her pageant to the Hall, to Mrs Bott's social-climbing delight, and the relief of Mr Graham Godwin, who yearns for peace and quiet. When he realises that he has William to thank for scaring away Miss Tomlinson and all the paraphernalia of her pageant, he invites him to go 'real grown-up fishing' with him – a prospect William finds even more attractive than a career in films. (*William and the Evacuees*, 2)

Goggles

One of William's schoolmates. (*William Again*, 8)

Golden Arrow, The

The official Scottish souvenir of the World Jamboree, held at Arrowe Park, Birkenhead, from 31 July to 13 August 1929. An exciting item for collectors of scouting memorabilia, with a garish colour cover of the campfire, this particular item had the distinction of publishing the wonderful

'William and the Sleeping Major' for the first time. There were no illustrations for the story in the *Golden Arrow*, but it was reprinted in the *Happy Mag* for November 1930 with a bonus – a picture of the Major asleep in the Bath chair, which never found its way into the book (*William's Crowded Hours*, 9).

How Gourock, the publisher, managed to scoop a new William story for such a relatively obscure publication remains a mystery. (D.S.)

Golightly, Miss Priscilla

The headmistress of Rose Mount, 'a large girls' school on the outskirts of the village'. Otherwise known as 'Golly', she is described as 'redoubtable': 'the Outlaws had learnt to confine their intercourse with her to a minimum' (*William and the Tramp*, 2). In *William and the Pop Singers*,

2, we are told that she is 'grim-faced, tight-lipped, with brisk staccato voice' and William has cast her in the rôle of 'a villain of the deepest dye' for a novel which he is writing. She appears again in chapter 4 of the same book, as well as in *William and the Masked Ranger*, 5, and *William the Superman*, 3. (She has the distinction of being at intervals the headmistress of both Joan and Violet Elizabeth.)

Golightly, Professor Justinian

The nephew of Miss Golightly, who has been virtually brought up by her. Despite his 'brilliant scholastic career', and the fact that he is to judge the historical essay competition which William's headmaster is urging his pupils to enter, he is a man after William's own heart. They meet hiding in a store-cupboard, both refugees from Miss

Golightly; and, after quickly establishing a rapport and eating every sultana in her house, end up by going to Hadley fair together, where William introduces the Professor to the delights of Monster Humbugs and the Wall of Death. (*William and the Tramp*, 2)

Gorton, Mr

Owner of local petshop in *William the Fourth*, 9. See also CATS.

Graham Graham, Mr

The president of the local Temperance Society of which MR BUCK is secretary. 'Mr. Graham Graham was tall and lank, with pince-nez and an earnest expression. Mr. Graham Graham's expression did not belie his character.' (*Still – William*, 2)

Great Man (1)

William's headmaster's cousin. See CARROWAY, MR AND MRS.

Great Man (2)

An unnamed Great Man from the Cabinet who comes down especially to address a political meeting at which William's father is to preside (see also DISCREPANCIES). He arrives by an earlier train than expected and, on his way to the village hall where the political meeting is to be held, is diverted by a sign pointing to the stable at the back of William's house which says: THIS WAY TO THE BLOODY HAND. He becomes the sole member of the audience of William's play because 'Most of the adults . . . were going to listen to the Great Man. Most of the juveniles were going to watch a football match.' The Great Man seems fascinated by the action of the play, which ends in an unrehearsed and exhilarating fight. The Master of Ceremonies (William, of course) introduces it as ' "The Bloody Hand," wrote, every bit of it, by William Brown – acted by Molly Carter an' Ginger an' Douglas an' Henry – they jus' learnt wot William Brown wrote.' The Great Man is so entranced by it all (presumably it is a wonderful change from cabinet meetings) that he loses track of time. The start of the political meeting has to be delayed; Mr Brown, going in search of the distinguished speaker, gravitates towards William & Co. in the stable, where he finds 'a wistful-looking old man on a packing case . . . an absorbed spectator of the proceedings'. (*William Again*, 1)

Green, Anthea

The small sister of CELIA GREEN who is a newcomer to the village. She wants to start a juvenile branch of the literary society run by Celia and persuades William to involve himself in 'detective journalism' in support of this. William is at first co-operative:

Since Joan had moved from the neighbourhood William had preserved intact his armour of woman-hatred, or rather of girl-hatred, but Anthea had found its weak spot. For there was a faint – a very faint – look of Joan about Anthea. She was small and dark, like Joan. There was a suggestion of wistfulness in her expression that brought the memory of Joan vividly to his mind.

Later, however, he begins to recognise a certain exploitativeness about Anthea:

He had a growing suspicion that he was going to be bossed and pushed around and dictated to.

Something in the very sweetness of this girl's face, the smoothness of her voice, warned him of the worst. As he looked at her, the resemblance to Joan seemed to be fading.

(*William's Treasure Trove*, 5)

However, he becomes involved with her again in *William the Superman*, 4, when he and Ginger decide to run a 'Cittisens Advise Burro' in the Old Barn. Anthea has been asked to Maisie Fellowes's party, and she can't face going to it in her well-worn 'silly old Austrian peasant girl's costume'. She expects that, if the C.A.B. is worth its salt, it will obtain a new fancy-dress costume for her. After several vicissitudes, William and Ginger *do*. They spot an attractive 'Gretel' dress (next to a Hansel costume which is not really connected with it) on a jumble-sale stall run by MISS MILTON. After a lot of bargaining, they buy it for the total of their combined resources – one and twopence half-penny. But when they triumphantly present the Gretel frock to Anthea she screams, chokes with rage, and abuses them. They have, unknowingly, bought back the 'hateful ole' dress which Anthea had sold earlier that day to Miss Milton for the jumble sale.

Green, Celia

See FILMS and ROBERT AND HIS FRIENDS.

Greenham, Peter

See FILMS.

Griffiths-Griffiths, Mrs

A very earnest Sunday-school superintendent who is in charge of a camp of boys near the village

'who've had no bad marks of any kind throughout the year'. She is a tall lady with white shingled hair, and is very keen on her Virtue Rewarded Camp, the inmates of which come from all over the country.

William and Ginger are in a quandary; with most of their friends away on holiday their band is much depleted – a fact known to the Laneites, who therefore choose that moment to challenge them to a fight. It seems impossible for William temporarily to recruit the good little boys from Sunday-school camp to his band, but – very tortuously – he manages to present them to the Laneites in a bellowing, charging mood, which is sufficient to make Hubert & Co. flee panic-stricken from their vantage point. The Sunday-school boys think that they have been taking part in some weird converting-the-heathen ritual, and they look forward to receiving for this a 'speshal' medal, mentioned by William, to wear next to their good-conduct badges: 'Their eyes gleamed. They thirsted for medals as a drug maniac for his drug.' (*William – The Bad*, 7)

Grimble, Horatio

An alias. See TRAMPS.

Grown-Up Friends

We are told in *William and the Brains Trust*, 1, that 'William had made many friends among the airmen' at Marleigh aerodrome. This, of course, was during the Second World War at a time when many social barriers were being broken down and there was in many aspects of life a strong sense of community solidarity. However, William's world is not noticeably one in which adults deeply appreciate him. He is essentially the eleven-year-old boy, and he never crosses the divide between the directness of boyhood and the complexities of the grown-up state. Those adults who *do* respond to him tend to be robust, eccentric or particularly warm-hearted. They are not, as a rule, concerned with image or status, for, as we know, without any deliberate plan to disrupt, William's flair for triggering off anarchic happenings is acute.

Amongst William's adult chums is Patsy, an A.T.S. girl stationed in his village (*William and the Brains Trust*, 9). 'She shared her sweet ration' with the Outlaws, 'she made bows and arrows for them – of a new and improved fashion . . . she had a method of building a wigwam that far eclipsed the one they had always used. She could climb trees with astonishing agility and run as fast as William . . . She took them to the Swimming Baths in Hadley, and taught them to play Water Leap Frog and Twisting.' Patsy is one of a type which recurs in the books: pretty, competent, and having a natural rapport with children does not 'talk down' to them. Others cast in a similar mould and numbered amongst William's friends are Miss Pollit in *William's Happy Days*, 5 (see ART AND ARTISTS), and Katie the land-girl in *William Carries On*, 3 (see FAIRIES, MAGIC AND THE SUPERNATURAL).

There is also a more mature and protective type of grown-up whom he befriends. MRS ROUNDWAY is the classic example of this type. Something between her maternalism and Patsy's and Katie's empathy with boyhood is conveyed in the person of Mrs Fountain, the expert cook and cookery writer in *William Carries On*, 1. She is slightly shy and vague but shows an interest in the Outlaws' concerns that is 'as unusual in a grown-up as it is flattering'. Not only is she intrigued by Red Indians and woodcraft 'and damming streams and climbing trees', she also invites William and his friends to wonderful home-cooked meals (even during wartime shortages). William, who is always loyal to his friends, is determined to help Mrs Fountain to get the commission to write the regular cookery page in *Woman's Mirror*. He takes the unusual step of helping to prepare the meal when the paper's editor, Mr Devizes, visits to sample Mrs Fountain's cooking at lunch. She has been saying how much she longed for lemons (impossible to obtain at that stage of the war) for flavouring. William, with the help of Violet Elizabeth, has abstracted some from Mrs Bott's unpatriotically hoarded supplies. He proudly puts one into the simmering soup. Only when the soup is served does everyone realise the ghastly truth; Mrs Bott's lemon hoard turns out to be soaps! Nevertheless the editor gives Mrs Fountain the job – and William half a crown for giving him his 'first good laugh since the blitz started'.

William's grown-up male friends tend to be men of action or at least of resource, though he is occasionally attracted in a rather patronising way to authors, artists and obvious 'intellectuals'. He quickly responds to a wide range of tramps, and the occasional charismatic burglar. A strong character himself, he likes to look after the underdog. ARCHIE MANNISTER (see also ART AND ARTISTS) is constantly championed by William and the Outlaws. Another put-upon friend whom he helps is Sergeant Malcolm who is small, anxious-looking, and at the beck and call of 'Capting-Fusspot' (Captain Fortescue), an arrogant and pompous young man whom William cuts down to size by making him look ridiculous in a nasty tangle with Farmer Jenks's nanny-goat, Letty (*William and the Brains Trust*, 2).

A very old soldier arouses his friendship in *William's Treasure Trove*, 4; this is Aaron Mason, who is seventy-eight years old and bored out of his skull in an old people's home. William undertakes to find him a job; he tries hard, without success, and eventually, much more by luck than by judgement, finds Aaron employment as gardener to GENERAL MOULT. It turns out that both of these retired military men are Boer War veterans. Aaron goes from strength to strength working for the General, to whom he becomes secretary-companion-valet-housekeeper. Like so many of William's grown-up protégés, he knows that he has in the leader of the Outlaws a true if unpredictable ally.

Hadlow, Ward

See FAIRMAN, MISS.

Hammond, Herbert

See TRAMPS.

Hampton, Sir Giles

At the time when William has been recruited by the Literary Society to provide the sound effects, etc., for its performance of *The Trial of Love* (see DRAMATICS), it becomes known that Sir Giles Hampton, one of the most distinguished actors in the country, is staying in the village. This causes much fluttering in the Literary Society. In the words of Miss Greene-Joanes: ' " . . . he's staying at the inn here" ' (after a nervous breakdown) ' "and he's supposed to be incognito, but of course he's telling people who he is because he's not *really keen* on being incognito. Actors never are really . . ." '

Sir Giles seems to be set in the mould of typical Shakespearian actor-managers of the late nineteenth and early twentieth centuries. William collides with him in the street, and Sir Giles asks – 'majestically' – if William knows who he is.

'No,' said William simply, 'an' I bet you don't know who I am either.'
'I'm a very great actor,' said the man.
'So'm I,' said William promptly.

As the conversation proceeds, it is difficult to decide who is the more egotistical, the actor-manager or the sound-effects boy!

At any rate, William whets Sir Giles's curiosity about the Literary Society's production, which he deigns to attend. At the end of the evening, he goes off chuckling about the grand finale (when William inadvertently soaks the heroine), and presents William with a new football. He also provides the Literary Society with the cinematograph they have been wanting, but have been unable to afford, for some time. Apparently the débâcle of the Society's 'little play' has completely cured his nervous breakdown, so William's efforts have achieved positive results both for the Literary Society and for the recuperating thespian. (*William – The Good*, 2)

Handkerchiefs

Mrs Brown's determination that William's appearance should be neat and tidy is unceasing, if abortive. Part of her effort is to equip him with clean handkerchiefs, which William puts to good, if unorthodox, use. A clean hankie is something to be broken in; *Just William's Luck*, 10, tells us that a freshly laundered one wears 'a superior, supercilious air', seeming to play its part 'reluctantly' in William's wide-ranging activities. However, once a handkerchief acquires a certain degree of degradation it becomes a trusted friend and ally.

William's Happy Days, 6, records that Mrs Brown's birthday present to him is a dozen new initialled handkerchiefs (the Brown family are not good at choosing gifts for their youngest member). The use to which William puts one of these is vividly described:

In the course of the morning it was used to staunch the blood from William's nose after a fight in the playground, to wipe the mud from William's knee after a fall in a puddle, to mop up a pool of ink from William's desk, to swaddle the white rat that William had brought to school with him, and as a receptacle for the two pennyworth of Liquorice All Sorts that had been Ginger's present to him. At the end of the morning its eleven spotless brothers would have passed it by unrecognised.

Happy Mag, The

That ever popular superstar of quality fiction, *Strand Magazine*, famous for Conan Doyle and P. G. Wodehouse, carried in the issue for June 1922 a full-page advertisement for a new magazine. It proclaimed its content to be 'full of humorous pictures, stories and sketches' and it warned that 'Whitsun holidays would be incomplete without a copy of it to hand'. The new magazine was the *Happy Mag*, and it was targeted unashamedly at the whole family. For Father in the first issue was an Edgar Wallace story, 'The Sentimental Crook'; for Mother 'Making George a Champion' by K. R. G. Browne ('He flung his arms about Jane and embraced her warmly, despite her frantic struggles'); for the teenagers, several humorous and romantic stories; and a two-page cartoon strip 'Peter Rabbit and His Baby Bunnies' for the very young at heart. Thomas Henry was already there, amongst others, with excellent cartoons: Little girl to artist (referring to her even smaller brother): 'Please, zur, do 'ee mind a takin' of our 'Orace's pikshur, 'e's so proud 'cos 'e's just gone inter trousis.'

Just – William, the first collection of stories from *Home Magazine*, was published in book form in May 1922, almost coinciding with the June birth of the *Happy Mag*. In December 1922 *More William* was published, along with the second printing of *Just – William*, and this marked William's move to the *Happy Mag* with 'Just William's Luck' (*William Again*, 9).

Only nine stories appeared in the *Happy Mag* before disaster struck. In the summer of 1923, Richmal Crompton succumbed to the crippling disease poliomyelitis and was consequently too ill to write. In fact she had written ahead of publication by several months, and the editor of the *Happy Mag* had three stories in hand: 'The Bishop's Handkerchief' (*Still – William*, 1), 'William the Showman' and 'A Dress Rehearsal'

(*William – The Fourth*, 10 and 14). These were published in the September, October and November issues of 1923. By December, Richmal had not recovered sufficiently to write, and it is appropriate that the first William story (reputedly) that she actually wrote, 'William Goes to the Pictures' (*Just – William*, 1) should be reprinted for this issue. It was illustrated with new pictures by Thomas Henry (never reproduced in the book). Thus, when all the illustrations for the first three books were 'brought up to date' for the 1950 edition, this story became the only one to have been illustrated by Thomas Henry three times.

Happily, Richmal was soon writing again. From then on she maintained an unbroken run of monthly William escapades (with an extra one every Christmas) until February 1934 – ten years and 132 stories later.

It seems significant that during 1924, the year following her illness, she produced another batch of marvellous characters who would sustain the village and the saga for the rest of her life. Just as the first four stories in *Home Magazine* introduced the Brown family, Joan, Jumble, the Outlaws and the Old Barn, so 1924 in the *Happy Mag* saw the introduction of most of our other favourites: Miss Milton and General Moult in 'Henri Learns the Language', Violet Elizabeth Bott (and the Botts) in 'The Sweet Little Girl in White', Farmer Jenks in 'William the Money-Maker', and Hubert Lane (but not yet the Laneites) in 'William the Match-Maker' (*Still – William*, 2, 3, 6 and 8 respectively).

If the *Happy Mag* was a rich source of amusement and pleasure for the family of the 1920s and 1930s, it is now an even richer source of William material, with treasures that have been virtually forgotten for over half a century. Almost every story which appeared up to the end of 1930 had an 'extra' drawing of William (usually as part of the story-title) that was not later reproduced in the appropriate book. This adds up to over a hundred 'missing' pictures, most of which are superb, and

many of which are reproduced in the *Companion* for the first time in hardback.

As early as 1923, Thomas Henry had also adopted the visual character of William for independent cartoons. These were at first black-and-white 'one-liners', which soon graduated into full-colour covers for the *Happy Mag*, as well as four presentation plates bound in with the Christmas 1925 issue. Just six of these colour covers were used (or adapted) for the dustwrappers for the books: *Still – William* ('Just His Luck!'), *William – In Trouble* ('Troubles Never Come Singly!'), *William – The Outlaw* ('William the Conqueror!' – changed to 'The Catch of the Season!'), *William – The Conqueror* ('The End of a Perfect Day'), *William – The Good* ('A Game of Patience!'), and *William – The Bad* ('Oh, Chris'mas!' – changed to 'Oh, Crumbs!'). There are no less than thirty others which have not yet been reproduced elsewhere.

From the mid-1920s, the black-and-white cartoons by Thomas Henry developed into double-page spreads of William adventures, such as 'William and Joan do their Best to keep the Christmas Party going all Night' (*Happy Christmas Extra*, 1926) and 'William Brightens Up a Frosty Morning' (*Happy Mag*, February 1927), a total of twenty-one adventures in all, plus several cartoons.

With the Christmas issue of 1926, another marvellous bonus appeared: an article 'By William' (written, of course, by Richmal Crompton), in which William gives his personal account of ideas and general grievances on the subject of 'I'll Tell You What's Wrong with Christmas'. In the January issue, 'New Year's Day' appeared, followed by ten others at roughly six-monthly intervals, the last being 'Home for the Holidays' with the *Happy Christmas Extra* for 1933. Several more such articles appeared in other publications, and a selection is being published in this Richmal Crompton Centenary Year, for the first time in book form, by Macmillan: *What's Wrong with Civilizashun.*

Only eight William stories appeared in 1934, and from 1935 to 1939 the annual average was ten – enough to keep the supply of books coming at the rate of one per year. Only one story remained uncollected in the books – 'William on the Trail' – and this was reproduced in a bibliography by Lofts and Adley (see WILLIAM IN PERFORMANCE).

Then came the war. Paper supplies were rapidly dwindling, and in an effort to economise the *Happy Mag* was reduced in size for the issues of April and May 1940. As the noose finally tightened on supplies, the magazine, along with many others, disappeared without warning. The last story to appear (in May 1940) was 'William Takes Charge' (*William and the Evacuees*, 1), which had its name changed to 'William and the Evacuees' for the title-chapter of the book.

For William, as well as for others, the war proved to be the end of an era. (D.S.)

Hart, Mrs and Susie

Mrs Hart and her small daughter Susie move into Elm Mead, which, while it was empty, had been a happy playground for William and Ginger. Not realising that it is now occupied, William and Ginger lure Hubert Lane into Elm Mead, intending to play ghost there, to study his reactions, which will provide copy for a story they are writing. (They have to have a villain for this purpose, and they decide that Hubert is 'the villainest one' they know.) Mrs Hart is so vague that Hubert's presence doesn't disturb her. She thinks that he must be the French boy she might (or might not) have invited to stay so that he can improve his English, and Susie can learn French. She addresses him, pseudo-French fashion, as 'Yubear'. Susie, who turns out to have good taste and judgement, dislikes Hubert, and he tries to bully her. She escapes

up a ladder to the loft, where William is concealed, and he and Susie have the satisfaction of emptying a bucket of none too clean cistern-water on to Hubert's 'puffy upturned face'. 'Yubear' rapidly departs, but William enjoys being at Elm Mead with Susie who 'though small and slight and of the sex for which William professed scorn and abhorrence . . . was an admirable playfellow'. (*William and the Moon Rocket*, 5)

'Hartsease'

See POEMS AND POETS.

Hassan

See CLIFF, MISS.

Hathaway, Angela

The sister of the MISS HATHAWAY who lives in William's village. (*William – The Rebel*, 4)

Hathaway, Miss

The occupant of Laurel Cottage, the high walls of whose garden fascinate William, who walks on them but on one occasion falls off, into Miss Hathaway's glass garden-frame. He hopes to apologise properly before she has time to tell his father, but she – or, rather, her maidservant – will not let him into the house. He hits on the idea of emulating Cleopatra, who rolled herself in a carpet to get into the presence of Caesar. William can't find an appropriate carpet, and has to make do with concealing himself in a very large dog-kennel. Unfortunately he is delivered to the wrong Miss Hathaway. (*William – The Rebel*, 4)

Hatherley, Marion and Miss

Spelt Hatherly in *Still – William*, 7. See FAIRIES, MAGIC AND THE SUPERNATURAL.

Hector and Herbert

Twins, whom William encounters and decides to 'evacuate' to his house, with chaos ensuing. (*William and A.R.P.*, 1)

Helston, Mr

Mr Helston is an extremely successful writer who comes to Clematis Cottage for a rest, under doctors' orders. He spends most of his time recuperatively fishing, and neglects the cottage, to the irritation of MISS MILTON, his near neighbour. The Outlaws have no objection to the state of his accommodation, but when Violet Elizabeth 'thteals' documents from his car (to make a story for the newspaper that William & Co. are producing) they are shocked to read what seems to be the typed confession of a very callous murderer. They arrive to search his cottage when he is out one day; Miss Milton and her cousin Julia have already gone into the cottage, unknown to Mr Helston, to clean it up. Thinking that the Milton cousins are burglars, William locks them in. Mr Helston arrives home with Mr Brown, his fishing companion for the day, to noise and chaos. Mr Brown points out to William that Mr Helston is not a murderer; the Outlaws have simply read a snippet of a novel on which he is working. He tells them all that Helston, under another name, is a very famous writer, and with journalistic aplomb William whips out 'the grubby piece of paper and much-bitten pencil that formed his editorial equipment' to interview him, and asks: 'What is the mos' excitin'

moment of your life?' Helston, hearing Miss Milton's hysterics still going strong, and observing William's features obscured by purple pencil-smudges, Violet Elizabeth's by soot, Douglas 'encased in his wastepaper basket' and Jumble chasing the stuffing of a broken cushion around the room, replies: 'On the whole, I think, this one . . .' (*William and the Space Animal*, 5)

Hemmings, Mrs Maggie

Sister of MRS ROUNDWAY.

Henri

See BUCK, MR.

Henry

See OUTLAWS, THE.

Henry, Thomas

Thomas Henry Fisher was the real name of the man who illustrated the William stories for over forty years with his distinctive signature: Thomas Henry. Like Richmal Crompton Lamburn he, too, dropped his surname to protect his real identity in the early days of his career. Thomas Henry feared that his freelance cartoons might be frowned upon by a possessive employer, while Richmal Crompton, as a teacher, feared the disapproval of the school authorities.

Thomas Henry was known to the editors he

worked with as 'Tommy Fisher', to readers of the cartoon strips 'Phipps and S.O.S.' in the *Nottingham Football Post* as 'T. F.', and to his younger relatives (predictably) as 'Uncle Tom'. Apart from the use of 'T. F.' and 'Thomas Henry', he always signed his landscapes and portrait sketches as 'T. H. Fisher', so anyone lucky enough to possess a watercolour of Norfolk or East Anglia thus signed may not realise the true identity of the artist. Certainly to William-lovers he will always be remembered as – simply – Thomas Henry.

When the first published William story 'Rice-Mould' appeared in February 1919 in *Home Magazine*, L. [Louise] Hocknell was the illustrator. The author and editor were apparently unhappy with these first pictures: they were well executed, but their charm failed to reflect William's anti-heroic qualities. A request went out to several established cartoonists for samples of drawings based on Richmal Crompton's character-descriptions, and Thomas Henry was chosen to illustrate the stories from then on. He was almost forty years old; Richmal Crompton was twenty-eight. It was the beginning of a writer–illustrator partnership that was to last longer than Charles Dickens and Phiz (twenty-three years), and W. E. Johns and Stead (twenty-four years), but not quite as long as Frank Richards and Chapman (over fifty years)!

Thomas Henry Fisher was the eldest of three sons and three daughters born to Mr and Mrs Fred Fisher. He entered the world at Eastwood in Nottinghamshire on 30 June 1879 in a house opposite the one in which D. H. Lawrence would be born some six years later. It is unlikely that the two boys ever met, because the Fishers moved to Nottingham in 1880.

Not much is known about Tommy Fisher's formative years, except that at the age of fourteen he became an apprentice lithographer with T. Bailey Forman & Sons, who were newspaper proprietors and general printers. They sent him to art school, where his marvellous talent rapidly developed. His earliest recorded work was reputedly his contribution to the famous sailor's head on the pack of Player's Navy Cut cigarettes. However, according to the manufacturer's own publicity, the head was registered in 1883, the lifebuoy (with Player's Navy Cut superimposed) in 1888, and the full trade mark in 1891 – when Thomas Henry Fisher was twelve years old. His family's suggestion that the sailor bore an uncanny resemblance to their Uncle Tom may be reasonable, but that his hand was involved in its original design seems out of the question. What *is* possible is that he may have adapted the design in some way, perhaps for colour reproduction, as part of his early apprenticeship.

In his spare time, he drew cartoons and submitted them to a wide range of popular magazines, signing them 'Thomas Henry' to avoid recognition by his employer, T. Bailey Forman. His first published illustration was for *Ally Sloper's Half Holiday* on Saturday, 20 February 1904, and his first contribution to the *Football Post* was on 17 September 1904.

In 1906 he married Gertrude Ellen Mensing, a daughter of the schoolmaster of the village school in Cotgrave. She gave him great encouragement, and together they built a house, including a garden studio, in the nearby village of Plumtree. In 1911 their only daughter, Marjorie, was born.

By as early as 1914, Thomas Henry had become a regular contributor to *Punch* (four cartoons that year), and by 1920 was producing cartoons and illustrations for *Boy's Own Paper*, *Tatler*, *London Opinion*, *Pearson's*, *The Royal*, the *Novel Magazine*, *The Captain*, *The London Mail*, *Strand Magazine* and many others. He was extremely prolific and earning enough in 1920 to offer 7*s* 6*d* to any member of the family who gave him a successful idea for a cartoon. A letter from the editor of the *Novel Magazine* declared in October 1922:

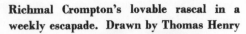

WILLIAM!

Richmal Crompton's lovable rascal in a weekly escapade. Drawn by Thomas Henry

Your work is so exactly what I want for the *Novel* and it is invariably so promptly delivered that I propose in future to pay 2 ½ gns instead of 2 gns per sketch.

The advance is not very substantial I'm afraid, but times are hard! Anyway please accept it as a sort of tribute to virtue and as a thank offering from a (sometimes) jaded editor!

A similar tribute to Thomas Henry's reliability came in a personal letter from the author Kenneth R. G. Browne on 10 December 1923:

I would like to take this opportunity of thanking you for the delightful way you have illustrated this series [in *The London Mail*]. After my experience of artists who apparently do not trouble to read the story they illustrate, it is a delight to find one who omits no single detail. If anybody has actually read any of these tales, I am quite sure that it was your drawings that impelled them to do so.

And another from Florence A. Kirkpatrick on 21 August 1924, referring to her book *Our Elizabeth Again*:

. . . out of nearly a dozen artists who have illustrated my various 'Elizabeth' stories and arti-

cles, you are the first to portray the type as I imagine it. The one on p.139 is particularly good. Most artists make her so intensely ugly and that was never my intention. Evidently you have a very keen sense of humour and your illustrations will greatly help along the book.

Thomas Henry's accuracy and brilliant interpretation of the humorous written word found no greater fulfilment than in the William stories. When William is 'trapped, trapped in a huge and horrible drawing-room, by a huge and horrible woman' (*William – The Fourth*, 2), Thomas Henry gives us a truly huge and horrible woman. When William scowls aggressively (*William – The Good*, 2), and we as young readers don't know exactly what 'scowling aggressively' means, the artist shows us exactly! And when Richmal Crompton asks for 'the hideous face of the goose upon its wobbling neck' (*William – In Trouble*, 1) to 'leer comically at the audience' it does just that.

Careful study of the early William illustrations, especially if one follows the sequence of their original magazine publication (see Appendix 2), reveals a character gradually developing before our eyes. As a result, some of the very early stories depict a William who bears scant resemblance to the William of the 1950s. It was for this reason that the publishers, Newnes, asked Thomas Henry to

Richmal Crompton as a young woman in the 1920s.

Thomas Henry in the early 1920s, around the time he began to draw William.

Happy Mag, December 1924.

Crusoe Mag, August 1924.

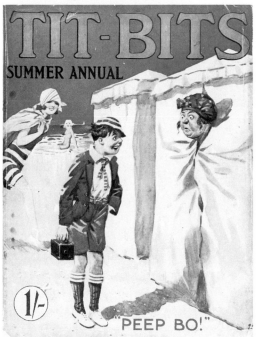

Tit–Bits Summer Extra, 1924.

Sunny Mag, January 1927.

A selection of vintage magazines, which feature colour 'William' covers by Thomas Henry.

Richmal Crompton in middle age.

Richmal's brother, John Lamburn *(left)* and her nephew, Thomas Disher *(right)*, both of whom provided inspiration for the William stories.

A wooden jigsaw by Thomas Henry; one of the comparatively few spin-offs from the 1950s.

The *Just William Magic Painting Book*, illustrated by Thomas Henry and published by BB Ltd, probably in the early 1950s.

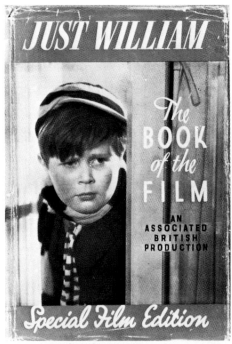

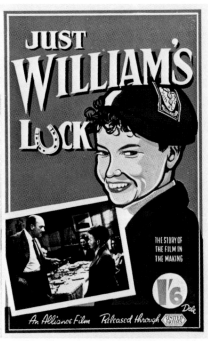

Dicky Lupino, the first film William, pictured on the cover of the book of the film *Just William* (1939).

The book of the 1948 film *Just William's Luck* starring William Graham.

John Clark, the first radio William (1945).

The first regular television William, Dennis Waterman, in the 1962 BBC series.

Richmal Crompton and Thomas Henry with some of their fans (Nottingham Book Fair, 1958).

William's most recent appearance on screen was in the 1977/8 LWT series, starring Adrian Dannatt with Bonnie Langford as Violet Elizabeth Bott.

do fresh drawings for the first three William books for the new edition of 1950.

Thomas Henry became a member of the Nottingham Society of Artists, and had a picture hung in the Royal Academy. Throughout the pre-war period, he continued his prolific output. He painted almost one-third of all the front covers for the *Happy Mag*, and usually illustrated at least one other story in addition to William in the same magazine each month. He illustrated many other children's books, as well as contributing hundreds of cartoons and front covers for a wide range of publications including *Boys' Budget*, *Blackie's Boys' Annual*, *Sunny Mag*, and many more (see MAGAZINES). His relationship with the *Novel Magazine* was to reach new heights in 1927, as it can now be revealed for the first time that Thomas Henry was the original illustrator for the Jane stories by Evadne Price. The first story, 'The Lion and the Mouse', was published in the *Novel* in November 1927. Even though the Jane books were eventually illustrated by Frank R. Grey (starting with the 1937 editions), more than fifty stories were first illustrated by Thomas Henry, from the start until at least November 1937 with 'Jane Sees the Phantom Light'.

In 1932, Tommy's world was shattered when Gertrude died of cancer. Marjorie was away at art school, and successive housekeepers were unsatisfactory. A year later, while on holiday in Newquay, he met Anne Bailey of Newstead, Nottinghamshire, an amateur operatic and musical-comedy 'star', many years his junior. They were soon married, and moved to a cottage at Old Dalby in Leicestershire where he was to spend the rest of his life.

As an individual, Thomas Henry was great fun to his family and friends, especially at Christmas when his nephews and nieces would gather round for a ghost story. But a publicity-seeker he was not. He was a very sensitive man in many ways, on one occasion fainting after a minor accident with his car. So shy was he in public that when he took on the duty of best man at his nephew Lionel Fisher's wedding he asked his wife Anne to deliver his speech (which she did).

If further proof were needed of Thomas Henry's retiring nature, it is that he met Richmal Crompton only once – at a luncheon arranged during the Nottingham Book Festival in 1958 – almost forty years after the beginning of their collaboration.

Thomas Henry was a good golfer, was excellent at bowls, and enjoyed the occasional rough shoot. He nearly always owned one or more English springer spaniels (which he would use as models when required), and his favourite places were Cornwall, the Cotswolds and Norfolk. He never used bad language, he liked a pint of beer (but was not a big drinker), and he loved his pipe and baggy plus-fours! He was an enthusiastic collector of antique furniture, was full of practical jokes (but never nasty ones), and occasionally played the violin in Old Dalby church, although he was not particularly religious. He became a freemason in June 1936, and his favourite artist was Cecil Aldin.

The Younger Brother (in an awestruck whisper). "SAY, 'ORACE, ARE YOU SURE WE'RE RIGHT FOR THE GALLERY? THERE'S A GENT BEHIND WIV SPATS ON!"

Then came the war, and with it the demise of most of the magazines that gave Thomas Henry his livelihood. The paper shortages forced him on several occasions to do his paintings on the back of Tate & Lyle sugar-bags. He continued to illustrate the slightly diminished output of William stories, and in 1947 began the famous strip cartoons of William Brown in *Woman's Own* that continued until his death some fifteen years later. Henry Ford then took over both the strip and the book illustrations.

Also in 1947, the following letter (dated 7 January) arrived from Austin Hatton, the features editor of the *Star* newspaper:

Miss Lamburn has consented to write 12 child stories for 'The Star' creating a new child character.

I wondered whether you, who shared in her masterly invention of William, would agree to do the illustrations for our series.

If it is at all possible, would you please let me know. I would also be grateful if you did not reveal the fact that we have got her to write this series for us . . .

This, of course, was Richmal's 'Jimmy'. Thomas Henry was then in his sixty-eighth year. He may well have felt that his work on the *Nottingham Football Post*, the strips for *Woman's Own* and the William stories were enough to keep him occupied but he accepted the assignment. In the end, however, Newnes decided not to use these drawings in the books, which were eventually illustrated by Lunt Roberts.

Richmal Crompton wrote thirty-eight William books in all, of which Thomas Henry illustrated thirty-three, and part of the thirty-fourth. He died of a heart-attack at the age of eighty-three on 15 October 1962, soon after he had returned from the pillar-box where he had posted his latest drawing for *William and the Witch*. (D.S.)

Heppleback, Mr

A glazier, who, because of William's awkward tendency to break windows with his bows and arrows, balls, conkers, etc., is fairly frequently called into the Browns' house. (*Just William's Luck*, 1)

Hetherley, Colonel

Retired 'Anglo-Indian' soldier, living at Reeth Lodge, whom at first the Outlaws consider to be 'a foreigner' (see NEW ELIZABETHANS). (*William and the Moon Rocket*, 6, and also mentioned in *William and the Pop Singers*, 2)

Higgs, P.C.

Police Constable Higgs enters the stories by name in the sixth book, *William – The Conqueror*, 9. (However, unnamed local policemen are called in as early as in the first book, *Just – William*, when in chapter 4 they are examining the Browns' conservatory after every flower has apparently been stolen from it. Actually William has picked and taken these to school as a love-token while briefly infatuated with one of his teachers, MISS DREW.

On his first appearance, the unfortunate Higgs is called upon to arrest Lady Markham for allegedly stealing Mrs Bott's pearls. It is all a misunderstanding, of course (see ANGELA (1)), but Higgs is put into an extremely awkward position: '. . . the village policeman was a youth who had lived on Lady Markham's estate all his life and looked up to her as lower in rank (and only *just* a little lower, even so) to the Queen alone. It was Lady Markham who had kept his grandmother out of the workhouse, had provided his mother with nurses and nourishment in her recent illness, and had been instrumental in getting him into his present position.'

P.C. Higgs plays a small part in six stories altogether. In *William and the Witch*, 3, the passage of time in his relationship with the Outlaws is noted. (He has, after all, known them for the best part of four decades, during which time *he* has matured, although *they* have remained firmly fixed as eleven-to-twelve-year-olds.) He is off-duty, and wanders up to a hoop-la stall which William and his friends are running: 'Outside his official capacity P.C. Higgs was a simple, friendly soul', and apparently, despite the 'intermittent feud' he has carried on with the Outlaws 'over the years', he still has 'a weak spot for them at the bottom of his heart'. Higgs is mentioned in the last of all the books, *William the Lawless*, 3, when the Vicar refers to him and 'all his kids'. Though obviously by then very much a man with family responsibilities, Higgs remains a constable. Possibly there is not enough crime in the village to make promotion easy even for ambitious members of the force, in spite of the activities of the numerous tramps, burglars, and con-men who crop up in the William saga! (The other books mentioning Higgs are *William's Television Show*, 4; *William's Treasure Trove*, 4; and *William and the Pop Singers*, 3. Many appearances are also made by unnamed policemen.)

History

The Outlaws' slender but colourful sense of history enlivens many of the stories, particularly when they are delving into the past for the purpose of putting on some fund-raising show or another. Meticulous research into any period is, in William's eyes, an irrelevance. Scrappy knowledge can easily be supplemented by drawing from his plentiful imagination. He comments, for example, that anyone can 'make up history people's clothes' for they 'jus' wore tablecloths and long stockings and funny things on their head'. He con-

fuses not only tablecloths with togas, but also one period with another (see HOWLERS).

In *William – The Bold*, 2, William is writing a play, and the Outlaws are exulting in the fact that, because Violet Elizabeth has gone down with the mumps, they now no longer need to have her in the part of Elizabeth I.

'I dunno that I want to have Queen Elizabeth at all,' said William. 'She wasn't very int'restin'. She didn't do anythin' but go trampin' about in puddles over people's coats . . .'

'She beat the Armada,' said Henry.

'No, she didn't,' said William. 'Nelson did that.'

'Drake.'

'Well, Drake then. But *she* didn't. I 'spect she jus' swanked about in an A.T.S. uniform, same as Ethel did in our war, but she didn't do any fightin'.'

As this conversation continues, the Outlaws confuse Shakespeare and Dickens, and the periods of Perkin Warbeck and George Washington. Their ignorance, at a time when schoolchildren were instilled with a strong, if sometimes simplistic, understanding of British history, is surprising. Some adults in the saga are similarly hopeless about the events of the past. In *William and the Evacuees*, 2, for example, Mrs Bott remarks that Botty 'nearly got a prize for history once . . . He'd've got it if he hadn't muddled up Nelson with Nero, or some such names.'

Hobbin, Mrs

At one time charwoman to the Browns, sometimes called Hobbin and sometimes Hobbins. See FAIRMAN, MISS. (*William – The Rebel*, 11, and *William – The Detective*, 8)

Holding, Mrs

See BERGSON, CLARENCE.

Holidays

' "Wouldn't it be heavenly," said William's sister, Ethel, "if someone would ask William somewhere for even a week?" ' The adult Browns' longing for William to go away, so that at least for a short period peace might reign in their home, is understandable.

William's holidays fall into three main categories:

1) those spent in his native haunts – wonderful respites from school, which he greatly enjoys;
2) enforced visits to relatives, which are nearly always extremely restrictive, and to be avoided at all costs, if possible;
3) trips to the seaside which offer on the positive side rock-pools and crabs, chances to fish, and Robinson Crusoe or pirate games. On the negative side, however, he misses his friends, Jumble, the vicissitudes of life in his village, and the woods, ditches, hedges and fields of the countryside that provide the setting for so many of his most memorable exploits.

Holidays can be long or short, and sometimes for William and his friends those that last just for one day are the most satisfying: 'The Outlaws swung happily along the road. It was Saturday. It was a holiday. All the world was before them . . .' (*William – In Trouble*, 2). Winter holidays as well as summer ones are bright with promise. In *William's Happy Days*, 1, the Christmas holidays have just begun; the Outlaws are spending these on home ground: 'They had made fires and tracked each other through forbidden woods, they had fished in forbidden streams, and they had discussed at length that insoluble mystery – why a

morning passes so much more quickly in holiday than in term time.'

Towards the end of their various holidays, the pendulum of the Outlaws' moods has swung completely from expansive optimism to gloomy grievance. With the thought of the beginning of term looming darkly over them, William, Ginger, Henry and Douglas aimlessly wander over the fields exchanging apprehensive and angry comments about 'Ole Stinks', 'Ole Markie', 'Ole Warbeck' and 'Monkey-Face', who are, of course, some of the teachers at their school (*Sweet William*, 2).

For William the worst kind of holiday (apart from some at the homes of obsessively house-proud and bigoted aunts) is that spent *en famille*, away from home but *not* at the seaside. Mr Brown on these occasions finds congenial occupation in river fishing, or simply burying himself deeper than ever behind his newspapers, recovering from the strains of the office and commuting. Mrs Brown enjoys shopping, and hotel life; she sometimes spends her time learning a new needlework skill, such as quilting. Robert and Ethel take out temporary membership of the local tennis club, and spice up their sporting endeavours with holiday flirtations, if 'the most beautiful girl in the world' comes along, or some strapping young man goes overboard about Ethel's Titian locks.

William is then stranded, and aggressively bored: 'What people came away for holidays *for* beat him. At home there was old Jumble to take for a walk and throw sticks for, and the next-door cat to tease and the butcher's boy to fight . . . Here there was – well, all he said *was*, he might as well be *dead*' (*William Again*, 3). It is a fairly safe bet, however, that once William has given utterance to his boredom adventure will be thrust upon him. In *William – The Rebel*, 8, he tries to concentrate the greater part of his energies upon fishing, but ends up having to cut down to size a horribly assertive young man, Archie, who sees himself not only as the greatest of all fishermen, but also as God's gift to the fair sex. In particular he wants to make an impression on Claribel, who is staying at the same boarding-house. Cast in a similar mould to Ethel, she is, as William can see at a glance, the sort of girl 'who makes things hum'. To avenge himself of the insults which Archie has heaped upon him, William contrives to put him always at a disadvantage with Claribel. He is considerably helped in his campaign by his understanding of Ethel's wiles and Robert's weaknesses, which he harnesses to good effect. For instance, when the great Archie nonchalantly stands in the water to demonstrate his fishing skills to Claribel, he suddenly loses his balance when his waders become flooded (William has punctured them with his pen-knife). His struggles to get back into the safety of the boat with Claribel reduce her pale pink organdie dress to a sodden mass. 'It's a miracle I wasn't drowned,'

gasps Archie. 'I wish you had been,' bursts out Claribel passionately. 'You've ruined my dress.' Archie's dreams of conquest are doomed, and William has managed to enliven yet another of his dreaded holidays away from home.

Home Magazine, The

William made his first appearance in print in the story 'Rice-Mould' (*More William*, 2) in the *Home Magazine* for February 1919. The mood of the period immediately after the First World War is captured on the cover of this issue, which shows a pretty lady being kissed by a handsome soldier, while a blue-eyed baby, wedged between them, gazes in blissful corpulence at the reader above the caption 'HOME – FOR KEEPS'. It behoves us cynics of the 1990s to assume that they are man and wife!

The magazine, published by George Newnes Ltd from 1893 to 1931, was aimed at the housewife and mother, with the usual articles on rug-making, bringing up children, cookery, and the wisdom of marriage, as well as a good proportion of fiction. It enjoyed several changes of name, having started as *Woman at Home (& Girl's Realm)*, to become the *Home Magazine (Woman at Home)*, and then, in October 1922, *The Ladies' Home Magazine*. This issue was also the last to contain a William story, 'Not Much' (*William Again*, 5), making a total of forty-one appearances in the magazine altogether. (For a full bibliography, see Appendix 2.) The publication later became *Home Magazine and Ladies' Field*, and was finally incorporated into *Homes and Gardens* in 1931, the unusual vehicle in which William was to make three further appearances during the Second World War.

Richmal Crompton (as R. C. Lamburn) had her first acceptance for the *Home Magazine* in August 1918 with a love-story, 'The First Arrow', illustrated by E. F. Sherie, followed in October by 'One

Crowded Hour', the acknowledged forerunner to the William saga. This story was illustrated by L. Hocknell, who also illustrated the first appearance of William in 'Rice-Mould'. Miss Hocknell's style, at its best with tearful seven-year-olds and pretty girls with dolls, was really too sentimental for the anarchic humour of the William tales. The editor must certainly have thought so, because by the following month THOMAS HENRY had been commissioned to produce drawings for the second story, 'The Outlaws' (*Just – William*, 8). It heralded the beginning of an association with Richmal Crompton that was to last until Thomas Henry's death in 1962 at the age of eighty-three.

Several William stories in *Home Magazine* contain pictures by Thomas Henry that have not been reproduced in the books. 'The Outlaws' (March 1919) includes a wonderful close-up of Mrs Butler's baby with the caption 'It was drenched with paraffin oil, and in its hand was the apple dumpling' (see BABIES). In 'Jumble' (June 1919) there are five cameos of William's beloved mongrel in various poses ranging from 'Just out of the ditch' to 'Eager, playful, adoring' (see JUMBLE). And in 'The Show' (July 1919) we see the first picture of William with his parents (and Aunt Emily), Mrs Brown looking particularly young and pretty (see BROWN FAMILY), while another depicts the fee-paying children clustered around the bedside of William's snoring Aunt Emily with the notice above her head 'FAT WILD WOMAN TORKIN NATIF LANGWIDGE' (see RELATIONS).

The *Home Magazine* for this period is almost impossible to find in the ephemera market, but if you should be lucky enough to find a copy you will enjoy, apart from its scarcity, the marvellous clarity of the original line-drawings.

After October 1922, the William stories moved to what was to be their home for eighteen years, the HAPPY MAG. (D.S.)

Home Notes

This little weekly magazine, crammed with knitting patterns, love-stories, the problem page, film gossip, recipes, baby advice and horoscopes, was William's last 'home' in magazines.

Richmal Crompton had been busy with scripts for the various radio series that began immediately after the war, with the consequence that no William book appeared in 1946 or 1947. In the meantime, Val Guest had written the screenplay for the film *Just William's Luck*, to be released in late 1947, and Richmal was involved in working this up into the book of the same name, the only novel-length William adventure. As a result, the production-line of short stories had slowed considerably.

It was welcome news when the following announcement appeared in *Home Notes* on 24 January 1947:

> If we said, 'He's an awful child, an incorrigible brat, what the French call an *enfant terrible*,' whom would you say we were talking about? Of course, it's that irrepressible young ruffian William! And here's a piece of good news about the young rascal – we shall be able to share in his adventures in next week's issue of 'Home Notes' – and there are more stories about William to come.
>
> Since Richmal Crompton's imagination first created the boy who has captured all our hearts – from the schoolboy of William's own age to the young in heart, if not in years – he has become as familiar as though he was fact instead of fiction . . .

The first story was 'William and the Witch' (*William – The Bold*, 4, as 'A Witch in Time'). Only three stories appeared in 1947, one in 1948, and two in 1949, followed by an average of three a year until the last on 9 September 1954, 'William's

Mistake' (*William and the Moon Rocket*, 8, as 'These Little Mistakes Will Happen').

By this time, the pattern of a new William book every other year had been set, usually with eight stories in each.

What is remarkable about *Home Notes*, and what makes it very collectable, is that all Thomas Henry's drawings are different from those used in the books. The scene may be the same in many cases, but the drawings for *Home Notes* are shaded half-tones, as opposed to the simpler line-drawings of the books.

Another issue of William interest (but not a story) is the *Home Notes* for 9 May 1947. In his gossip column, Collie Knox mentions that he sat next to Richmal Crompton at a Foyles luncheon:

Authors are seldom as their readers imagine them. Miss Richmal Crompton, whose *Just William* stories have won millions of reading and radio fans, is no exception. She, too, is quiet of voice, and retiring of manner.

'Parents write to me,' she said, 'and call me to task for the naughtiness of their children. Their efforts to emulate my William's adventurous spirit are not always appreciated in the home!'

Miss Crompton possesses a keen insight into the child mind, coupled with a love for children. She has evolved a 'character', thereby doing what most writers long to do.

Accompanying the paragraph is a delightful picture of Richmal Crompton with her brother John (the original 'William'), along with radio producer Alick Hayes and the radio 'William', John Clark.

(D.S.)

Homes and Gardens

Until September 1941, *Homes and Gardens* contained no fiction at all. However, a desperate editor, obviously badly affected by the privations of the Second World War, was moved to write most apologetically in the editorial for that month. The Government, he said, had forbidden anyone to build new houses, and no one had any money to buy new furniture. This, coupled with the fact that most gardens had been dug up to plant vegetables or for the breeding of chickens and rabbits, had made his life as editor of *Homes and Gardens* somewhat tricky. What people needed, obviously, was fiction. Fiction to take their minds off their homes – and their gardens.

So fiction it was. But it wasn't until June 1943 that 'William's War-time Funfair' appeared, followed by 'The Outlaws' Report' in May 1944, and 'Aunt Florence, Toy-Maker' in November 1945 (*William and the Brains Trust*, 4, 7 and 10).

It seems rather odd that just these three stories should grace *Homes and Gardens* during the period in which William was already resident in *Modern Woman*. It was even more odd that all three were illustrated, not by Thomas Henry, but by an artist called Gaffron, especially as Thomas Henry must have been preparing *his* drawings for them pending the publication of *William and the Brains Trust*. He must have been working on the book well in advance of publication in April 1945. He was also concurrently illustrating those stories that were appearing in *Modern Woman*. Presumably, this is one of those little mysteries that will never be solved.

Gaffron was a very accomplished artist who designed all the covers for *Homes and Gardens*, commencing with the 'new format' issue of September 1941, and continuing throughout the war and beyond, at least until 1947. The covers were marvellous but, needless to say, the attempts at William and Ginger were doomed to failure. Gaffron, like any other interpreter, was up against Thomas Henry's characterisations of almost thirty years' standing. Not an easy act to follow.

After the war, *Homes and Gardens* (probably

with much relief) went back to homes and gardens; *Modern Woman* (presumably) went to find more modern women; and William (by now a seasoned traveller) went to HOME NOTES. (D.S)

Houses and Gardens

William's own house and garden are spacious – both before and after the family's removal in *More William*, 10. In fact his first house and the second, The Hollies, in which he seems to have remained for the rest of the saga, have so much in common that one wonders why the Brown family decided to move from one to the other. From the stories it is possible to build up a detailed picture of William's

home (see WILLIAM'S HOUSES); it is true that over the years there seems to have been a *psychological* shrinking of The Hollies, and certainly the domestic staff became considerably reduced (see SERVANTS), but there never was any shortage of space in William's physical environment. The Browns' lifestyle seems to have required morning room, dining-room, drawing-room and library-cum-study, as well as kitchen, scullery, bathroom and bedrooms, of course. William also had a play-room in the early days which housed his 'engine and books and things' (*More William*, 6) but he doesn't appear to have spent a great deal of time in it. (Neither, surprisingly, do we hear much more about this engine, which must surely have been an object of great pride to him.) William is

essentially, of course, an outdoor boy, and the Browns' 'disused coach house', summerhouse, stables and wood-shed would be happier areas for his activities than a conventional playroom. Most of all the OLD BARN is a happy compromise between indoors and out and, being situated away from any grounds owned by the Outlaws' families, a place of refuge from adults – a splendid head-quarters for the secret worlds of imagination that William occupies for long stretches at a time. Empty houses and gardens are always potential special places for the Outlaws, providing both the setting and the inspiration for some of their most adventurous games and most lurid fantasies.

Generally speaking, William prefers other gardens to his own, which suffers the limitation of having an ever watchful gardener for whom any lively boy is a *bête noire*. It is also neat and tidy and far less conducive to exploration and adventure than gardens which lie empty and happily neglected: 'The house next door had been unoccupied for so long that William had begun to look upon its garden as his own property.' It is, apparently, not much more than 'a waste expanse of old tins, broken pots, and the heterogeneous collection of rubbish that marked a long period of To-Letness', but it is his 'stronghold', which he peoples in his imagination with picturesquely attired brigands who spring into action at his command (*William – The Pirate*, 5). The Outlaws find and temporarily take over other empty houses from time to time, and most of these have gardens that beg to be played in.

The thrill of stumbling upon an empty house comes vividly across in *William and the Witch*, 2, when the Outlaws (playing truant from Violet Elizabeth's party) find an unoccupied property in the woods. The possibilities of the 'empty, dust-laden hall and bare uncarpeted staircase' are gleefully pointed out by William. There are lots of games they can play there – 'Better than any ole Postman's Knock' (which might well be in progress at that moment at the party from which they have escaped). The height of joy is their discovery of a rat in residence.

In *William's Happy Days*, 7, a whole page is devoted to William's description of the ideal house that he will buy once he becomes a millionaire. This will dispense entirely with carpets 'or anythin' like that' so that there will never be complaints about boots not being wiped. It will accommodate a regular window-mender so that William can break ten windows a day if he likes. The garden will not be cluttered with flowers but allowed to go wild, with 'elephants an' lions an' tigers an' giraffes an' things like that' all living wild (but tamed to an extent by William). The house will contain a sweetshop. All the Outlaws will live together in it, and 'a real train' will run through all the passages and rooms, 'with real coals', to be driven by the Outlaws when it is too wet to go out and play with the animals. The final touches to William's dream house are switchbacks instead of staircases, swings on the roof and a water-shute from there down to a pond in the garden, and one room devoted entirely to insects, with 'snails an' caterpillars crawlin' all over the walls, so that we can watch 'em'.

Howlers

Howlers, particularly historical ones, frequently embellish the stories. In *Sweet William*, 6, for example, when, after hearing about Pitt and Wilberforce freeing the slaves, William embarks upon a career as a reformer, he calls himself 'Hole' when he cannot quite remember Pitt's name. He is more generally responsible for the misplaced phrase or statement than the simple howler. When a school lecturer mentions the possibility that 'the plays of Shakespeare were written by Bacon' and goes on to mention Hamlet, it is inevitable that William should tangle things up: ' "When I called him Ham, you said it was Bacon, and now you're calling him Ham yourself . . . I tell you what," said William confidingly, "let's say Eggs for both of them." '

When Henry, who has a real interest in archaeology, tells them about the Piltdown Man hoax, the Outlaws decide to devise their own historical trick. They have acquired a collection of dully domestic Victorian and Edwardian letters, and decide to enliven these for the potential historical researchers by adding postscripts dealing with interesting and exciting events from the past. Their postscripts are masterpieces of anachronism: Henry at least tries to refer only to events which took place in, or within a decade or so of, the period of the earliest letters: 'The Black Hole of Calcutta took place yesterday and tomorrow six hundred are going to ride into the Valley of Death.' William's footnotes, however, 'spanned the whole field of history with wild abandon': 'Henry VIII got married to the third of his six wives this morning'; 'I went down to Hastings yesterday to watch the battle. Harold looked as if he'd got an arrow in his eye'; 'I helped Guy Fawkes carry gunpowder into the House of Commons last night. We nearly got caught by a policeman'; 'I was helping to put out the fire of London all yesterday. I feel rotten this morning. I think I must have caught the plague' (*William and the Masked Ranger*, 1).

Illness

There is little serious illness in the stories; the village naturally has its crop of ancient, infirm, deaf and somewhat senile characters; various genteel ladies develop headaches, while servants and others from the 'lower orders' occasionally have 'queer turns'. Women and girls from all strata of society (and at times even strong men) have hysterics as the result of some action or other of William's. Mr Brown sometimes suffers from a

minor disorder of the liver, but generally speaking the Browns enjoy rude health. William in particular is rarely confined to the sickroom, although over-eating of dubious sweetmeats and rich food takes its toll from time to time, when he is literally sick or afflicted with slight indigestion. His worst bout of genuine illness is probably influenza (*William's Happy Days*, 4: see BOOKS), but on one or two occasions he invents imaginary maladies in an endeavour to get out of going to school or attending some other equally unpleasant function (see BELL, DR). (*William – The Fourth*, 3, tells us that in the privacy of his bedroom William practises the churchyard cough which proves an asset to him on many occasions.)

He uses illness inventively as an excuse for getting Ethel out of a social engagement which he thinks she doesn't wish to keep (actually, she does). In a spirit of pure helpfulness he tells Mrs Morrison that Ethel 'can't come to-night' because she has epilepsy and 'a bit of consumption too'. Later on Ethel is distraught about the rumours concerning her health which are sweeping through the village, and even the normally sanguine Mrs Brown demands a little testily: 'But William . . .

how did you think it was going to help *anyone* to say that Ethel had epilepsy and consumption?' (*Still – William*, 4).

Illustrators

William's first illustrator was Louise Hocknell, of whom we know virtually nothing. She was producing excellent drawings in *Home Magazine* in 1919, and illustrated other stories by Richmal Crompton, usually with a romantic or emotional content. But her pictures for 'Rice-Mould' did not anticipate the reckless style required for a boy of William's dark potential. When this story was reprinted (*More William*, 2), it contained fresh illustrations from THOMAS HENRY, who had taken over from the second story in the magazine and continued to be, in effect, the 'only' William illustrator.

In an odd interlude, however, another artist attempted three William stories, in the wartime HOMES AND GARDENS. This artist was Gaffron, and he designed all the covers for the magazine during this period. It remains a slight mystery why Thomas Henry was not asked to illustrate these stories for *Homes and Gardens*, especially as he was in any case concurrently illustrating them for book publication.

William's last illustrator, Henry Ford, is also something of a mystery. He took over from Thomas Henry within months of the latter's death in 1962, completed the illustrations for *William and the Witch*, and took over the strip cartoons for *Woman's Own*. He deliberately emulated the style of Thomas Henry to create the minimum disturbance of the genre, and even his signature bore an uncanny resemblance to that of his predecessor.

There were no more 'official' illustrators. Arthur Ranson had a brief 'Look-In' in the *Junior TV Times* as part of London Weekend Television's merchandising of the television series in 1977, while cartoonists in the national press have often used William's image to underline a telling political point. Notably, Chic Jacob in the *Observer* successfully cast Margaret Thatcher as Violet Elizabeth and Willie Whitelaw as William (leader of the Wetlaws), and Low in the *Daily Express* put Harold Wilson in the star role. Doubtless there were others, and doubtless there are many more to come. (D.S.)

Improvisation

The Outlaws are masters of improvisation – Mrs Brown is constantly in despair because William has used yet another pair of garters for catapults – which is frequently necessitated through lack of funds and facilities (see also GAMES AND TOYS, FANTASY AND IMAGINATION). In *Sweet William*, 7, for instance, they plan to use masks for one of their nefarious exploits, and William says that those who do not own masks can have black handkerchiefs tied over their eyes:

> 'All my handkerchiefs are white,' said Ginger . . . 'At least . . . they are when they've been washed.'
>   'Well, you can black one, can't you?' said William impatiently. 'What's ink for?'

It is also, of course, for blacking the flesh revealed by large holes in the Outlaws' socks.

Insects

Insects and 'creepy-crawlies' are always a source of great interest to William, who finds it difficult to understand that others do not necessarily share his enthusiasm for them. For example, in *More William*, 8, he befriends Bettine Franklin, a small dark-haired girl in his class who admires him in a discreet from-the-sidelines manner. William magnanimously decides to give her a present, and presses a centipede into her hand, explaining that she will find it 'jolly int'restin' and that she should put it in a matchbox with holes to give it air. 'And because she loved William, she took it without a shudder.'

In *Still – William*, 14, insects are once again a yardstick of his affection for one of the fair sex. This time it is 'JOAN', the little girl next door, who is receiving William's attentions:

'. . . I like you better than *any* insect, Joan,' he said generously.
    'Oh, William, do you really?' said Joan, deeply touched.

William explains that he is going to marry her when he grows up so long as she will not expect him 'to talk a lot of soppy stuff'.

Earlier in the same chapter William is lovingly tending his collection of woodlice, centipedes and earwigs, and the 'star' of them all, Albert, the stag beetle who, at least in the eyes of his owner, is clever enough to respond to training and be taught tricks. His mother has just discovered the collection in William's sock-drawer, which is not only their home, but also their larder, so that crumbly bits of bread and little pools of marmalade adhere not only to the insects but also to socks and hankies. Needless to say, even Mrs Brown's large fund of tolerance is taxed by this, though William quite genuinely cannot understand her irritation. Albert, after disturbing a Bible class, and then a French lesson, is eventually 'took off' William, who has to console himself with a rather special earwig called Fred.

The disruptive aspects of William's various insect collections are blithely exploited in many of the stories as a means of debunking pompous or pernicious adults. A good example occurs in *William – The Fourth*, 10, when, for safe-keeping, William hides his current collection of beetles, caterpillars, ants and cockroaches under the sofa in his living-room where, unknown to him, the Society for the Encouragement of Higher Thought is scheduled to meet. Its pretentious president, Miss Euphemia Barney, chooses to position herself on the sofa and, of course, the insect collection, which starts by nipping and stinging the president, soon throws all the Higher Thinkers into total confusion (see AUTHORS).

Isaacs, Mr

Mr Isaacs, the owner of the village sweetshop, is at the centre of one of the most bizarre and out-of-character episodes of all the William stories. In *William – The Detective*, 6, he is the victim of the Outlaws' Jew-baiting activities. See also ANTI-SEMITISM, POLITICS AND POWER and XENOPHOBIA.

Isabella

A pupil from Rose Mount School, who becomes the self-appointed squaw of the Outlaws when they decide to enliven an enforced nature ramble by playing Red Indians. They dislike her on sight for her assertiveness, and William tries to scare her off by twisting his face into 'a startling expression of ferocity', brandishing his tomahawk and threatening to scalp, skin, roast and eat her: ' "That's cannibals," said the little girl placidly. "You've got mixed. Red Indians don't eat people." ' William is so nonplussed by this knowledge of Red Indian lore by a mere female that when he tries 'to resume his expression of ferocity' all he can manage is 'a squint and bared clenched teeth'. (*William – The Explorer*, 2)

James

A chauffeur/coachman who, in *William – The Pirate*, 4, is a rival of George the baker's man for the affections of William's Aunt Jane's pretty maid, Molly (see GEORGE, 3).

Jameson, Jameson

Jameson Jameson first comes into the stories in *William – The Fourth*, 1, when we are told that his 'parents had perpetrated on him the supreme practical joke of giving him his surname for a Christian name'. He is the founder of the Society of Reformed Bolshevists (see POLITICS AND POWER) and a good friend of Robert's, despite their occasional rivalry over a girl or some prestigious position in the local community (*William – The Pirate*, 11). Like Robert, his attentions shift from one pretty girl to another; Ethel, of course, inspires in him the statutory brief infatuation that is her due from every unattached young man in the village.

Jameson Jameson is mentioned in nineteen of the stories, although in *Sweet William*, 3, he is mistakenly called Victor throughout. In the beginning he is nineteen and three-quarters, and senior to the then seventeen-year-old Robert. In *William – The Rebel*, 12, however, he appears to be one month younger than Robert. He is last mentioned in *William and the Witch*, 3. See also ROBERT AND HIS FRIENDS.

Jameson, Victor

Younger brother of Jameson Jameson, approximately the same age as William, and a consistent friend of the Outlaws, though never admitted to the intimacy of their group. His occasional rivalries with them are good-natured rather than malevolent. His first appearance (like his brother's) is in

William – The Fourth, 1, and his last is in *William the Lawless*, 6. Altogether he is mentioned in thirty-three stories.

Jenks, Farmer

Farmer Jenks is first mentioned in *Still – William*, 6, when he is described as 'the Outlaws' most implacable foe'. Jenks's fury when the Outlaws trespass on his fields is vitriolic, and his threats of retribution are dire. William's favourite is that Jenks will 'cut his [William's] liver out': 'He could not resist haunting Farmer Jenks' lands because the chase that always ensued was so much more exciting than an ordinary chase. "Well, he's not cut it out *yet*", he used to say proudly after each escape.'

Happily William's liver remains in place and intact to the end of the saga, even though Farmer Jenks is mentioned in forty-six of the stories, and in the last of the books, *William the Lawless*, 3, is still 'growling' and using – according to Miss Milton – 'shocking' language about a dog (fortunately not Jumble) that he claims to have caught chasing sheep in Three Acre Meadow. See also Jumble.

'Joan'

That 'Joan' was William's 'best and earliest love' cannot be disputed. However, the conception of 'Joan' as a single 'little girl next door' with a curiously variable surname – Clive/Crewe/Parfitt, which reverts finally to Clive – raises distinct difficulties.

In his early years, before he attained the age of eleven, still living in the house where he was born (see WILLIAM's HOUSES) and sandwiched between the Merridews and the Clives, William enjoyed the loyalty of Ginger on one side and the adoration and unquestioning obedience of Joan on the other.

While regarding her as 'his' Joan, William reacted towards her with no great emotion until the arrival of her golden-haired cousin Cuthbert and her apparent transference of affection to him aroused William's intense jealousy: 'Previously he had received Joan's adoration with coldness, but previously there had been no rival' (2.6). Several times in these early stories Joan Clive is graphically described as having blue eyes and bright golden curls (1.1, 2.6, 2.14). It is very difficult to see how an identification of Joan Clive with Joan Crewe (to whom William declares his desire for eventual marriage in 5.14) can be physically possible, seeing that Joan Crewe (as we are told repeatedly) has dark eyes, dark curly hair and a dimpled oval face. When one considers William's somewhat juvenile behaviour in the Joan Clive stories (and the absence of any indication that the Outlaws as yet exist as an *organised* group), one may perhaps wonder whether these early stories reflect the period when William was rather younger than his customary eleven years. It is conceivable that some considerable time before the Crewes took up residence in the village, Joan Clive, together with her mother and six-foot-six father James Clive, had removed from the village and out of William's life, so that by the time Joan Crewe came on the scene the details of Joan Clive's appearance were no longer very clear or significant in William's memory and that he recalled only her devotion with particular pleasure.

One cannot of course simply ignore the discrepancy in 3.14 where the Joan Clive with whom William is 'shipwrecked' is said to have *dark* curls. But one may fairly argue that a single discrepant statement may be classified as a narrator's slip. The *repeated* statements in several independent stories regarding Joan Clive's blue eyes and golden hair cannot so easily be disregarded.

In 4.8 the dark-eyed, dark-haired, dimpled, shy and 'rather silent' Joan Crewe takes the Outlaw oath and is admitted as the only female member.

She subsequently distinguishes herself as the ideal loyal squaw. William receives her devotion and acceptance of male domination as gladly as he accepted that of Joan Clive. But this time he responds emotionally (5.14). Joan Crewe, not Joan Clive, is William's 'best and earliest love' who sets the 'type' of girl towards which William manifests a constant susceptibility.

Unfortunately for William, Joan Crewe's residence in the village does not have the permanency of that of the other Outlaws. After the episode with Mr Galileo Simpkin in 7.2 she disappears from the scene, not returning until 8.5 after an absence so prolonged that the Outlaws celebrate her return with their 'Mammoth Circus' organised in secret at Rose Mount School. The last we see of Joan Crewe is in 9.7 where she points out a fairy-ring to William. In 12.8 we are told that she has long since left the village. The passage in question is a confused one. 'There had only been one serious love passage in his life, and that had been when he had lost his heart to Joan, the little girl next door, who had long since left the neighbourhood. Though William had forgotten her [!], he would occasionally meet [a girl] whose likeness to Joan would stir a tender chord . . . the dimpled face and dark hair that always made him think of Joan.' William seems to have forgotten the golden-headed girl next door (Joan Clive) who left long ago. Clearly he had not entirely forgotten the dark-headed Joan Crewe who had never lived next door and had departed somewhat more recently. Although in William's young memory there may be some kind of superimposition of the image of Joan Crewe on the more vaguely recalled image of Joan Clive, more probably the words 'the little girl next door' are a narrator's error unless of course she is anticipating an event as yet in the future and to be described below. At all events the appearance of Angela in 12.8 recalls Joan Crewe to William's mind.

Had it not been for the war, Joan would never have returned to the village. The sensation the news of her intended return provokes in the Outlaws indicates that she has by no means been forgotten. She returns to the village – from London – as Joan Parfitt, which suggests that in the interim her mother has been widowed and married again, divorce at that date being a much less likely alternative. The bombing of Mr Parfitt's London warehouse has suggested that the village may be a safer location for his family. Joan and her mother take Lilac Cottage but are obliged, because of a supposed unexploded bomb, to stay for a time at Miss Milton's. There is subsequently even thought of sending Joan to the safety of a residential school in Scotland. However, this comes to nothing. Joan's reference (24.4) to the Miss Peache episode (12.7), which she could only have heard about from William, indicates the enthusiasm with which he acquainted her with his adventures during her absence.

By the end of the war the Parfitts seem to have contemplated permanent residence in the village. They purchased the house next door to the

Browns' – since the gate could be seen from William's bedroom window (27.4) it must have been the house on the east side, once occupied by the 'gorilla' neighbour (14.5) – and presumably lived there for a time, to judge from the wording of Joan's pleading letter to William in 27.4. However, when, after a substantial absence, Joan and her mother wished to return, they found that the unfurnished tenancy they had granted to MISS EVESHAM involved them in legal difficulties, and it was only William's intervention that persuaded her to abandon her tenancy. Presumably, therefore, when Joan was composing her verses for the Outlaw victory celebrations ('The Battle of Flowers': 27.5) she was then in point of fact 'the little girl next door', although the text gives no indication of this. By the end of this story William stands staring and pondering on the incomprehensibility of the female sex. The attachment is beginning to wear a little thin. We are told in 28.2 that 'Joan's father went abroad on frequent business trips and Joan and her mother generally accompanied him, so that the friendship was never put to any great strain, but at present the family was in England and Joan was attending Miss Golightly's school' (i.e., Rose Mount). One would suppose from the text that they have sold the house next door to The Hollies, which may have represented too permanent a base, and are living elsewhere in the village in the road 'leading to the Church Room'. The events of 28.2 can be dated fairly exactly as Henry has lately seen the film *Scott of the Antarctic*, released in 1948. This story seems to end an era in William's life: 'Suddenly, rather to his own surprise, William found that he didn't care. He didn't even want to reinstate himself in Joan's eyes. He thought of her party . . . and found that he didn't want to go to it. The demands of womankind in general and Joan in particular were incessant and exacting.'

By 33.5 Joan's family had removed from the village. The romance was over. I doubt whether William ever married Joan.

In 28.2 there is a final discrepancy. Joan's mother is referred to consistently – and astonishingly – as Mrs Clive. Whatever else may be questioned, this is evidently a narrator's slip of the tongue. 'Clive? Did I say "Clive"? I meant *Parfitt*, of course!' (K.C.W.)

Jocelyn, Mr

Appears briefly in *Still – William*, 11, when, dressed as a toreador at the Botts' fancy-dress dance, he is mistaken by the Outlaws for a ruthless politician and shut up in the coach-house. William realises his error when someone describes Mr Jocelyn to him: 'He's a writer, I believe. Nobody important.' (Richmal putting her tongue in her cheek at her own expense, perhaps?)

Jones, Carolina

A small girl in the village who first comes into the stories in *William and the Evacuees*, 1. Docile and full of admiration for William, she has only to shake her pretty ringlets, flutter her long lashes and put a smile on her cherubic lips to spur him to further efforts (to get the village children the perks which the evacuees have). She continues fairly regularly to appear in the books as one of the audience for the Outlaws' shows and public exploits, being last mentioned in *William the Superman*, 1, when the Outlaws are no longer concerned with the problems of the Second World War but with those of rebuilding society in the aftermath of a possible atomic war. Carolina (sometimes Caroline) crops up in eight stories altogether.

Jones, Farmer

Mentioned in *William – The Fourth*, 3, and in *William Does His Bit*, 3.

Jones, Mr

A refugee clown from Budapest ('Jones' is obviously a name adopted since he has been in England). See EGERTON. (*William – The Explorer*, 3)

Jones Minor

One of William's schoolmates. (*William Again*, 8)

Jumble

Canines frequently crop up in the saga (see DOGS), but the only regularly recurring doggy hero is Jumble, the apple of William's eye, and the pet who comes into his life in the first book, *Just – William*, and who does not make his final bow (or bark) until *William the Superman*, the penultimate book in the series. The out-of-sequence publication in book form of some of Richmal's magazine stories has been mentioned previously; nowhere

does it strike a more irritating note than in the case of Jumble, who takes part in one of the Outlaws' adventures in *Just – William*, 7, *before* his official coming into William's life, which is described in detail later in the book in chapter 12. Child readers of the book must have found this difficult to understand. Later generations of William fans in particular would be unlikely to know that chapter 7 ('William Joins the Band of Hope') was published in the August 1919 *Home Magazine*, while chapter 12 ('Jumble'), which deals with his advent, appeared in the same magazine two months earlier in June.

Although Jumble wagged his way into the stories in a disorderly manner, there is no doubt that he was from the beginning a perfect complement to William. He is robust and wholehearted rather than fearfully bright: in his first appearance in *Just – William* he is rabbiting in the woods with the Outlaws and joyously but ineptly chasing a butterfly and a bee and scratching up a molehill. He ends up being stung by a wasp.

His real début (in chapter 12) illustrates his irresistibility to a small boy. William is in one of his occasionally gloomy moods (because his father has just confiscated his bow and arrows) when he becomes aware of something 'coming down the road. It came jauntily with a light, dancing step, fox-terrier ears cocked, retriever nose raised, collie tail wagging, slightly dachshund body a-quiver with the joy of life.' Jumble gives an inviting bark of welcome, William's drooping spirits lift, and an immediate dog-and-boy rapport is established. We are told that Jumble is one of the few beings who fully appreciate William, and certainly William totally appreciates Jumble.

He had 'sometimes practised privately in readiness for the blissful day when Fate should present him with a real live dog of his own. So far Fate, in the persons of his father and mother, had been proof against all his pleading.' Even after Jumble's advent there are some difficulties in establishing

William's ownership of him, but once this crisis is overcome Jumble is resolutely there to stay. He becomes not only William's but also the Outlaws' frequent companion. Indeed, Jumble (whose thought processes are often described) feels that he has a right to be included in most if not all of the Outlaws' exploits: 'When Jumble was sent home he retired to the ditch till the Outlaws had proceeded some way and, he hoped, forgotten about him (Jumble was as great an optimist as his master), then he emerged from the ditch and followed again, keeping a discreet distance' (*William – In Trouble*, 5).

Generally Jumble quivers 'to the tip of his nondescript tail with expectation' whenever William is around. There are, however, moments when despite adoring each other 'William and Jumble . . . got on each other's nerves'. In *William's Happy Days*, 9, William is in the mood for rabbiting, but Jumble isn't: he keeps bringing sticks for William to throw, but William has no appetite for this, 'and so relations became strained'. When William tries to play Red Indians, Jumble has set his heart on hide-and-seek instead. Eventually they are reduced to William strolling 'aimlessly along the road, dragging his toes in the dust', while Jumble ferrets in the ditch 'pretending that he is out by himself'.

However, earlier in the same book (6) all is harmony between them until William, on his birthday of all days, has temporarily to part with Jumble who needs residential veterinary treatment after hurting his foot in a rabbit-trap: 'a birthday without Jumble was, in William's eyes, a hollow mockery'. Jumble's enforced absence triggers off a series of animal-orientated incidents involving Ethel and her current admirer, Mr Dewar, and the dancing class which William under maternal pressure reluctantly attends (see Dogs and Dancing Classes). William endures a lot of frustration in this chapter, but all losses are in the end restored when his pet is returned, whole and happy again, from the vet's:

The joy of walking along the road again with his beloved Jumble at his heels was almost too great to be endured . . . His heart was full of creamy content.

He'd got Jumble back. That man [Mr Dewar] was never coming to the house any more.

He wasn't going to any more dancing-classes.

It was the nicest birthday he'd ever had in his life.

Sadly this is not the only occasion when William is 'dogless and disconsolate'. In *William – The Rebel*, 1, Jumble is involved in a skirmish with Wotan, a rather unsympathetic Alsatian which Ethel is looking after while its real owner (another of her male admirers) is away on holiday. Jumble has the right of long-term residence in the Brown household on his side, but Wotan has the might of weight and size and viciousness on his. Jumble has once again to be temporarily hospitalised at the vet's while his side is stitched up; the vet 'had much past experience of William's amateur surgery' and knew that in the early days of the dog's recovery he would do better away from his master's affectionate but over-zealous attentions.

Salt is poured into William's psychological wounds every time he sees the obnoxious Wotan lording it over the household, and Ethel (who doesn't really like dogs at all) fussing over the Alsatian and striking elegant poses with him in the manner of an actress in a film she has recently seen. Poetic justice comes when Tinker, a sturdy and belligerent small white dog reminiscent of Jumble in appearance, attaches himself to William and gets the better of Wotan in a fight, just when Ethel is taking him – groomed, perfumed and beribboned – to take part in a dog show. Tinker is claimed by his rightful owner, a handsome young man who quickly succumbs to the charms of Ethel's 'blue eyes and red-gold hair': ' "I adore dogs," said Ethel unblushingly . . .'

William is delighted to see the last of Wotan, but

despondent without Tinker until, suddenly remembering that his period of separation from Jumble is due to end, 'whistling loudly and untunefully, he set off down the road at a run towards the vet's home'.

Unfortunately Jumble is in the wars yet again in *William and A.R.P.*, 4. He gets hit by a passing car: 'It wasn't really Jumble's fault, because he'd just seen a rat on the bank on the opposite side of the road and he naturally couldn't be expected to think of two things at once.' In this instance the damage is not long-lasting, even though Jumble's cries of pain and anger rend the air, and the blood is unhygienically wiped from his leg with a hankie of William's 'already so highly variegated with mud and ink that a little blood more or less made no difference'.

The next chapter brings one of the greatest crises in Jumble's (and William's) life. Inspired by seeing a film about sheep-dogs, William decides to become a dog-trainer, with Jumble, of course, as the potential 'world's prize sheep-dog'. Recognising that practice will be required, William decides that he and Jumble will work on the sheep of his long-standing enemy Farmer Jenks. Jumble goes berserk with the heady joy of the chase, terrorising the 'big, ponderous, slow-moving white things' which he would never have dreamt of chasing if not urged on initially by William. When Farmer Jenks comes upon the scene of devastation he not unnaturally attributes malicious intent to William. He demands that the provisions of the law be enforced: damages (of £5) must be paid by William's father, and the sheep-harassing dog must be destroyed! Neither William's desperate pleas, nor those of his neighbour, Farmer Smith, who is sympathetic towards William, can move Jenks. William is distraught, and almost in tears, begging his father not to carry out the sentence of doom on his beloved pet: 'He didn't do anything wrong at all. He was only obedient same as you're always wantin' me to be. It would be a jolly sight fairer to have *me* destroyed. Why don't you have *me* destroyed?' Even the adult Browns, who had always protested dislike of 'that wretched dog', are strangely depressed that he must now disappear from their lives, but they cannot alter the situation. In despair William runs away with Jumble, prepared to become exiled from everyone and everything he has known and loved for the sake of his pet. Through one of those happy coincidences which crop up at critical moments in the saga he encounters a Miss Wortleton, a benign spinster who runs an animal sanctuary in her house at Marleigh, and who insists on giving Hector, a *real* sheep-dog, to William. And Hector springs into action when Farmer Jenks is having terrible problems in rounding up a large herd of sheep for market. Thanks to circumstances and to the skilful negotiations of the friendly Farmer Smith, Jumble is reprieved, and Jenks, who is in urgent need of a new and efficient sheep-dog, buys Hector for a price that covers the damages due from Jumble's earlier depredations *and* leaves William with a profit of ten shillings.

Jumble plays a part in many memorable incidents in the stories, generally from the side-lines. However, in *William – The Explorer*, 3, his master is determined to push him into the centre of events: ' "I think it's time Jumble *did* something with his life," said William.' The Outlaws point out that he's 'done enough', recently chewing up Mr Brown's slippers, illicitly eating a steak pie, and giving Miss Milton's cat a nervous breakdown by chasing it. But William, expounding upon Jumble's 't'rrific intelligence', wants his pet to have a career! Vainly Ginger, Henry and Douglas point out that Jumble is not the easiest of dogs to train; recent efforts to make him into a surrogate greyhound, a regimental mascot and a stand-in St Bernard have all been failures. Nevertheless William sets his heart on training Jumble to become a police dog. He doesn't succeed, of course, but the episode ends with Jumble (and

William) savouring a moment of glory when at a children's party entertainment a brilliant clown temporarily co-opts Jumble into his act.

After sharing so many of his master's adventures, it is significant that the last mention of Jumble in the stories shows him still gamely backing up William. The Outlaws have been involving many of the village children in an attempt to lay the foundation of a new civilisation (in the event of society being wiped out by a nuclear war: see WARTIME). Things go awry, and the hysterical wrath of a group of mothers is about to fall upon William and Co. who therefore slink unobtrusively away. Jumble abandons the pleasures of a dog-fight in order to join them and, 'realising that danger and disgrace' are threatening his master, he hastens 'to put on the Faithful Hound look that had got him out of many a tight corner' (*William the Superman*, 1).

Katie

Farmer Jenks's land-girl (*William Carries On*, 3). See FAIRIES, MAGIC AND THE SUPERNATURAL.

Kellyngs, Mr

Mr Kellyngs, in *William and the Tramp*, 7, is a harmless writer/naturalist who is staying for a while at Honeysuckle Cottage where he is writing a book. The Outlaws are, as so often, intrigued with ideas of spies and spying. It is 1952, and their thoughts are also running on atom bombs. They have formed a Secret Society 'for puttin' down crim'nals', and decide to concentrate on 'the new sort that go off to Russia with sci'ntific secrets'. Ginger expresses doubts that any such criminals/spies live in their neighbourhood, but William (quite accurately) says with his consciously 'hoarse ironic laugh': 'Well, it's news to *me* . . . that there's anythin' about this partic'lar place that stops crim'nals coming to it.'

Mr Kellyngs is marked out as the 'atom bomb stealer'. He is waylaid, and brought to the Old Barn, where William, dressed up as Stalin, tries to persuade him to hand over the atom bomb secrets: 'Hist! Not a word! Give me the papers and begone!' The quiet but humourless Kellyngs begins to fume with anger, but, spotting a spider which Ginger has acquired from the grocer's boy (who found it in a crate of bananas), he becomes overjoyed; it is the tarantula that he has been wanting for years! The Outlaws' disappointment that he is not a spy is tempered by relief, succinctly voiced by Douglas, that 'he didn't wade in our blood, anyway'.

Kidnappings

William is tempted both by impecunious circumstances and by some of the thrillers that he reads (see Books) to organise kidnapping attempts from time to time. The most interesting of these occurs in *Sweet William*, 3, when in fact the Outlaws require money for an unselfish reason – to support the pet housing scheme of a lady whose blue eyes and golden hair move them deeply. Their plan is simplistic: they will 'jus' go away an' hide somewhere an' write kidnappin' notes' to their fathers. They decide to start with Mr Brown and concoct a missive which threatens that William will be put to death with 'horryble torchure' unless £100 is left 'imedatly' just inside the entrance to the Old Barn. Unfortunately they entrust the ransom note to little Johnny Smith, who drops it in the brook, realises that it is too defaced to be read, but fails to inform the Outlaws of this. Gloomily they wait, hidden, but with the barn in their sights, until it becomes obvious that Mr Brown is not prepared to part with £100 in order to save his younger son. They won-

der whether they have set the stakes too high: perhaps they should have suggested forty pounds – or thirty – or twenty – or even, as William says 'coming down suddenly to hard facts', half a crown. ' "Or even sixpence," said Ginger wistfully.' With little expectation of results, they despatch a second ransom note – which reaches the wrong Mr Brown: Robert. That blameless youth is fearful that a well-meaning note he has written might lay him open to a blackmail attempt. The second ransom note is so ambiguously worded that William is not mentioned – so Robert thinks that his fears have been realised. He creeps nervously after dark to the proposed rendezvous (the hole in the churchyard wall) and pushes through it all the money he has: 'It's only one pound, four and fivepence halfpenny, but I promise to bring the rest as soon as I can . . . And

I've brought my watch and my camera and the new horn I'd just got for my motor cycle . . .'

William is deeply and desperately moved by what appears to be such devotion to him on Robert's part (especially as his father apparently places no value on him). He firmly tells his friends that they will keep only two and six of Robert's money for the charitable housing scheme; the rest will be returned. He makes many resolutions about being nicer to Robert in the future – to noble self-sacrificing Robert! The two brothers have a hilarious at-cross-purposes dialogue, during which Robert realises that he is not under a blackmail threat and that somehow he has been conned out of two and sixpence by his younger brother. William, too, realises that Robert is not quite so devoted to him as he had imagined.

Whenever the Outlaws try to kidnap children younger than themselves, disaster follows; babies in particular have a nasty way of getting the upper hand and making the kidnappers dance attendance on the victim. So, too, does little LADY BARBARA D'ARCEY, who wears out William & Co. with her demands (*William – The Fourth*, 6). When William eventually and with relief returns his victim to the bosom of her family, he is hailed as Barbara's gallant rescuer. His mother and sister are taking tea with the d'Arceys: 'Mrs. Brown and Ethel beamed proudly. "And he *pretends*," said Mrs. Brown, "not to like little girls . . ." '

The Outlaws are not the only residents of the village who *appear* to have kidnapping ambitions. In *William Carries On*, 7, Mrs Bott is worried because Violet Elizabeth seems to have disappeared. Actually she is playing hide-and-seek with William in Miss Milton's house, unknown to its owner, who is at the War Working Party meeting. On their way to their various homes after the meeting, these stalwart ladies – MISS MILTON, MRS BOTT, MRS BROWN and MRS MONKS (the Vicar's wife) – call at Miss Milton's to collect some more oiled sea-boot stocking wool. Mrs Monks finds a

dirty cobwebby Violet Elizabeth asleep in the loft. At the time, Miss Milton and Mrs Bott are in the middle of a long-drawn-out quarrel, and Mrs Monks presumes that this is a kidnapping and a horrible revenge on Miss Milton's part: 'Still, Mrs. Monks had read books on psychology and knew that elderly spinsters did queer things.' (Fortunately Miss Milton eventually emerges from the episode with her reputation untarnished, and her feud with Mrs Bott at an end.) See also KISSES.

Kirkham, Mr

Mr Kirkham is referred to as the Mayor of Hadley, in *William and the Moon Rocket*, 6, and *William and the Pop Singers*, 2. We know little about him apart from William's somewhat contradictory comments in these two books. In the first he says that Mr Kirkham is 'jolly nice. He once bought me an ice-cream.' In the second he suspects the Mayor of being a criminal (or at least an imposter who has killed off 'the real' Kirkham). See also NEW ELIZABETHANS.

Kisses

Although there are many romantic moments in the stories (featuring participants of Robert and Ethel's generation), there is more emphasis on verbal than on physical wooing. If and when kisses occur, these are discreet rather than passionate.

On the whole, William does not have the cute or prepossessing appearance which might tempt old – or young – ladies to kiss him. For this he is profoundly grateful, as kisses are anathema to him. Nevertheless a few perverse females try to subject him to this ignominy. LADY BARBARA D'ARCEY, his kidnap victim in *William – The Fourth*, 6, is unimpressed by his assuming the role of Rudolph of the Red Hand: ' "Well, I'll *kiss* you, dear Rudolph

Hand," she said, "if you like." William's look intimated that he did not like.' He does, however, have to endure a kiss from Lady Barbara's grateful mother, when he returns her.

The most notorious kiss in the stories is, of course, that which Violet Elizabeth forces him to give her on their first encounter, when the fluffy six-year-old female completely breaks the will of the eleven-year-old 'desperado, and scorner of girls' (*Still – William*, 3). See BOTT, VIOLET ELIZABETH.

William has at least one felicitous kiss. At the end of his first encounter with DORINDA LANE she fulsomely expresses her admiration of him: ' "I think you're the bravest person in the world, and I think your magic's *wonderful* and I love you *ever* so much." She raised her face and kissed him. She was unexpectedly pleasant to kiss . . .'

Klein, Mr Adolph

Described in *William and the Space Animal*, 7, as 'the head of one of the lesser known film companies', Adolph Klein sees himself as someone rather more important than, say, Samuel Goldwyn or Louis B. Mayer. Ordered rest and country air by his doctor, he has rented Marleigh Manor for a period from Sir Gerald and Lady Markham. At first he finds country life boring, because his 'sole subject of conversation was Mr. Adolph Klein, and no one in this benighted place seemed to be interested in it'. An exception is William, who, hoping to get Ethel a job in films (see BROWN FAMILY), is vitally interested in Mr Klein and his doings. William asks if he 'axshully' makes films, and with Klein's terribly long and overpoweringly bombastic reply, prefaced by 'I *am* the films', William realises that he has 'for the first time in his life . . . met his match in eloquence'. In Klein's view he is, like his films, 'staggering, stupendous, epoch-making, colossal'; to most of the villagers, he appears as a brash, flashily dressed figure, with a prominent nose, 'short sighted eyes (framed in enormous horn rims) and lips pursed over a huge cigar'. Even when he decides to carry on the tradition of the fête customarily held at Marleigh Manor by the Markhams, Klein decides that it should 'outshine every other fête that had ever been held. It was to be a mixture of an Olde English May Day and a continental carnival, with a smattering of the Festival of Britain and a Hampstead Heath Bank Holiday.'

Knights

The mythology of the Round Table and the quest for the Holy Grail were dear to Richmal's heart, and she used them (as she did so many of her precious causes) to excellent comic effect in the William stories. Struggling one day to inspire her class with enthusiasm for Tennyson's *Idylls of the King*, MISS DREW explains that a knight is a person who spends his time 'succouring the oppressed':

> 'Suckin' wot?' said William, bewildered.
> 'Succour means help. He spent his time helping anyone who was in trouble.'
> 'How much did he get for it?' asked William.

Despite this unpromising beginning, William's latent chivalrous impulses are deeply stirred by Miss Drew's retellings of tales of knightly courage. Naturally he then has to emulate the exploits associated with the Round Table.

His excursions into Arthurian adventure are amusingly chronicled in *More William*, 4, and even more atmospherically in *William – The Bad*, 1. In this episode the Outlaws form themselves into the Knights of the Square Table (a packing-case in the Old Barn has to serve instead of the traditional Round Table), and they put up a notice to attract clients:

They have unusual success in righting the wrong of their first caller – a pleasant young man whose girlfriend ('damosel') has huffily, after a tiff, done him 'much despite' by going off with a fat-headed chump ('false knight') named Montmorency Perrivale. The Outlaws make short shrift of the young man's rival (who is portrayed as the typical, bemonocled, gullible would-be-sophisticate of the between-the-wars period).

Vague echoes of the Arthurian legends can be found in further stories (for example, in *William's Television Show*, 5, new and attractive additions to the juvenile population of the village are Launcelot and Geraint, the Thompson twins).

Knowle, Professor

See DRAMATICS.

Lambkin, Gregorius

See APRIL FOOL'S DAY and NEIGHBOURS.

Lamburn, Richmal Crompton

See CROMPTON, RICHMAL.

Lane, Dorinda

Dorinda is yet another little girl with dark eyes, curly dark hair and dimpled cheeks who appeals to

William. Rather dauntingly she turns out to be a cousin of HUBERT LANE, William's greatest enemy, but he is still determined to capture her attention and respect. He has a hard time at first, inflicting his company on Hubert and Dorinda as they walk through the village. However, he manages to make good one of his rash boasts about having unusual prowess; because Dorinda is interested in fairy-stories William claims that he is a magician. He is instructed by her to command a large room full of food to appear, and he does so! (Unknown to Hubert and Dorinda, the Women's Guild is holding a cookery exhibition in the village hall on that day. William performs his magic just as they reach the hall, and fortunately it is at a moment when the food has been laid out but is temporarily unattended.) Hubert, Dorinda and William tuck in, despite the latter's apprehension that they might at any moment be discovered. Dorinda is impressed, but remains imperious and demanding: 'insatiable as all her sex', she demands from William further

proof of his magic powers. When she asks him to turn a lamp-post into 'a prince in a cloak of gold and a diamond crown' William informs her 'rather curtly' that he can only perform one spell each day. He is not allowed to rest on his laurels, however. To make quite sure of diverting Dorinda's interest from Hubert to himself, William has to prove his pluck by facing FARMER JENKS's bull and chasing it. Hubert, green about the gills and 'boo hooing' with fear, has cravenly run away, and William is prepared to face being savaged rather than to share Hubert's shame. Amazingly, the bull *does* run away from William when he starts to chase it. Fate is again on William's side, for Sammy, this particular bull, is a mixed-up animal who is 'as sweet tempered as a lamb and loves a romp like a puppy'. Unaware of Sammy's amiable disposition, Dorinda tells William the hero that she likes him '*heaps* better than Hubert' (*William's Crowded Hours*, 6).

Dorinda is a spirited character, who might have been developed as a long-term friend of William's, but in fact she comes into only one more story (*William – The Pirate*, 2). She is again staying with her aunt in the village (though no mention is made of Hubert), and she is now described as 'the temporary possessor of William's heart, a hard-boiled organ that generally scorned thraldom to any woman'. She is in fact rather more docile than in their first encounter, with admiration of William spilling over. She is to attend a performance of *Hamlet* at his school, and William, cast as a non-speaking attendant at the court of Elsinore, is determined to dazzle Dorinda by playing the star part. To prepare himself he learns only one speech ('To be or not to be', of course) by heart, confidently prepared to extemporise the rest. The fact that another boy, Dalrymple, is supposed to be playing the Prince of Denmark does not deter William from launching immediately into the famous soliloquy as soon as he gets in front of the audience. His refusal to come off, despite being chased around the stage by his frantic form-master, reduces Shakespeare's noblest tragedy to knockabout farce; and Dorinda appreciates it – and William – no end!

Lane, Hubert

Hubert, the long-standing enemy of the Outlaws, is mentioned in fifty-five of the stories, starting with *Still – William*, 8 (1924), and ending with the last William story to be published: *William the Lawless*, 6 (1970).

When he first appears Hubert is not particularly antagonistic towards William and his friends:

Ginger and Douglas and Hubert Lane, all loudly and redolently sucking Bulls' Eyes, were coming down the road. Hubert Lane was a large fat boy with protruding eyes, a superhuman appetite and a morbid love of Mathematics who was only tolerated as a companion by Ginger and Douglas on account of the bag of Bulls' Eyes he carried in his pocket. He had lately much annoyed the Outlaws – by haunting the field they considered theirs and, in spite of active and passive discouragement, thrusting his unwelcome comradeship upon them.

The unwelcome comradeship, of course, is not thrust upon them for much longer. Hubert quickly loses his special interest in Mathematics; he also abandons the spectacles which are mentioned later on in *Still – William*, and by the next book, *William – The Conqueror*, 8, is described as 'William's school-fellow and mortal enemy. Between William and *his* friends and Hubert Lane and *his* friends raged a deadly feud.'

Except for one or two very shaky respites there is no let-up in this ongoing feud. It is not just rivalry between two gangs but something much deeper.

Hubert, egged on and supported by his doting mother, however outrageously he behaves, is basically the coward who bullies whenever he finds himself in a position of strength; he lies, cheats, manipulates, and buys the allegiance of his followers with his liberal supply of pocket-money and the treats and goodies showered upon him by his parents. William holds the Outlaws together by sheer force of personality, and the loyalty which, though unheralded and unsung, always remains strong enough to bind the four boys together. (JOAN, of course, is also a loyal member of the Outlaws – the only female of the group – but her presence and participation are necessarily spasmodic.)

Occasionally there are suggestions that a truce should be called between the two gangs, but Hubert and his followers never honour their side of the bargain if the Outlaws agree to this (see CHRISTMAS). The pattern of each gang trying to 'one-up' the other and to win on the psychological front, with the occasional pitched battle in between, is generally maintained. However, the feud between the Outlaws and the Laneites is from time to time exacerbated by the intervention of a third party. Hubert's Uncle Charlie, for instance, who prattles on about being the 'eternal boy' (and is a horrible object lesson in the awfulness of this kind of retarded development), gets 'a lot of boyish fun out of the Outlaws v. Laneites feud'. It is always at the expense of William & Co., who cannot immediately find a way of retaliating against Mrs Lane's obnoxious brother, who could, of course, bring to bear against them the whole weight of adult 'moral' authority, if seriously challenged. But William finds a way of making Uncle Charlie a laughing-stock when he comes to their school to give a talk on his travels, which is to be illustrated by the Laneites, wearing appropriate costumes. William manages to lure Hubert & Co. away so that the Outlaws can hold the stage (screened off from Hubert's uncle's view) in wildly unsuitable and comic garb: for example, Ginger as a Laplander appears in Ethel's bathing dress, with his nose reddened and a wicker plant-pot on his head. Uncle Charlie is in a cab on his way to the station and his home-going train before the day is out, and before the story of his blighted travel-talk can spread all round the village (*Sweet William*, 8: see also EGERTON and LANE, HUBERT'S UNCLE).

Things are going badly for the Outlaws again in *William and the Evacuees*, 6, when the Laneites have been augmented by two older youths – 'sons of an old school-friend of Mrs. Lane' – who are staying for a while in the village. Also a few occupants of a camp for the unemployed, recently opened in the neighbourhood, are 'formidable toughs' who enjoy chasing the Outlaws out of some of their traditional haunts. William sets his hopes on his father's cousin – a Mr Ticehurst – who is visiting from Africa. He turns out to be a bit of a wimp, who can't stand the sight of boys fighting. However, when he is set upon by some of the toughs and robbed, he is stung into action. He pays Jimmy Hayes, a retired lightweight boxing

champion known as the Human Tornado, to dress up in his clothes (tropical jacket and terai hat) and, when accosted by the toughs, to give them a beating they will not forget. The plan works: Jimmy Hayes's despatch of no less than six of the campers is observed by both the Outlaws and the Laneites from a sufficient distance for them to think it is Mr Ticehurst who is so masterfully cutting the toughies down to size. William collects a great deal of reflected glory from the incident, which deters Hubert & Co. and the campers from subsequent attacks on the Outlaws.

There is a short period in the 1960s when William's and Hubert's enmity seems muted. In *William and the Witch*, 3, William, in Archie's car, passes Hubert on the road:

William leant out of the window and pulled his Face. Hubert pulled his own Face back. There was no malice in the exchange. It was simply a display of craftsmanship by brother artists. Hubert's Face was not in the same class as William's (William's Face had made strong men blench) but, as William generously admitted to himself, it wasn't bad. For a fleeting moment he was almost tempted to wave to him, but he resisted the temptation. Life without Hubert as an enemy would be unendurably dull . . .

The last reference to Hubert (in *William the Lawless*, 6) shows William preparing to return home from the seaside and looking forward to future contacts with Hubert, the feud having 'taken a new turn just before the holiday started'. The nature of this new turn is not specified.

Lane, Hubert's Uncle

A 'breezy, hearty' but 'detestable' man who considers himself 'good with children'. When Roxana Lytton plans a party for her cousin Egerton

(*William – The Explorer*, 3) 'a half-hour's talk' from Hubert's uncle is planned as part of the organised entertainment, which is planned to keep the young guests as quiet as possible (see EGERTON and LANE, HUBERT).

Lane, Mr and Mrs

Parents of Hubert, who are blindly uncritical of him. Mrs Lane is saccharinely sweet but extremely shifty. Mr Lane is the kind of man who always writes strong letters to the fathers of the Outlaws when Hubert whines a little more strongly than usual about some real or imagined injury they have inflicted upon him. Like her only offspring, Mrs Lane first appears in *Still – William*, 8. She is referred to in thirty-two stories, plus being part of 'the Lanes' in *William the Lawless*, 1, whose garden gnome is appropriated by the Outlaws for the beautification of the garden of a supposed pensioner. Mr Lane is first mentioned in *William – The Conqueror*, 11, and in thirteen episodes altogether.

Lane, Queenie

Queenie is the stubborn, ferocious and distinctly unfeminine-looking cousin of HUBERT LANE, who, a year or two older than him, virtually takes over his gang when she comes to stay. This is at a time when both the Outlaws and the Laneites are suffering harassment and humiliation from the Red Heads, a gang of rough and tough older boys who are camping on FARMER JENKS's Four Acre Meadow.

Henry very reasonably suggests that the Outlaws and the Laneites should call a temporary truce and join up against the intruders; but William, who hates Queenie with a peculiar intensity, will only permit this if assured that she will play no further part in Hubert's gang. With characteristic and unendearing chauvinism, William categorises all 'rotten ole' girls as 'cowardy custards', who spoil everything they join. Queenie doesn't lightly forget such insults. She pretends to withdraw (but actually remains very active in the gang), and Outlaws and Laneites have some success in keeping the campers at bay. But, alas, Queenie is biding her time. She is conducting secret negotiations with the Red Heads to have the hated William taken prisoner and shut up in a semi-derelict cottage called Fairmead. There, William and his rescuer, Ginger, hear its owner, Cross-Eye Smith, discuss with his son Rube a plot to burn down the cottage and claim the insurance money. The inadvertent revelation of this later on to a representative of the insurance company brings to both William and Ginger the reward of brand-new bicycles – to Queenie's fury and frustration! She somehow blames Hubert for her enemies being thus fulfilled, and the episode ends with her turning on her cousin, and their howls rending the air as they engage in a fearfully savage fight. The moral of the story seems to be that girls are actually more nasty and spiteful than boys. When, for example, one of the Red Heads is taken prisoner by the joint forces of the Outlaws and the Laneites, William's bark (as inquisitor) is worse than his bite, but Queenie presses for their captive's teeth to be yanked out, for pins to be stuck into him and for his hair to be pulled. Similarly, when she connives with the Red Heads for William to be captured, she hopes to see him 'torchered'. (*William and the Evacuees*, 8)

Lane, Tarquin

Tarquin is described as 'Mrs. Lane's nephew', but as he is definitely a Lane it must be her husband to whom he is connected by blood (and Hubert, of course). Tarquin is grown-up, large, athletic, with a hearty false charm; he is an artist but, unlike ARCHIE MANNISTER, the local painter, is always smartly and confidently dressed. Even his startlingly luxuriant moustache appears to underline his self-assurance. Tarquin and Archie are contenders for the commission of painting a mother-and-daughter picture of MRS BOTT and VIOLET ELIZABETH. The Outlaws are determined that Archie will get the job. Hubert Lane is equally

anxious that his cousin will succeed. At a preliminary interview Tarquin tells Mrs Bott that her face shows ' "intelligence of a high order, nobility, sensitiveness, integrity, generosity, broad-mindedness, culture, idealism, courage, honesty, capability and – and charm. Above all – charm." ' When he stops for breath, Mrs Bott purrs: ' "You've got me a treat." '

Honest Archie, however, is realistic, and answers Mrs Bott's ' "Now look at my face an' tell me honest what you see" ' by remarking about it (rather as William might have done), ' "It's fat . . . it's got a double chin. Well, three, actually . . ." ' and other accurate but unflattering things.

In the end Mrs Bott drops the portrait idea (see BOTT, VIOLET ELIZABETH), and Tarquin, with a farewell twirl of his trendy moustache, turns out to be not so dreadful a character as one might suspect an adult Lane to be. (*William and the Witch*, 5)

Language

It is not easy to convey the natural language of childhood through the printed word without caricature or sentimentality. Richmal Crompton hit upon a simplistic method of presenting William's special brand of jargon, logic and eloquence. His monologues and conversations may not be in strict accordance with street or playground speech, but they vividly suggest the authentic atmosphere through dogged repetition and skilful use of stylised colourful phrases and rhetorical questions. Very soon after his character was established (in *Just – William*) his loquaciousness was subjected to narrative analysis: 'There was no doubt that when William condescended to adopt a phrase from one of his family's vocabularies, he considerably overworked it.' His 'dreaded eloquence' is one of the crosses which his family has to bear. When, for example, William brings home a ferret instead of a cat as a present for Ethel from her current admirer, he trusts to the suggestibility of repetition to save the day:

> William's face was expressionless.
>
> 'All I can say is wot he told me,' he said in a monotonous voice. 'He said it was a valu'ble white cat, in a highly nervous state.'
>
> '*This*?'
>
> 'It may have got a bit mixed up on the way, but that's what he said. He said that it was a valu'ble white cat, in a highly nervous state.'
>
> 'You needn't keep on saying that,' said Ethel, irritably.
>
> 'It's wot he said,' said William, doggedly. 'He said distinctly that it was a valu'ble white cat, in a . . .'
>
> 'Be quiet, William!'
>
> (*William Again*, 6)

In *William's Happy Days*, 2, William desperately hopes that the power of words will dissuade his father from implementing the headmaster's diabolical suggestion of holiday coaching:

> 'In the *holidays*,' he exclaimed wildly. 'There's *lors* against it. I'm sure there's *lors* against it. I've never heard of *anyone* having lessons in the holidays. Not *anyone*! I bet even slaves didn't have lessons in the holidays. I bet if they knew about it in Parliament, there'd be an inquest about it. Besides I shall only get ill with overworkin' an' get brain fever same as they do in books, an' then you'll have to pay doctors' bills an' p'raps,' darkly, 'you'll have to pay for my funeral too. I don't see how *anyone* could go on workin' like that for months an' *months* without ever stoppin' once an' not get brain fever and die of it. Anyone'd think you *wanted* me to die. An' if I did die I shun't be surprised if the judge did something to you about it.'
>
> His father, unmoved by this dark hint, replied coolly, 'I'm quite willing to risk it.'

Rhetorical questions form a strong plank of William's logic; his family, and to an extent his friends, have learnt the wisdom of ignoring both these and some of the questions which he poses 'more from an ineradicable propensity' for asking them than because 'he really wants to know':

> His pocket money was mortgaged for a month to come in order to pay for the crockery he had broken while training to be a juggler. 'Well, they've all gotter learn, haven't they?' he had protested, when sentence was passed on him. 'Gosh! D'you think jugglers can throw up plates like that without practisin'? D'you think they're *born* throwin' up plates like that? They've gotter break a few plates an' things practisin'. Stands to reason . . .'
>
> (*William and the Evacuees*, 7)

William is frequently characterised as the master of misinterpretation, of conscious – or unknowing – obstructionism:

> ' . . . which of our grand national buildings have you seen?' said Mr. Cranthorpe-Cranborough . . .
>
> 'I've never been to the races,' said William sadly.
>
> (*William – The Outlaw*, 6)

Leopold

A member of one of William's secret societies. See ALBERT (1).

Lewes, Mr and Mrs

The Vicar of West Mellings and his wife. (*William – In Trouble*, 8)

Lewes, Sir Ross

'The most famous actor of his day', now retired, who agrees to judge the best child performer in some nursery rhyme scenes produced by Miss Milton to mark the 1951 Festival of Britain. William becomes involved only through maternal coercion. During the performance he abandons his bit-part to lead a wild chase of children and pets across the stage. Sir Ross unreservedly awards him the prize because he embodies 'the whole carefree spirit of vagabondage . . .'. (*William and the Tramp*, 6)

Liquorice Water (also spelt Licorice and Lik'rice)

The favourite beverage of William and the Outlaws, liquorice water is mentioned in twelve of the stories. It was not – like home-made sherbet and fizzy lemonade – a drink well known to, or much used by, children of the 1920s and 1930s (when it was most featured in the saga). The fact that it *is* home-made is established in the first reference to it (*Just – William*, 8): 'This beverage was made by shaking a piece of licorice in water.' Simple enough, but whether the water has to be hot or cold for the initial mixing is not specified. The resulting brew obviously varied in strength and quality. In *William – The Gangster*, 5, the Outlaws are providing liquorice water in bulk for the 'Nit' (Night) Club which they and Violet Elizabeth organise in the Old Barn: 'Douglas was anxiously inspecting his jugs of liquorice water. So pale had it looked that he had had recourse to the dubious expedient of colouring matter. He had on the impulse of the moment dissolved a cake of black paint from his paint box in each jug.' Not surprisingly this brings about the early break-up of the nightclub through nausea on the part of several patrons.

Liquorice water comes into its own in *William's Happy Days*, 10, when William is taking an interest in the psychically inspired photography of Auriole Mannister and the visionary painting of her twin brother Tristram (see Art and Artists).

To keep the other-worldly inspiration flowing, Auriole tries to lubricate it with an appropriate drink. She and Tristram are giving up stimulants which 'dull the psychic faculties'. They try liquorice water provided by William, which Auriole pronounces as 'very nice . . . A pure herbal drink', and Tristram as 'quite delicious'. William is commissioned to make bulk supplies for them: 'He was more thrilled by this than by anything else that happened in this fascinating household. He'd never before met a grown-up who did not look upon liquorice water as a messy juvenile concoction to be thrown away with contumacy whenever discovered.'

Loch Ness Monster

Mentioned twice (but not actually participating in the action of the plot) in *William – The Detective*. In chapter 2, William (having been totally immersed in a muddy ditch and then having to climb over a pile of coal) encounters a young woman who screams that she's been terrorised by something that is '*Just* like the Loch Ness Monster'. In chapter 10 a conversation about the Loch Ness Monster ('still well to the fore in the news') inspires 'in William's bosom an insatiable desire to capture a prehistoric monster'.

Lomas, Miss

Ran a Sunday school for the Sons and Daughters of Gentlefolk which William attended for a short time – until she had a nervous breakdown, soon after he joined (*William – The Conqueror*, 8). Her Bible class is also mentioned in *Still – William*, 14. *William and the Brains Trust*, 9, contains a reference to 'ole Miss Lomas', whose rabbits William has accidentally let out. Possibly this is the same Miss Lomas, and she has decided that breeding rabbits is rather more satisfying than imparting religious knowledge to children. See also DOBSON, MISS DOREEN.

Love, Miss Arabella

Arabella Love is a well-known musical-comedy actress who comes to stay at the holiday resort of Sea Beach while William is there. He is without his family. His mother has gone into a nursing-home – for a slight (unspecified) operation – and he has been sent to stay with Mrs Beacon, an old friend of Mrs Brown's, 'in order to relieve the domestic strain'. Pulling the communication cord on his way there, and thus fortuitously preventing a fellow-passenger from being robbed and assaulted, he has been treated as a hero. He is irritated to realise after a few days that he is no longer 'news'. Miss Love, 'a platinum blonde with a ravishing smile and an apparently inexhaustible wardrobe', *is*. To hog the limelight once again, William follows Miss Love into the sea, swims after her and pretends to 'life-save' the actress. She and the few onlookers, however, are convinced that *she* has saved *him*. William tries again – this time to pretend to rescue a friendly Labrador dog (whom he first pushes off the edge of the jetty into the water). The next day he is thrilled to see photographs of the dripping dog and himself. He is not so happy about the caption, however: DOG RESCUES SMALL BOY. *And* it turns out that the canine in question belongs to Miss Love! (*Sweet William*, 10)

Lytton, Roxana

See ROBERT AND HIS FRIENDS.

Macnamara, Dahlia

See ROBERT AND HIS FRIENDS.

Magazines

William stories appeared in many magazines over the years, chronologically in *Home Magazine*, the *Happy Mag*, *Tit-Bits Summer Annual*, the *Golden Arrow*, *Modern Woman*, *Homes and Gardens* and *Home Notes* (see under individual headings, and Appendix 2 for a full bibliography).

Thomas Henry drew hundreds of William cartoons independently of the books, some in strip format for *Woman's Own*, some as double-page 'adventures', and over forty in full colour on the covers of other magazines (or as presentation plates), in the *Happy Mag*, the *Tit-Bits Summer Annual*, the *Sunny Mag* and just a few in *Crusoe Mag*, which later became the *Golden Mag*.

The *Crusoe Mag* had just one William cover (August 1924), with the caption 'What are You Staring at, Boy!' spoken by a couple with green paint on their backs, as William stands grinning, holding a 'Wet Paint' sign hidden behind his own back.

The *Golden Mag* had two: for September and November 1926. The first, 'The Motor Boat Now Going', with William cutting the rope prematurely with a knife, and the second declaring, 'Darling, Nothing Shall Ever Part Us!' as William sends a mouse along the garden wall that separates the spooning couple. (D.S.)

Maidstone, Colonel

Ethel is adversely comparing her long-term boyfriend JIMMIE MOORE with Colonel Maidstone, a 'quiet, retiring middle-aged man', who has recently taken The Limes furnished, and who knows 'how to do things properly' when he takes a girl out. By this Ethel means that the Colonel spends money freely on taxis and trimmings, which Jimmie doesn't. The admiring and impeccable retired military gentleman, however, turns out to be an imposter (unmasked indirectly by William: see WAKELY, CHIEF CONSTABLE) who is really a successful black-marketeer. For once the spoilt and spiky Ethel has been exploited: as the Chief Constable eventually explains, it is the racketeer's policy to take a furnished house in the country and to attach himself 'to the most ordinary and innocuous family in the neighbourhood (the Browns tried not to flinch at this) . . . and if there's an attractive unmarried daughter' to pay 'marked attention to her. Then there's no mystery about him. He's accepted as an ordinary member of the community . . .'. (*William – The Bold*, 2)

Malcolm, Sergeant

See GROWN-UP FRIENDS.

Mannister, Archie

First mentioned (as Tristram Mannister) in *William's Happy Days*, 10, and then as Tristram Archibald Mannister in *William – The Bold*, 1, but 'known to the whole neighbourhood as Archie', this resilient character appeared or was referred to in some nineteen stories, the last of all being *William the Lawless*, 5. He mellows from being the freakish twin brother of Auriole (see ART AND ARTISTS) into an engaging if inept personality. Artistically he belongs to the 'aggressively modern' school of painting, although he can use conventional methods 'when hard pressed for cash' and having to produce calendars, Christmas cards, etc. At the end of the saga he is living in 'a tumbledown cottage' which is simply called 'Archie's

cottage'; he started off, like so many of the artists and authors who come to William's village, in Honeysuckle Cottage.

William and the Outlaws always feel protective towards Archie (see GROWN-UP FRIENDS); in *William and the Witch*, 5, they decide to advertise his talents, and daub his car with pictures and slogans which, although embarrasssing to Archie, bring about good results in a commission for work he really likes (painting pictures of gardens) from Sir Gerald and Lady Markham.

Archie is, in effect, the village's permanent artist; he also becomes one of Ethel's long-term admirers, wildly idealising her, lacking the sophistication which might attract her, yet offering the dogged devotion she is sometimes happy to fall back on.

Markham, Sir Gerald and Lady

See V.I.P.s.

Markham, Ronald

Son of SIR GERALD AND LADY MARKHAM, a Cambridge undergraduate, who appears only in *Sweet William*, 5. At a college 'rag' he has acquired a 'real policeman's helmet' which William lusts after. (He gets it, too.)

Markham, Walter

A nephew of SIR GERALD AND LADY MARKHAM. William is asked to the Markhams' grown-up Christmas party one year (to Robert and Ethel's chagrin) to be a companion to Walter who is 'of William's age, but not after William's heart'. He is 'an earnest intellectual boy, whose chief interest lay in his collection of wild flowers, and who shuddered with horror when William mentioned the white rats that he had bought with a recent tip'. (*Sweet William*, 5)

Marks/Markson, Mr

See FINCH, MISSES and SCHOOLS.

Martin, Anthony

See ANTHONY MARTIN.

Mason, Aaron (renamed Bill by General Moult)

See GROWN-UP FRIENDS.

Masters, Colonel Alexander

First mentioned in *William*, 7, as 'a choleric old gentleman who lived with his sister at the other end of the village'. Every November he gives an 'elaborate firework display' to which he invites some of his friends among whom he does *not* include the Outlaws. Nevertheless, one year when William & Co. face a parental ban on the purchase of fireworks they manage to appropriate those which are waiting to be used at the Colonel's display. But, as they prepare to let them off in the field behind the Old Barn, their fathers come to prevent them. They stay – entranced by the sight of the fireworks – and have a wonderful time with their sons' Catherine wheels, Roman candles and rockets. However, they get more than they bargain for. The Colonel, spitting with fury, comes in search of his fireworks (which only passed into the Outlaws' hands because his sister, MISS MASTERS, was so nervous about the dangers of these explosives). The old warrior prepares to extract terrible retribution from the Outlaws' fathers (who, naturally, he thinks have stolen his fireworks), and William fuels his fury by pointing out that the guy which is waiting to be burnt is an effigy of the Colonel himself.

William knows this, of course, because the offending guy was made by the Outlaws.

The Colonel (sometimes referred to as Lieutenant-Colonel) crops up again much later in the saga, but he and his daughter Diana (see ROBERT AND HIS FRIENDS) are then described as 'new people' to the locality, so perhaps this Colonel is not the same as the firework enthusiast. (*William's Treasure Trove*, 1; *William and the Pop Singers*, 4; *William – The Explorer*, 4)

Masters, Miss

Mild inoffensive sister of COLONEL ALEXANDER MASTERS. (*William*, 7)

Mayfield, Professor

The Professor writes books on economics, and is the father of Rowena, for whose affections Robert and Oswald Franks are battling (see ROBERT AND HIS FRIENDS). Professor Mayfield is so anti-social that he bars visitors from the house, and it becomes an understood thing that whichever of Rowena's admirers could wangle an invitation from her father would be at a distinct advantage as a suitor. William, who really likes the lively and sympathetic Rowena, is determined to help Robert's cause. He finds his way into Professor Mayfield's presence unorthodoxly – through a skylight and covered in green paint – but is welcomed because the Professor wants William's 'fiendish grin' to be used in the illustrations of Tonando – a leading character in the space fiction for the younger reader that he writes under the name of Martin Morrow. The Professor takes warmly to William, and then agrees to invite Robert to tea – to lunch – and to dinner! (*William's Television Show*, 3)

Mayfield, Rowena

See ROBERT AND HIS FRIENDS.

Mehitavel, Marmaduke

Alias. See TRAMPS.

Mendleson, Felicia

See ROBERT AND HIS FRIENDS.

Mercer, Honoria

See ROBERT AND HIS FRIENDS.

Merton, Dorita

See ROBERT AND HIS FRIENDS.

Merton, Lord

A member of the Cabinet who, in Mr Brown's opinion, is ruining the country by his economic policies. When he attends the Botts' New Year fancy-dress party as its distinguished guest, his evening – thanks to William – ends in humiliation and physical assault. (*Still – William*, 11)

Miller, Frankie

A small, stout, snub-nosed boy of seven who sometimes forms part of William's audience. (*William and the Evacuees*, 1; *William's Television Show*, 8; *William the Superman*, 1)

Milton, Miss

Miss Milton's rarely used Christian name, Mildred, is given in *William and the Space Animal*, 5, but she is generally always addressed and spoken of as Miss Milton. She comes on the scene in *Still – William*, 2, as the occupant of one of the four houses which comprise Jasmine Villas (Mr Burwash, Mr Luton and Mr Buck reside in the others). Miss Milton is the archetypal between-the-wars village spinster, with sufficient money not to work, enough time on her hands to be something of a busybody, an antipathy towards children and pets of the boisterous kind, and generating an atmosphere of vinegary fustiness. Small wonder that in her first exploit she is not amused when HENRI, a visiting French boy, claims to have seen Mr Luton propose to and kiss her. (He has actually been watching one of the Outlaws' games, in which Joan plays Miss Milton and Ginger Mr Luton.) Miss Milton's reactions tend to be over the top. When Mrs Brown and Mrs Frame hear that Mr Luton apparently has designs on Miss Milton, they feel bound to point out that Luton already has a wife, from whom he is not divorced, and that he therefore shouldn't have kissed Miss Milton. Quivering with rage, Miss Milton gives two piercing screams and denounces the ladies who are trying to help her as 'Slanderers . . . vampires . . . liars . . . hypocrites . . . snakes in the grass'. Her screams continue to rend the air, even after Mrs Brown and Mrs Frame have fled, trembling, from her wrath.

In *William and A.R.P.*, 1, her slightly impaired hearing is referred to. William has 'evacuated' Hector and Herbert, seven-year-old twins from Hadley, and billeted them, temporarily and surreptitiously, in the cellar of his home. Miss Milton turns up at his house when the twins are having a noisy potato-fight in the cellar; it takes some time for the sounds to filter, in a muffled way, into Miss Milton's hearing range. When they do 'her plain, matter-of-fact, pince-nezed face' lights up in

'happy ecstasy' because she thinks she is developing a capacity for psychic hearing (being 'the seventh child of a seventh child', etc.).

Miss Milton (together with Mrs Brown, Mrs Bott and Mrs Monks) is at the centre of most of the groups in the village which work for various good causes. She is particularly associated with the arranging of white elephant stalls. As she points out in *William and the Moon Rocket*, 8, she never gives money to children 'on principle', though sometimes as a reward for some special service rendered by a juvenile she will make a gift of some 'little thing'.

She is quite frank about having a horror of children (in *William Carries On*, 2), when she lets Mrs Parfitt and Joan occupy her spare bedroom while

they are waiting for an unexploded bomb which has landed near their home to be dealt with. Miss Milton, having already driven away her quota of evacuees by her fearful meticulousness, makes life miserable for the Parfitts. 'Only that morning Miss Milton had reproved her [Mrs Parfitt] for drawing her bedroom curtains an inch further back on one side than on the other and had asked her to see that Joan did not put her hand on the baluster rail going up and down stairs, as she had found several finger marks on it.'

She lavishes some love on what William describes as her 'rotten ole cat', and on a Pomeranian dog. The pet which perhaps best suits her somewhat frosty personality is Charlemagne, her parrot (*William and the Moon Rocket*, 8). He is described as 'a decrepit fowl of mildewed moth-eaten appearance, who was content generally to doze away his time in the intervals of devouring huge slices of the sponge cake for which he had a morbid passion'. He has a fine flow of dubious language, an embarrassment to his fastidious mistress.

Altogether Miss Milton is mentioned in fifty stories. The last reference to her occurs in the penultimate chapter of the last book (*William the Lawless*, 5). Her sensible clothes have been very slightly allowed to move forward with the times; there is even one episode in which she strives to look and feel very much younger. In essence, however, she is still the same suspicious repressive character as she was when she first encountered William in the early 1920s.

Miss Milton (aunt of)

Unnamed genial aunt of Miss Milton who asks William to help her prepare a list of foodstuffs suitable for a children's party to be given by Miss Milton, which he will be attending. (*William – The Showman*, 8)

Miss Milton (mother of)

Presumably Mrs Milton. This lady is mentioned in *William and A.R.P.*, 1, and on other occasions as 'the seventh child of a seventh child', which is why Miss Milton feels that she must have inherited propensities for psychic experiences.

Milton, Miss Julia

The cousin of Miss Milton, who looks very much like her, but is amiable, and fond of children. She appears in *William Carries On*, 7, and *William and the Space Animal*, 5.

Modern Woman

In spite of the demise of the *Happy Mag* in May 1940, and her wartime duties in the A.F.S., Richmal Crompton still managed to write a further thirty-one stories up to 1945. The editors of George Newnes Ltd must have been anxious to find a new vehicle for the first publication of William stories, and until quite recently its identity remained in obscurity for researchers. It was only my chance acquisition in 1986 of an issue of *Modern Woman* containing a William story, and a subsequent investigative visit to the British Library, that finally located the first appearance in print of the stories which were later collected together in *William Does His Bit*, *William Carries On* and *William and the Brains Trust*, together with the story 'The Battle of Flowers' included in *William – The Bold*.

Like *Home Magazine*, where William made his first forty-one appearances, *Modern Woman* was directed entirely, as its name implies, towards the feminine domestic market. It is therefore not really surprising that this magazine should have held its secret for over forty years, as it hardly came in the domain encompassed by serious literary research.

In August 1940 the first contribution, 'Boys Will Be Boys', was announced in the editorial: 'Richmal Crompton introduces her notorious boy to *Modern Woman* readers in a riotous story of peaches and the cream of a joke.'

The publication continued to host new William stories every month until October 1941, and then every two or three months until his last appearance in May 1946 with 'The Pageant' (*William – The Bold*, 5, as 'The Battle of Flowers').

Although most of the stories appeared in the magazine in slightly abridged form, this last story is notable because the version in *Modern Woman* contains a poem written by Violet Elizabeth Bott, not used in the book, which carries this disclaimer from Violet Elizabeth: 'I've not made a piethe of poetry about mithe, but I could if I tried.' Well, it wasn't about mice, but she did try, and in *Modern Woman* it ran as follows:

> 'I am ole Germany,
>   Beat in the war,
>   A goothe that won't go goothe-thtepping
>   Any more.'

She pointed to Hubert, who wore a row of medals on his coat.

> 'Here'th ole Goering,
>   He ithn't purring
>   Any more.'

She next pointed to Bertie Franks, who had a short moustache corked upon his upper lip.

> 'Here'th the ole Fuehrer,
>   He won't go to Nur –
>   – nburg any more.'

Next she waved her hand airily to Claude Bellew, a thin under-sized member of Hubert's gang.

> 'Here'th ole Goebbleth the liar,
>   He won't thay London'th on fire
>   Any more.'

A wave of both hands included the rest of the Hubert Laneites.

> 'And here'th the ole German prithonerth,
>   Their generalth too,
>   Looking juth like the monkeyth
>   You thee in the zoo.'

The original version then goes on to explain how the Hubert Laneites had been duped into donning the garb of Nazi leaders:

For Violet Elizabeth had joined them, offering to organise their pageant, act the part of Britannia, and even help them capture the Outlaws for German prisoners. She had cast Hubert Lane for the part of Churchill, stipulating that he must have a row of medals, which, she assured him, Churchill always wore. So Hubert, who was rather stupid, procured the medals. She then assigned to Bertie Franks the part of Mr. Eden and had corked his moustache herself, assuring him that the likeness was now so perfect that no one could tell the difference. Claude Bellew, she had said, must be Monty, Georgie Parker and the rest of them British soldiers. Instead of which, she had shamelessly delivered them into the hands of their enemies . . .

Only three stories in *William and the Brains Trust* remained unaccounted for, and for these William was literally to go back to his roots: for in 1931 *Home Magazine* had been incorporated into HOMES AND GARDENS, and it is there that we need to look. (D.S.)

Molly

The lively-natured maid of William's Aunt Jane who is particularly kind to William (and Jumble). She has two suitors, George and James, and William sees to it that Molly becomes engaged to the former, whom he greatly admires. (*William – The Pirate*, 4)

Money

Money, and the difficulty of extracting this from mean parents and other adult relatives, is a constant theme of the William stories. Certainly for middle-class parents the Browns are not over-generous in the pennies they hand out to William for

performing errands and other small tasks. (Ethel could be particularly mean, offering only a half-penny when the going rate would surely have been at least a penny.) Of course the Outlaws are not always the most efficient of workers:

> 'Huh!' said William contemptuously . . . 'Weed all day for a penny an' then get the penny taken off you 'cause you pulled up a few flowers by mistake.'
>
> 'Yes,' agreed Ginger. 'Chop up firewood all day for a penny an' get it taken off you 'cause you chopped up the wrong stuff by mistake.'

One of William's favourite hobby-horses is that of the large school fees on which his father wastes his money: 'Grumblin' about school costin' so much an' still makin' us go there! Seems batty to me' (*Sweet William*, 3).

Pocket-money is very modest, and often mort-

gaged much in advance because of the Outlaws' unfortunately well-developed tendency to break windows and other objects in the course of their activities. There is, however, compensation to be derived from parting tips given by friends and relations – or by fathers who are overjoyed to see their guests departing prematurely.

Monkey Brand

Unnamed schoolmate enemy of William's. (*William – The Fourth*, 14)

Monkey-Face

One of William's teachers (of Latin) who is obviously no favourite of his. (*Sweet William*, 2 and 5)

Monks, Mr and Mrs

It is appropriate that in a village like William's the Vicar and his wife should play a prominent part in affairs. However, the fact that in many of their appearances they are referred to as 'the Vicar' and 'the Vicar's wife', without being given personal names, emphasises the fact that they are stereotypes rather than realistic characters. It doesn't even necessarily follow that every reference to 'the Vicar' or 'the Vicar's wife' is to Mr and Mrs Monks; vicars and their ladies could well be part of the shifting population of the village, but if this is so they seem sufficiently similar to be interchangeable (rather like so many of the girls who inspire romantic passion in Robert Brown: see ROBERT AND HIS FRIENDS).

The Vicar is first mentioned in *Just – William*, 5, and his last appearance is in *William the Lawless*, 3. The Vicar's wife makes her entrance in *William – The Fourth*, 3, and her final bow or curtsy in

William the Lawless, 4. (In *William – The Rebel*, 11, her Christian name is given as Elfrida.) They seem to be childless, apparently by choice. We are told in *William – The Conqueror*, 8, that the Vicar hates boys, and in both *William's Crowded Hours*, 7, and *William – The Showman*, 6, that Mrs Monks 'dislikes children'.

There are certainly times when she dislikes William, and the feeling is mutual. In *Sweet William*, 7, for example, when the Outlaws decide to institute St Mars' Day because St Valentine's Day is so sickening, she is one of the first of the grown-ups whom they list to be 'scored off': ' "All right," said William. "Yes, we'll put her down . . . she took away my caterpillar, jus' 'cause I was teachin' it to walk along my pencil when she was tellin' us about someone called the Leak of Nations, an' I bet she's not rememberin' to feed it reg'ly. . ." '

In *William and the Brains Trust*, 8, we learn that, although Mr and Mrs Monks seem to lead lives of unblemished respectability, 'William, whose taste in literature tended to the lurid, had always cherished the suspicion that this blatant appearance of respectability hid some secret career of crime. He had – at different times and without success – tried to prove that they were spies, murderers and traffickers in drugs.' Now he suspects that Mrs Monks is a member or the head of a gang of toy-stealers (this is at a time when metal – such as that of toy soldiers – is desperately scarce and valuable).

Even when William is not conducting an active campaign against the Vicar and his wife there is something unsatisfying about his relationship with them. The Vicar is vague and colourless; Mrs Monks is assertive, but so preoccupied with the sales of work that she so much relishes, and other exemplary activities and causes, that she really has no time for other than the most superficial contacts with individual parishioners.

Monkton-Bruce, Mrs Bruce

Secretary of the Literary Society who tries with little success to arrange a really interesting programme of activities: 'She'd written to ask Bernard Shaw, Arnold Bennett, A. Einstein, M. Coué and H. G. Wells to come down and address them and it wasn't her fault that they hadn't answered. She'd enclosed a stamped addressed envelope in each case.' At any rate she has William to liven things up (see DRAMATICS). (*William – The Good*, 2, and *William – The Rebel*, 12)

Montacute, Miss

Short, tubby, 'usually clad in tweeds and twin sets', she runs the Extra Dimension Community which needs Perfect Harmony in which to thrive. She has therefore abandoned the city and recently come to live in William's village, where 'the aura' is supposed to be beneficial. (*William the Lawless*, 5)

Montagu, Miss

A temporary neighbour of William's, who rents Mrs Frame's house for the whole of August. She resents William from the moment he sits on the fence between them and tries to establish friendly relations. She sends a string of complaining letters to his parents about William's singing, whistling, general noisiness and his looking at her over the fence. She confiscates arrows and balls which land in her garden, and even Jumble's collar, which falls off the fence, where William has put it, into her garden. This is the last straw. At midnight William manipulates the catch on Miss Montagu's dining-room window with his penknife, and retrieves his confiscated possessions. He is wearing a long overcoat and a black mask. Miss Montagu, in abject terror, disturbs him, and he threatens her

with his toy pistol and gets away. The next day
Miss Montagu can talk of nothing else but her midnight adventure: '*Three* great *giants* of *men*.
They've *ransacked* the place – they've stolen all
my jewellery. They – they covered me with
revolvers and threatened to take my life . . .'

A little later on, when Miss Montagu is recuperating in her garden deck-chair from the excitement
of her constant retelling and embroidering of her
adventure, she becomes aware of 'that wretched
boy' next door, sitting on top of the fence and –
horror of horrors – holding all the objects she has
confiscated from him! William spells out his
terms; if she continues to complain about him to
his parents, he will tell everyone what really happened when he visited her house to reclaim his
possessions: she will be a laughing-stock! Miss
Montagu gets the message. She assures William
that her nerves have now quite recovered, that no
noise from his garden will disturb her, and that if
any of his things should land in her territory he
may come over to fetch them. 'Then, with great
dignity, she got up and swept into the house.
William watched her retreat with apparent uncon-
cern. " 'K you," was all he said.' See also
NEIGHBOURS. (*William – The Conqueror*, 6)

Montpelimar, Madame

A phoney psychic who persuades MRS BOTT that
she can guide her into developing her latent clair-
voyant gifts. Flattered at being considered an 'old
soul', Mrs Bott installs the occultist at the Hall.
Madame Montpelimar enjoys sharing Mrs Bott's
'far from meagre' wartime meals and her drives
through the village in the Rolls. The fact that the
villagers do not give her psychic guide the respect
which Mrs Bott feels is her due is a constant irri-
tant; nevertheless Madame Montpelimar wears
'the satisfied smile of one who has been on her
beam ends and has found a mug in the nick of
time'. She is unprepossessing in appearance –
small, stout, frowsy, sallow and gipsy-looking. She
sports 'dingy and ancient garments' of the floating
variety, and has lots of greasy-looking dull-brown
hair that is coiled into a bun.

Madame Montpelimar begins to feel that the

hours of boredom she suffers from Mrs Bott's company warrant more than just getting her keep and a few car-rides; she had hoped to con her hostess out of considerable sums of money, too, but Mrs Bott's gullibility does not extend that far. Madame Montpelimar decides to filch the diamond brooch that is left carelessly about her hostess's bedroom and 'boodwor'; she manages to put the blame on William (who has climbed surreptitiously into the Hall to reclaim a penknife confiscated by Mrs Bott). For once William is at a loss to solve his problems, and it is JOAN who cannily sorts matters out, unravelling the mystery of the whereabouts of the brooch when she also unravels the psychic's plentiful coils of hair which have made a perfect hiding-place for the lustrous loot.

Madame Montpelimar – 'alias Princess Borinsky, alias Lady Vere Vereton, alias Baroness Gretchstein, alias Mary Smith' – is removed to the police station; Mrs Bott tearfully offers William fantastic sums in compensation for wrongfully accusing him of theft (which, to his chagrin, Mrs Brown refuses); William tells Joan that she did jolly well, and that he couldn't have done better himself. It is good to see the docile Joan playing such a positive rôle. (*William Carries On*, 4)

Moore, Jimmie

Jimmie (or Jimmy as his Christian name is sometimes spelt) is an admirer of Ethel who occupies a special position. When she meets him 'for the first time in her life' she is 'in love'. This is recorded in *William's Crowded Hours*, 8. Jimmie loves her, too, and their relationship flourishes over several stories, despite Jimmie's meanness with money and his jealousy of the many other young men in Ethel's past (and those who hope to be part of her future). Jimmie is next mentioned in *William – The Showman*, 10. Ethel now has two extremely ardent suitors, Richard and Charles, running 'a neck-to-

neck race for her favour'. We are told that 'Jimmie Moore, her chronic local admirer' has been 'completely ousted'. He is, however, only biding his time. Ethel sets 'a love test' for Richard and Charles to help her decide which one she will partner to the Tennis Club's Annual Tournament Dance. The test consists of their giving up the chance of competing in the Men's Singles Championship in order to sit with Ethel, who pretends to be laid low with a headache. Neither suitor turns up because, on their way to Ethel's house, William diverts them with a love test of his own making: that of rescuing Ethel who, he says, has fallen in the river.

Ethel is decidedly piqued when neither Richard nor Charles turns up at the time stipulated in her letter to them about the love test, but the canny Jimmie presents himself at the right moment and triumphantly takes her to the tournament (and, one imagines, to the dance afterwards).

Nevertheless the path of Jimmie's true love certainly runs rough! In *William and A.R.P.*, 8, he has another rival: Dr Horace Ashtead, a young assistant to DR BELL. The pretentious Ashtead's incorrect diagnosis of William's feigned illness removes him from Ethel's list of hopefuls and shuffles Jimmie back into favour. He is grateful to William, even though he knows that his debunking of Ashtead has been unintentional, and he gives him the badminton racket on which he has set his heart.

William and the Brains Trust, 6, mentions that Jimmie is away in the Navy while the Second World War is being waged. Ethel is pining, not so much for Jimmie, but because all the eligible young men of the village are away on active service (see WARTIME).

Hostilities are over in *Just William's Luck*, and in chapter 8 we find Jimmy (now spelling his Christian name differently) still established as the 'most persistent' of Ethel's numerous admirers. His stinginess is mentioned again, and the fact that he has 'a good position'. (We are never told the nature of his work. It is curious that the jobs of Ethel's admirers and Robert's friends are rarely mentioned, let alone described in any detail.) Ethel is having her customary fun in playing off one beau against another. Jimmy really puts up with an awful lot!

In *William – The Bold*, 2, Ethel is bemoaning Jimmy's lack of style (and expenditure) on a London trip which he arranges for them both. She compares him adversely with the sleek and secure middle-aged COLONEL MAIDSTONE (who turns out to be a racketeer).

Jimmy seems more like a friend than a lover in *William and the Space Animal*, 7, when he just drops in for the evening. (Possibly he is now so fed up with Ethel's jibes about his supposed meanness that he no longer bothers to take her out.) He is last mentioned in *William's Television Show*, 7, when he heads Ethel's guest-list for the party which she and Robert are planning for their parents' wedding anniversary.

Then, apparently, the Jimmy–Ethel romance fizzles out. It seems sad that the only young man Ethel has ever been in love with didn't achieve a more dynamic relationship with her; but, of course, Ethel's rôle in the saga – like that of many nubile soap-opera heroines – really demands that she never settles into married domesticity. One permanently sock-mending and 'yes-dear'-ing woman (Mrs Brown) is enough in any long-running drawing-room comedy. See also ETHEL AND HER FRIENDS.

Morency, The Honourable Marmaduke

One of MRS BOTT'S first aristocratic acquaintances, the Honourable Marmaduke represents (to her) the first rung on the social-climbing ladder. He is 'not an earl exactly' but distantly related to one, and at any rate he is 'County'. 'So far County had

persistently resisted the attempts of Mrs. Bott to "get in" with it.' Her mind leaps forward to one of his nephews ('he himself would be rather too old') marrying Violet Elizabeth later on ('Ivory charmeuse for Violet Elizabeth of course and the bridesmaids in pale blue georgette') and to all the relations standing in the way of the earldom being killed off by earthquakes, floods and so on.

Mrs Bott's roseate dreams are sharply interrupted when she and the Honourable Marmaduke come across a notice guiding them to a field where William and the Outlaws are holding their version of the Wembley Exhibition. Her companion thinks this promises to be 'rather jolly, what?', so Mrs Bott concurs: ' "Yars," she said in her super-county-snaring accent . . . "We always trai to taike an interest in the activities of the village." ' The exhibition consists of four small blacked-up boys (representing the children of the Commonwealth and Empire) in a variety of strange garments. Mrs Bott, still anxious to impress her aristocratic acquaintance, comments on the quaintness of the exhibition: 'I do wish my little gurl was heah . . . But I don't let her mix with common children. She's so carefully gorded . . . She's a beautiful chehild . . . She'd be *sow* int'rested . . .'

Bang on cue a shrouded figure throws off its covering and leaps into the air. Like the others it is liberally covered with blacking but, *un*like the others, it is dressed in stays and small frilled knickers: ' "I'm a Nindian. I'm a Nindian," ' squeaks Violet Elizabeth as her mother's screams rend 'the very heavens' (*Still – William*, 6).

The Honourable Marmaduke Morency takes it all in his languid stride, we gather. He is mentioned again in *William's Crowded Hours*, 8, when the Outlaws, on one of their money-making stints, have the bright idea of selling old photographs (see FUNFAIRS AND FÊTES). Glory Tomkins is furious to find a photo of Marmaduke (her current escort) inscribed 'To Ethel the Only Girl in the World for Marmaduke'. With a cry of rage she looks around for Marmaduke and finds him 'an innocent smile on his lips, regardless of his doom'. He is last mentioned in *William and the Brains Trust*, 6, as having joined the Navy during the Second World War.

Mortimer, Miss

See DOGS.

Morton, Mrs

See DRINK.

Moss, Mr

See SWEETS AND SWEETSHOPS.

Moston, Emmeline

See ROBERT AND HIS FRIENDS.

Moston, Mr

Father of Emmeline Moston, and owner of The Elms at Marleigh. He becomes very tetchy when Robert's and Jameson Jameson's rivalry for his daughter's affections results in a certain amount of damage being done to his property. (*William – The Pirate*, 11)

Motorcycles

Motorcycles (solo or with pillion or sidecar) were popular means of transport in the 1920s and 1930s, but (like pedal cycles) they do not figure prominently in the stories. Robert is the proud owner of one in *William – The Bad*, 9; in *Sweet William*, 1; in *William – The Dictator*, 6 and 10, and in other episodes. (In *William Does His Bit*, 5, he is supposed to have given up his motorcycle.)

Moult, General

General Moult is mentioned in thirty-three of the stories, during the run of which he ages somewhat and celebrates both his eightieth and ninetieth birthdays. He starts off in *Still – William*, 2, as 'fat and important-looking' but with a certain breeziness. He soon settles down, however, into being the stereotyped retired military gent of peppery temper and static opinions. General Moult, who shows little interest in the company of women, is a rather lonely character until fairly near the end of the saga when, through William's indirect intervention, he meets AARON MASON, who, like the General, is a Boer War veteran. Theirs is an instant

rapport; old campaigns are discussed with relish, and Aaron (renamed Bill by Moult) becomes his batman, gardener, Man Friday – but above all his friend and companion.

Moult has little time for the modern boy, but William is not a particular enemy of his. They tangle occasionally, but grudges are not generally carried forward into the next encounter. Indeed, General Moult often seems to forget who William is: boys to him are collective rather than individual. He is slightly deaf and short-sighted, but he takes on a new lease of very active life during the 1940s. He spares time from playing golf and rearranging his private Boer War museum to throw himself wholeheartedly into the Home Guard when, after two years of the Second World War, he decides that it is not after all just 'an insignificant skirmish' (*William and the Brains Trust*, 3). A 'mock invasion' is planned, and the General organises the village children as helpers, offering his much-coveted South African ostrich egg as a prize to the child who makes the most valuable contribution to the manoeuvre. William is desperate to win it, although it seems that all the advantages lie with Hubert Lane, but by plenty of luck, and very little judgement, William triumphs, and the egg is his.

In *William's Treasure Trove*, 4, 'Old Mouldy' is eighty (it is in this story that he discovers Aaron Mason). In *William the Superman*, 2, he is fast reaching his ninetieth birthday (although he seems to think he is still eighty: there is just the suggestion of senility about him, and he has become a touching rather than a comic Blimpish figure). Plans are made in secret by a group of ladies for a wonderful ninetieth-birthday party for the General in the village hall. Aaron Mason explains to the Outlaws that a cloud hangs over his employer, who has been trying – without success – to have his South African war memoirs published. The General is so depressed that he thinks a particularly malevolent witch-doctor, whom he once arrested, has put an evil spell on him. On his birthday, however, he receives an enthusiastic offer from a publisher. He is then asked by Miss Milton, on the pretext of fixing the window-catch, to drop in at the village hall. When he does so, it is to rousing cheers, songs and smiles from 'his neighbours . . . his friends . . . his well-wishers . . . He hadn't realised till this moment how much he valued them.' 'For He's a Jolly Good Fellow', 'Happy Birthday to You' and ' The Boys of the Old Brigade' are enthusiastically if inharmoniously rendered. The shell of the General's 'crustiness' crumbles and 'tears of emotion' stand 'in the dim, red-rimmed eyes'. When Aaron/Bill asks how he is feeling, General Moult replies: 'I don't think I've felt so happy since – since the Relief of Mafeking.'

This is the high spot of his involvement in the stories, although he crops up again (back to his usual barking and spiky form) in *William the Lawless*, 1, 3 and 5.

Murdoch, Georgie

Another example of the Perfect (or Perfectly Awful) Child who comes to the village and makes the Outlaws' lives a misery. White-suited, well mannered, smarmy and a cissy in every respect, Georgie becomes the idol of all the local mothers and spinsters when his family takes up residence at The Laurels. Eventually Ginger, Henry and Douglas – sick to death with having this paragon held up to them for emulation by their mothers – give William an ultimatum. Either he squashes Georgie to psychological pulp or he (William) can no longer be considered a fit leader of the Outlaws. William accepts the challenge; Georgie gets 'sickniner an' sickniner' by the day, and when the children are asked to present scenes from British history at a posh garden-party he insists on having the best parts. William appears to be amenable to this; he persuades Georgie to enact an episode in

the life of King John (*after* he 'loses his things in the Wash'), and to allow his perfect person and white sailor-suit to be slightly muddied for authenticity. Actually William daubs him lavishly with mud, and inveigles him into believing that King John has two courtiers named 'Dam and Blarst'. (Georgie's weakness is that he will never admit his ignorance; therefore William's gems of historical misinformation are accepted by him.) Thus it comes about that an unusually filthy-looking Georgie (in the belief that he is addressing his faithful courtiers) declaims 'Oh, Dam and Blarst' in front of an audience of shocked and shattered erstwhile admirers. Afterwards even his wonderful manners and charming smile cannot erase 'the memory of that mud-caked little horror uttering horrible oaths'. Georgie simply has to go. His parents sell their house, take their leave and tell their new neighbours that there isn't a boy in William's village 'fit for Georgie to associate with'. William has well and truly salvaged his honour, and his position as the Outlaws' leader. (*William – The Outlaw*, 3)

Mush, Miss Gregoria

See APRIL FOOL'S DAY.

Mutch, Miss Gregoria

A gossip-spreading lady in *William – The Rebel*, 12, who possibly is meant to be the same character as Miss Mush!

Neighbours

Over the years, the Browns have many neighbours, partly because the sub-letting of properties (on both long- and short-term agreements) was common in the period between the two world wars, and partly perhaps because William could hardly have been a restful neighbour. The shifts of residents on either side of William's successive homes (see WILLIAM'S HOUSES) include his great friends Joan and Ginger (and of course their families), Mrs Frame, Miss Montagu, Mr Gregorius Lambkin and Miss Gregoria Mush (see APRIL FOOL'S DAY) and Miss Amelia Blake (see CATS).

There is also the nastiest neighbour of all, the nameless 'gorilla' of *William – The Pirate*, 5, whom William eventually contrives to drive to distraction (by making his doorbells peal constantly, through a primitive form of remote control). See also DOGS.

New Elizabethans

In celebration of the coronation of Elizabeth II (see QUEENS) William and the Outlaws decide that, in Henry's words, they 'ought to be doin' somethin' about bein' New Elizabethans'. Their idea is to emulate Drake and other sea-captains from the time of Elizabeth I, and to 'take treasures off foreigners' and give them to the country. It proves dif-

ficult to find foreigners in the village (see HETHERLEY, COLONEL), so they decide instead to find a new country (by digging) and, in fact, uncover the valuable collection of silver which belongs to Mr Kirkham, the mayor. He decides that the proceeds from the sale of this should be used to help the country, and the Outlaws can say how this money should be spent. At the end of the episode, they are allowed to play a game on Mr Kirkham's dartboard, in the middle of which Ginger notices that Hubert Lane, who has been away, is now back. With Elizabethan images still very much in his mind William grins, and pauses in the business of dart-throwing: ' "There's time to finish the game an' beat the Laneites, too," he said.' (*William and the Moon Rocket*, 6)

Newnham, Sir Roderick

A well-known London actor who is to be the guest artist in the play which is to be produced for the opening of the Hadley New Theatre. He does not endear himself to the local inhabitants, as he refers to Hadley as a 'one horse town' and to its best hotel's meals as 'pig swill'. Surprisingly, though they contemplate taking Sir Roderick down a peg or two, the Outlaws do not go out gunning for him. See also BOSCASTLE, GUY. (*William and the Masked Ranger*, 6)

Old Barn, The

The Outlaws are a very fortunate group of small boys in having the Old Barn as their headquarters; it is a secret-refuge childhood fantasy come true. They put it to good use over the years when it is, by turns, a nightclub, a newspaper office, an exhibition hall, a circus, a theatre, a political office, the Court of the Square Table, and the venue for many other functions.

There are some traumatic moments in *William and the Masked Ranger*, 3, when it appears that the very existence of their hidey-hole is under threat, but fortunately the developers do not move in, and the Old Barn is still sturdily (if rather crumblingly) standing when it is last mentioned in *William the Lawless*, 5. See also OUTLAWS, THE.

Olympic Games

Mrs Brown, having been used as a model by a visiting cosmetics demonstrator, looks good, and suddenly wonders if she has wasted her life. She thinks of various places and events that she wishes she had been to: these include the South of France, Ascot, a Buckingham Palace garden-party, and the Olympic Games. The Outlaws decide to put on an Olympic Games for her and, practising throwing the hammer in the garden of Brent House, William stuns a burglar. The grateful occupant, Mr Tertullian Selwyn, offers William almost anything he wants as a reward. William wants to give his mother 'a thoughtful act' for her birthday, so he asks Mr Selwyn to help with the cost of curing the dry rot in the platform of the village hall, something dear to Mrs Brown's heart. She doesn't get her Olympics, but she does receive Mr Selwyn's

undertaking that he'll cover all the expenses of the platform's repair. (*William's Television Show*, 4)

Optimism

William's optimism is satisfyingly unquenchable. He is the sort of boy who will happily spend a lot of time building a rabbit-hutch in the hope that fate will one day supply a rabbit; basically he has enormous trust in positive aspects of life, and belief in the power of his own will, and imagination.

In *William Again*, 4, we realise that for William, under parental pressure, church-going is as fixed a routine as the stars in their courses. Nevertheless William optimistically endeavours to break the pattern:

'I'm not going to church this morning,' Robert happened to say, carrying a deck-chair into the garden.
 'An' I'm not, either,' said William, as he seized another chair . . .

Although ultimately resilient, his hopefulness receives frequent knocks from his family, as this episode illustrates. He patiently explains to his 'tophatted and gloved' father that he'd *like* to go to church, he is disappointed not to go, but that as he has been 'took ill' suddenly he'd 'jus' like to go an' lie down qui'tly – out of doors':

 . . . his Pegasean imagination soared aloft on daring wings – 'I feel's if I might *die* if I went to church this mornin' feelin' 's ill as I do now.'
 'If you're as bad as that,' Mr. Brown said callously as he brushed his coat, 'I suppose you might as well die in church as anywhere.'

When William's optimism *is* allowed to dictate events, it is of course not uncommon for things to go awry, but William is equipped to cope with this:

'There was something to be said for being in bed and asleep when his father came home.' Retribution, put off to the following day, is apt, as he knows, to lose its edge.

In *Sweet William*, 10, he finds himself suddenly demoted from hero to victim (see LOVE, MISS ARABELLA), having apparently had to be rescued from drowning. He is on holiday at the seaside and in the week left before he has to go home he asks himself, baffled, if there is anything he can possibly do to change the situation: '. . . his incurable optimism rose to answer the question . . . He was a hero, and he must, by some means or other, win back his heroic status.'

Just occasionally William is caught in the reverse mood of hopelessness, which is as dark and dull as his optimism is bright:

The only possible solution of the situation, he decided, was for the end of the world to come now at once, but William had learnt by experience that that event never takes place when summoned.

'No,' he said to himself bitterly. 'No, if it comes at all, it'll prob'ly come when I've jus' caught a fish an' before I've had time to show it to anyone, or when someone's jus' brought [sic] me an ice cream an' before I've had time to eat it . . .'

(*William's Happy Days* , 8)

Orford, Lieutenant

A Hitler look-alike. See WARTIME.

Outlaws, The

Although it appears as the eighth story in *Just – William*, 'The Outlaws' was the second of the William stories to be published (in *Home*

Magazine, March 1919: see Appendix 2). As well as William, of course, this features Ginger, Henry and Douglas, so that all the Outlaws, with the exception of Joan, have then come on to the scene. (Joan takes the Outlaws' Oath in *William – the Fourth*, 8. She is the only female member, and their ranks are then complete; no further members are ever admitted, not even the pushy Violet Elizabeth. Although Joan *is* an Outlaw, her spasmodic appearances in the stories – because her family moves, and she goes away to school, and so on – mean that generally when the Outlaws are mentioned it is William, Ginger, Henry and Douglas who are being described.) The Old Barn, which of course is the headquarters of the Outlaws, is first referred to (in the *books*) in *Just – William*, 5.

The Outlaws are bound from the beginning by a strong sense of loyalty, and the knowledge that most of their dealings are best kept from the eyes of adults: 'In their shrinking from the glare of publicity they showed an example of unaffected

modesty that many other public societies might profitably emulate.' Richmal made excellent use of the childhood group or gang, conveying the genuine atmosphere of its allegiances and ambitions, its solidarity and its rivalries.

Shoving and jostling each other, both physically and figuratively, William, Ginger, Henry and Douglas rarely express their mutual affection overtly. Any remotely sentimental or 'soppy' talk would be anathema to them, but they remain through almost every one of their hundreds of joint exploits completely supportive of each other. Though closely knit, they have distinct personalities and, in certain areas, differing values. William – resilient, assertive, optimistic and splendidly imaginative – is the almost-never-questioned leader. However, occasionally when several of his schemes and stratagems have gone badly awry he has to pull a particularly attractive plum out of the pie to prove that his rightful place is still at the top of the heap. (Henry, the oldest of the Outlaws, has vague ambitions to challenge William for the leadership but, lacking William's panache and inspiriting optimism, he knows that he will never take over.) Ginger is the faithful lieutenant and William's very special ('best') friend. There is a particular empathy between William and himself, even to the fact that they both have unruly hair that is – in varying degrees – carroty in colour. Their closeness is enhanced by the fact that for the first ten years or so of their lives they live in adjoining houses (see WILLIAM'S HOUSES).

Henry is the best-informed of the Outlaws, sometimes a bit of a know-all. He is conscientious, too – for example, taking the trouble to look up the spelling of every word of an important Outlaws letter in the dictionary. He enjoys airing his knowledge and pursuing research into a subject. Douglas has a pessimistic and an I-told-you-so streak in his make-up which is not always appreciated by the others, especially by William.

When the four Outlaws have to split into two sets of partners, there is generally a pairing-off of William and Ginger, and Henry and Douglas. Despite their deep sense of loyalty to the group, William has put the needs of a little girl who attracts him before those of the Outlaws (see ANGELA (2): *William's Happy Days*, 8), and their solidarity again seems under threat when the phlegmatic Douglas surprisingly defects briefly while in the throes of an infatuation in *William and the Masked Ranger*, 4. (There are suggestions that Douglas is a weaker character than his friends. In *William and the Space Animal*, 7, we learn that 'Douglas was a well-meaning boy but he had no initiative. Without William to tell him what to do, he just didn't know what to do.')

William, of course, has a surname; Ginger has two (Flowerdew and/or Merridew: see DISCREPANCIES); neither Henry nor Douglas is ever given the distinction of a surname. It is a curious fact that Ginger, Henry and Douglas each has an elder brother (Hector, John and George respectively) of an age to be a friend or rival of Robert, and a suitor of Ethel. Henry suffers the additional handicap of having a young (unnamed) sister who is sometimes described as a baby (confined to a pram) but occasionally seems to be at least a toddler, with toys and sundry pieces of useful apparatus that the Outlaws are glad to be able to 'borrow' from time to time. See addendum p. 218.

The Outlaws' Named Relatives

Book	Character
8.9	Douglas's Aunt Jane
31.8	Douglas's Uncle Ernest
6.2	Flowerdew, Miss (Ginger's aunt)
23.8	Flowerdew, Mr
6.2	Flowerdew, Mrs
7.3	Flowerdew, Mrs
24.4	Flowerdew, Mrs
8.7	George (Douglas's brother)

9.6	George (Douglas's brother)
13.8	George (Douglas's brother)
26.8	George (Douglas's brother)
35.1	George (Douglas's brother)
3.12	Ginger's cousin George (twin)
3.12	Ginger's cousin John (twin)
17.11	Ginger's cousin Miss Carrol
13.4	Ginger's cousin Percy Penhurst
15.5	Ginger's Aunt Amelia
14.1	Ginger's Aunt Arabelle
10.6	Ginger's Aunt Emma
10.6	Ginger's Aunt Jane
8.9	Ginger's Uncle George
10.6	Ginger's Uncle George
10.6	Ginger's Uncle John (1)
10.6	Ginger's Uncle John (2)
8.7	Hector (Ginger's brother)
9.6	Hector (Ginger's brother)
9.9	Hector (Ginger's brother)
10.1	Hector (Ginger's brother)
13.8	Hector (Ginger's brother)
26.3	Hector (Ginger's brother)
26.8	John (Henry's brother)
25.6	Merridew, Hector
31.7	Merridew, Hector
36.2	Merridew, Mr
24.10	Merridew, Mrs
36.2	Merridew, Mrs
26.9	Merridew, Richard (Ginger's cousin)
10.1	Merridews, The
28.1	Merridews, The

Parfitt, Joan and Mrs

See 'JOAN'.

Parker, Frankie

'A small snub-nosed freckled boy with a perverted craving for cocoanut ice' (*William – The Showman*, 5). He also appears in *William and the Space Animal*, 1, as an 'expert swopper': 'I'll swop a Nougat Square for two of your Treacle Dabs, 'cause they're smaller, aren't they?' and so on. He has a brother, Freddie, and they play very small parts in several stories.

Parker, Georgie

A small boy who confuses evacuation with vaccination (*William and the Evacuees*, 1). Also appears in *William and the Tramp*, 6.

Parsons, Frankie

A small boy who is a fairly regular member of the audience for the Outlaws' entertainments, etc. He is self-assured and a bit of a know-all. He first appears in *William's Television Show*, 5, and finally in *William the Superman*, 6.

Patsy

See GROWN-UP FRIENDS.

Peache, Miss Victoria

See AUTHORS.

Pennyman, Mr and Mrs

A Ruskinite married couple who temporarily occupy the Hall in *William – The Bad*, 10. They are the kind of harmless 'lunies' that particularly appeal to William. 'Dressed in classical robes with fillets about their heads', Euphemia works her loom while Adolphus plays 'unmelodiously but evidently to his own entire satisfaction upon a flute'. Shocked by 'the ugliness of modern life', the Pennymans hope to bring back everyone (or at least the inhabitants of the village) to 'the morning of the world'. They are food and dress reformers, and believe in making everything that is in common use in their home with their own hands. The re-education of the villagers does not proceed too well: classes in hand-weaving and vegetarianism are sparsely attended, so the Pennymans launch their Merrie England campaign, which fails because the villagers resent the substitution of milk and nut cutlets for strong drink and roast beef. The appeal of country dancing is also eclipsed because the Charleston and the Blues are being taught in the neighbouring country-town. As a last-ditch attempt to revivify the eternal values, the Pennymans arrange a May Day masque, with Euphemia as the May Queen, Adolphus as St George and William and their prissy Kate-Greenaway-garbed nephew Pelleas as the dragon. The two boys dislike each other on sight, fight each other inside their shared dragon-skin, and then William ferociously battles with Adolphus. The audience cheers deafeningly as St George is pursued relentlessly by the dragon.

The Pennymans give up re-establishing the morning of the world; they decide to accept but to purify modern civilisation, and form the League of Perfect Love (*William – The Detective*, 7), for the protection of wildlife. However, the first meeting of the League is disrupted by William who, unknowingly, releases several rats into the room. He also tangles with the Pennymans in chapter 5 of the same book.

Perkins, Mr

A teacher at William's school, known as 'Ole Warbeck'. (*Sweet William*, 2 and 4)

Perkins, Section Officer

See A.F.S.

Pinchin Major

One of William's schoolmates. (*William Again*, 8)

Pocket-Contents

William's pockets are used to capacity. In *Just – William*, 1, we learn that the contents of one include sweets (Gooseberry Eyes), 'a penknife and top and a piece of putty'; in chapter 4 of the same book he catches a lizard on his way to school and puts it in his pocket, but later finds that the lizard has 'abandoned the unequal struggle for existence among the stones, top, penknife, bits of putty, and other small objects that inhabited William's pocket. The housing problem had been too much for it.' In *William – The Rebel*, 2, on one of those occasions when he plans to run away and seek his fortune, he puts as many meat pasties from the larder as he can into his pockets. Later, when he devours them, 'one had broken into tiny pieces in his pocket, but William was no whit disconcerted by this. He ate every fragment, including a piece of string, some bits of crayon, a small piece of rubber, and a generous sprinkling of ants' eggs, a packet of which, destined for his goldfish, had lately broken in his pocket. Cheered and refreshed by this mixed diet, he sets off once more.' In *William and the Witch*, 3, 'he brought from his pocket a handful of assorted objects, including a length of string, then carefully detached the string from a blob of Plasticene, a liquorice bootlace, a piece of sticky paper, a crumbling dog biscuit, a couple of corks, the top off a milk bottle and the wishbone of a chicken'.

Poems and Poets

The William saga is sprinkled with consciously awful pieces of doggerel, and it seems that Richmal wrote poems (and about poets) with some relish (see FRANKS, OSWALD). In *William and the Space Animal*, 5, the Outlaws make one of their several attempts to start a newspaper. Henry points out that 'there's got to be a po'm in a newspaper'. He thinks this should be about spring; William favours one about adventure; Douglas thinks the subject of the poem should be food; while Ginger insists that it should concern itself with love: 'All great po'ts wrote po'ms about love. Shakespeare did an' so does that woman called Hartsease that writes po'ms in the *Hadley Times* . . .'

They decide that each of them should write one line on the subject he fancies. These will then be combined into a composite poem. The Outlaws are very proud of the result, which reads as follows:

Flowers come springin' out in the spring,
An' Shakespeare wrote about love an' said it
was a jolly good thing,
An' I'm goin' to be the first one to shoot myself
to the moon,
An' choc'late creams taste better than lollipops
though they get finished more soon.

Politics and Power

Politics, and the drive for power of those who practise it, provides caustic and comical moments in the stories. As Richmal points out, William has many of the qualities that would make an excellent politician. In *Sweet William*, 6, Mrs Monks, the Vicar's wife, seems also to be pointing this out to him. She is trying to persuade him to join a society she has just started for the children of the village (the S.E.F.C.R.C.: Society for Educating Future Citizens in the Responsibilities of Citizenship).

William is not particularly interested until she says: 'You see, dear boy . . . when you're grown up, it's you who will govern the country.' William is 'galvanised into sudden interest. "Crumbs!" he said. "I didn't know that." ' He thinks he's been chosen to govern in the manner of dictators such as Hitler and Mussolini, not understanding the difference between the 'collective responsibility' that Mrs Monks is outlining and an individual one. Neither does he wish to wait until he is twenty-one, as the Vicar's wife suggests; he decides to exercise his political powers immediately. His first act as a reforming politician is to free the slaves (Mrs Monks has been talking about Pitt and Wilberforce) and, although no one apart from himself understands what he is doing, or talking about, at least he ends up by having an enormous (but illicit) afternoon tea (see FOOD).

He sees himself as Prime Minister in *William – The Bad*, 3. Party politics are very much to the fore, and the ever knowledgeable Henry patiently explains to his friends the stances of the major parties, each of which in its own way wants to make the country 'better'. The Conservatives want to do this by keeping things 'jus' like what they are

now'. The Liberals want to make things better by 'alterin' them jus' a bit, but not so's anyone'd notice', the Socialists 'by taking everyone's money off 'em', while 'the Communists want to make things better by killin' everyone but themselves'. Each of the Outlaws adopts the rôle of a party leader, William becoming the top Tory, winning a 'general election', becoming 'Prime Minister', and getting back for the juvenile population the use of the pond which MISS FELICIA DALRYMPLE has claimed as her property. Then he is 'sick of pol'tics altogether. There isn't any *sense* in 'em. I'd sooner be a Red Indian any day.'

Nevertheless, several books later he is dabbling again in political matters. In *William and the Brains Trust*, 7, inspired by the Beveridge Report, the Outlaws make one of their own. Their 'rights' are set out in detail (and in their idiosyncratic spelling). These include 'as much hollidays as term . . . no afternoon school . . . sixpence a week pocket munny and not to be took off . . . No Latin no French no Arithmetick . . . As much ice creem and banarnas and creem buns as we like free . . . No punishments and stay up as late as we like.'

William has the responsibility of seeing that an Act of Parliament is passed to endorse their report. He doesn't succeed, but he does get an invitation for the Outlaws to see a pantomine at Christmas. There is an appreciative 'Gosh!' and a 'Hurrah!', and we are told that the Outlaws have acquired a certain 'philosophy of life'; they have realised that 'a pantomime in the hand is worth a dozen Acts of Parliament in the bush'.

William's most amusing excursion into politics occurs in *William – The Fourth*, 1, when he becomes the only member of the junior branch of the Society of Reformed Bolshevists. Robert and his friends have formed themselves into the Society of Advanced Bolshevists, but they do not want juvenile members, so William happily becomes the president, secretary, committee and member of his own political group. As Richmal comments, like many better-known politicians he is interested mainly in the sound of his own voice, so he doesn't mind conducting all of the society's business solo. However, he grasps the basic 'Bolshevist' message that everyone has 'gotter be equal' and decides to broaden the membership of his party to make it more powerful. The concept of equality appeals to his new members, who appropriate the cameras and watches of their elder brothers (the members of the senior branch of the Bolshevists). As Robert, made sadder and wiser by the incident, explains to Mr Brown: 'It's all right when you can get your share of other people's things, but when other people try to get their share of your things, then it's different.'

Pollit, Miss

See ART AND ARTISTS and GROWN-UP FRIENDS.

Polliter, Mr

Relief history-master at William's school. See WARTIME.

Pomeroy, Philippa

See ROBERT AND HIS FRIENDS.

Poppleham, Ella

A small girl from the village, associated peripherally with some of the Outlaws' schemes, mainly as part of the audience. First appears in *William and the Evacuees*, 1 and finally in *William the Superman*, 1.

Porker, Mrs

A large, unpleasant, rich lady, temporarily occupying the Hall, and trying to make life miserable for Miss Rossiter, whose family lived there for hundreds of years (obviously pre-Bott) but who have fairly recently had to sell it. With a little pseudo-psychic interference, William puts things right! (William's Happy Days, 9)

Privet, Miss

A paying guest at the Browns', arranged by William, unknown to his parents, who confuse her with the Aunt Susan they are expecting from Australia. (William – The Explorer, 5)

Protest Marchers

Chapter 5 of William and the Pop Singers deals with two groups of protesters. One is based in the village and 'organised' by Miss Thompson who is absent-minded but incredibly good-natured. The trouble is that her branch of the Society for the Preservation of Animal Life exists only in her imagination, and Mr Meggison is coming down from headquarters to address what he fondly envisages as an active lively group. Fortunately William leads a band of Protest Marchers, who are dying for a cup of tea, into Miss Thompson's garden just in time for Mr Meggison's visit. The Protest Marchers seem to be campaigning for Freedom in general, but as they have Hannah, a pig, as their mascot Mr Meggison is convinced that they represent his particular movement. Hannah turns out to be so disruptive that Mrs Thompson manages to convince Mr Meggison that it might not be a good thing to continue the local branch – so she gets off the hook. The Protest Marchers are happy because they get their tea; they also manage to sell Hannah,

who is becoming a nuisance, to Farmer Smith, and they think they have made their mark because 'a boy' (William) has asked all of them for their autographs. (He has actually had them all sign some questionnaires for which a researcher friend of his is desperate to find signatures.)

Queens

Given William's attitude towards life, it is not surprising that, in his eyes, leaders and figureheads are usually seen to be male. (Even when he temporarily assumes the rôle of dictator, it is noteworthy that he has to be 'Him Hitler' because 'Herr Hitler' suggests the femininity which he despises: see Anti-Semitism.) Nevertheless he has a strong feeling for Elizabeth II: 'Since watching the Coronation on television, William had been consumed by a secret fervour of loyalty. As liege man of life and limb, he would have yielded place to no one.' The Queen becomes the focus for his patriotism when the Outlaws decide to become New Elizabethans (*William and the Moon Rocket*, 6). See also NEW ELIZABETHANS.

At the more local level, there are of course May Queens but they, and the May Day rituals generally, are in William's opinion pretty 'soppy'. In *More William*, 8, it is a streak of anti-feminism, as much as a dislike of the greedy Evangeline Fish, that prompts him to depose her from queenship (even before she is crowned) and make himself the May King (see FOOD).

Redding, Mr

A spy for Germany during the Second World War. William thinks he's a 'bird-man' (a naturalist) but indirectly helps with his unmasking. (*William and the Evacuees*, 3)

Relations

We are told that as well as his mother, father, sister and brother

> William was blest with many relations, though 'blest' is not quite the word he would have used himself. They seemed to appear and disappear and reappear in spasmodic succession throughout the years. He never could keep count of them. Most of them he despised, some he actually disliked. The latter class reciprocated his feelings fervently.
>
> (*William – The Fourth*, 5)

Although this was written comparatively early in the saga, it seems that Richmal already felt that

William's aunts, uncles, cousins, great-aunts and -uncles and second cousins and so on were getting out of hand. Subsequently she often reintroduced relatives who had already been established in earlier stories. However, she also brought in new characters, whose links with the Browns varied from the close to the tenuous, and to baffle readers still further she repeated certain names (i.e., aunts Jane, Lucy and Florence) although the characters to whom these referred varied so much in different episodes that one feels that William must have had (at least) two aunts Jane, Lucy, Florence, etc.

Great-Aunt Jane represents a good example of this kind of complexity. She crops up in *William Again*, 2 (as the gutsy old dear whom William figuratively saves from the jaws of death: see FRANCIS), and in *William – The Fourth*, 5 (as the coconut-shying, roundabout-riding sin-obsessed character). Although they look alike in Thomas Henry's illustrations, these two redoubtable old biddies are distinct from each other, because each is meeting William for the first time. (There are other Aunt Janes, too.)

Of course, Richmal made good use of stereotypes, and many of William's relatives fall within this category. Some are nervous, some aggressive, but they have many attributes in common: 'The aunts sat round the drawing-room fire talking and doing crochet-work. In this consists the whole art and duty of aunthood. *All* aunts do crochet-work' (*More William*, 1). And, of course, mend socks! (Richmal herself was a happily devoted aunt, and perhaps this is why she writes so zestfully about aunts, and so often sends them up!)

Later on, another auntly duty is mentioned: William's father's aunt is 'an old lady who neither liked nor understood boys, but she was very correct and had prided herself from earliest youth on doing the right thing. And the right thing in the case of a boy was a tip' (*William*, 10). Unfortunately, as William bitterly and frequently points out, aunts and uncles are generally less understanding, and

addicted to sending him, when politeness necessi-
tates a present, direly dull things such as 'pencil-
boxes, and story-books about curious, exemplary
boys, and boxes of crayons and pens and things'
(*William Again*, 6).

William has a preponderance of aunts, but his
male relatives can be as great a burden as some of
his female ones. There is, of course, MR
CRANTHORPE-CRANBOROUGH, 'a very distant
cousin of William's father', who trades on the relationship to try to obtain William as a new pupil for
his school; there is also Uncle George (see
ANIMALS) whose efforts to make William conform
to his ideal of quiet and serious boyhood seem
unquenchable, until he felicitously swallows his
godson's frog. William doesn't have much luck
with godparents: his godmother is that 'huge and
horrible woman' MRS ADOLPHUS CRANE.

On the whole, if visiting aunts, uncles and
cousins leave William alone, or are reasonably tolerant towards him, he plays the game with them.
When Cousin Mildred arrives, 'elderly and very
thin and very tall' and wearing 'a curious, long,
shapeless garment of green silk with a golden gir-
dle', she is flatteringly deferential towards him.
This is because she lusts after psychic revelations

(so far denied her) and William, inspired by his
lurid reading and unbridled imagination, convinces
her that he is on intimate terms with rattling 'skele-
tons. And ghostly arms beckonin' an' all that.'
Being 'a sportsman' he feels eventually, 'after the
gift of an exceptionally large tin of toffees', that he
must admit her to what she calls 'the elect' and
arrange a psychic experience for her. Swathed in
his sheet he appears in her bedroom, emits 'a sound
faintly reminiscent of a sea-sick voyager' and
'speaks', in response to Cousin Mildred's plead-
ings that he should, in ghostly language: ' "Honk.
Yonk. Plonk," he said firmly.' It is enough to transport her into 'ecstatic joy' (*More William*, 7).

Most of his female relatives are less easily gratified. His mother's Aunt Emily, for example,
comes for a week's visit, stays indefinitely, and
seems all the time to feel that she is not getting
quite the attention that she deserves. She claims to
be fragile (though she is actually extremely hefty).
Every day she snores noisily throughout a rest
upstairs between her hearty lunch and her hearty
tea. Her size, appetite and fearfully penetrating
snore, which suggests a raging lion in pain, fascinate William. He decides to harness the snore to
helpful effect by making it an auditory-off-stage
feature of the Outlaws' current 'Wild Animal'
show for the local children. Stimulated by his audience's delighted response, he opens up Aunt
Emily's bedroom, and, for a penny a time, permits
his public to file past her enormous frame ('In
sleep Aunt Emily was not beautiful'), which is clad
only in a blouse and striped petticoat. Ever more
daring, he puts notices against items on her dress-
ing-table: 'FAT WILD WOMAN'S HARE, FAT WILD
WOMAN'S KOME, FAT WILD WOMAN'S TEETH', etc.
Aunt Emily snores through it all, as the audience
keep filing in and paying their pennies for repeat
performances. When she suddenly awakens on
the 'top note of a peal that was a pure delight to
her audience', she shakes William till his teeth
rattle, acidly instructs Mr Brown 'to procure a

conveyance' for her and complains bitterly to him about how William has insulted her. Mr Brown concurs that it is '*disgraceful!*' but, watching the cab bear her away, he presses a half-crown into William's hand (*Just – William*, 5).

The most satisfactory of his relations in William's eyes is almost certainly his Cousin Dorita, a lively and interesting character who sadly appears in only one episode (*Just – William*, 9). Together they foil the family's plan to force them to attend the wedding of their Cousin Sybil, wearing the humiliating attire of white satin: ' "We was walkin' round the room an' we sat down on the Chesterfield and there was this stuff on it an' it came off on our clothes," explained William stonily and monotonously and all in one breath.' In their ruined page and maid-of-honour garb, William and Dorita are left alone while everyone else takes off for the wedding. They play a riotous game of mountaineering on the staircase, using mattresses from their own, Mr and Mrs Brown's, and Cousin Sybil's beds. Dorita tells him that if she ever marries she'd as soon marry him as anyone, and William gallantly replies that he 'wu'nt mind' so long as it could happen 'in ornery clothes'. Dorita is clearly a girl after his own heart.

A list of William's relations, both appealing and obnoxious, is given below.

Book	Character
17.4	Aggie, Cousin
17.4	Aggie, Cousin's boy
10.6	Aunt (William's)
1.3	Aunt (William's)
20.7	Aunt Belle Holewood
20.9	Aunt Belle Holewood
3.9	Aunt Ellen
1.5	Aunt Emily (Mrs Brown's aunt)
5.9	Aunt Emma
5.11	Aunt Emma
2.1	Aunt Evangeline
16.5	Aunt Florence
20.5	Aunt Florence
23.3	Aunt Florence
25.8	Aunt Florence
25.10	Aunt Florence
27.7	Aunt Florence
33.2	Aunt Florence
16.4	Aunt Florence Brown
36.6	Aunt Hester
2.1	Aunt Jane
2.2	Aunt Jane
14.3	Aunt Jane
14.4	Aunt Jane
16.6	Aunt Jane
4.2	Aunt Julia
3.11	Aunt Lilian (Mrs Brown's sister)
20.7	Aunt Louie
20.9	Aunt Louie
21.8	Aunt Louie
22.6	Aunt Louie
2.1	Aunt Lucy
3.2	Aunt Lucy
21.6	Aunt Lucy (Ethel's godmother)
29.3	Aunt Maggie
1.1	Aunt Susan
1.6	Aunt, an
9.1	Aunt, an
9.1	Aunt, an
9.8	Aunt, an
10.10	Aunt, an
11.2	Aunt, an
11.6	Aunt, an
13.4	Aunt, an
13.5	Aunt, an
13.6	Aunt, an
14.10	Aunt, an
14.10	Aunt, an
15.4	Aunt, an
16.8	Aunt, an
19.4	Aunt, an
19.10	Aunt, an
21.5	Aunt, an

22.3	Aunt, an
23.1	Aunt, an
27.5	Aunt, an
26.4	Aunt, an
27.1	Aunt, an
28.5	Aunt, an
30.2	Aunt, an
37.7	Aunt, an
19.6	Auntie Flossie
17.11	Aunts
20.2	Aunts (various)
2.1	Barbara (cousin)
38.6	Brown, Mr's Aunt Amelia
6.3	Brown, Mr's brother
5.9	Brown, Mrs's aunt
24.4	Brown, Mrs's cousin
37.4	Brown, Mrs's cousin
4.7	Brown, Mrs's cousin's son
23.10	Brown, Mrs's favourite sister
32.5	Brown, Mrs's mother
4.2	Crane, Mrs Adolphus (William's godmother, Mrs Brown's second cousin)
7.6	Cranthorpe-Cranborough, Mr (distant cousin)
1.9	Dorita
21.6	Ethel's godmother (Lucy)
9.7	Flavia, Cousin
3.2	Francis (William's cousin)
9.7	Frederick, Uncle (Brown)
3.11	Grandfather Moore
15.12	Grandmother
1.9	Grant, Sybil
12.2	Great-Aunt Augusta
3.2	Great-Aunt Jane
4.5	Great-Aunt Jane
4.5	Great-Aunt Jane's father
32.5	Great-Aunt Susan
4.2	Great-Uncle Joshua
5.11	Jimmie
2.1	Jimmy
2.1	Jimmy's mother
1.9	Michael
2.7	Mildred, Cousin
8.8	Robert's godmother
22.6	Ticehurst, Mr (Mr Brown's cousin)
22.8	Ticehurst, Mr (Mr Brown's cousin)
2.11	Uncle (South Africa)
9.6	Uncle (William's)
8.9	Uncle Charles
5.9	Uncle Frederick
6.7	Uncle Frederick
4.2	Uncle George
2.5	Uncle George (William's godfather)
4.2	Uncle James (paternal)
5.9	Uncle Jim
3.2	Uncle John
4.12	Uncle, an
6.6	Uncle, an
7.7	Uncle, an
9.2	Uncle, an
10.3	Uncle, an
16.1	Uncle, an
22.3	Uncle, an
27.3	Uncle, an
2.8	Uncle, an old
16.3	William's godmother
26.12	William's grandfather

Reports

School reports occasionally influence the action of the stories, although on the whole they are regarded by both William and his family as simply a rather unpleasant fact of life:

. . . there was a certain monotony about William's reports. Masters who had a delicate shrinking from the crude and brutal truth wrote, 'Fair'. Those who had the courage of their convictions wrote, 'Poor'. The mathematical master, who was very literal, wrote, 'Uniformly bad.'

The horror and disgust of William's father at these statements was generally as simulated as William's penitence. They knew their respective *roles* and played them, but they had gone through the scene too many times to be able to put much spirit into the parts.

William – The Conqueror, 3.

See also *William's Happy Days*, 2.

Robert and His Friends

Unlike Ethel's, Robert's age fluctuates. It shifts upwards and downwards between seventeen and twenty-one, although, apart from a short period of military service (see WARTIME), he remains a perpetual student, with no noticeable increase in psy-

chological maturity throughout the thirty-eight books. Robert's guiding passion is for beautiful girls, but these seem to stay for the brief period of the relationship firmly on the pedestals on which he places them, so that little intimacy occurs. Generally speaking, his 'goddesses' are all cast in the same mould: physically stunning, they have no serious interests; they are imperious, jealous and demanding, ready always to soak up flattery and quick to take offence. Robert has quite a lot to offer these tetchy lovelies but, unsophisticated and shy, he fails to realise this. We are told that he is one of the most personable youths in the village, and his interests are assorted and energetically pursued. He is at various times secretary or treasurer of local sports and drama societies; he also has 'high-brow' aspirations, as shown when he reluctantly takes William on a promised trip to a pantomime and, to suggest his superiority to the proceedings, determinedly reads Chekhov during the performance (*William – The Pirate*, 7); also, of course, he supports such short-lived intellectual groups as the Society of Advanced Bolshevists (see POLITICS AND POWER) and the Society of Twentieth Century Poets (see FRANKS, OSWALD).

William's intervention in Robert's romantic life is generally disastrous; he confuses discarded loves with the current one, concocts atrocious but well-intentioned amorous verses to the wrong girl on several occasions and, of course, constantly embarrasses Robert, when he is seeking to impress some new idol, by his mere scruffy, tactless and ubiquitous presence.

Generally speaking William holds all the bright young things who attract Robert in contempt; he senses the 'bossiness' that lies just beneath the apparently fragile femininity, the vanity and self-absorption. Nevertheless there are occasional exceptions. One of these is Miss Cannon, the first embodiment on record of 'the most beautiful girl' Robert has ever met in his life. She comes to tea, but before entering the house encounters William

and stays in the garden to play Red Indians with him. William, like Robert, then falls victim to her charms and, during the agonisingly polite and embarrassing tea-party which follows, insists on sitting in on, and interrupting, Robert's fumbled efforts to converse meaningfully with her. When the family tries surreptitiously to remove William from the love-blighted scene, his response is to declare in a sibilant whisper that becomes a stentorian blast: ' "I wasn't doin' any harm . . . only *speaking* to her! . . . Is no-one else ever to *speak* to her . . . jus' 'cause Robert's fell in love with her?" ' (*Just – William*, 2).

It is a long time before Robert finds another girl-friend whom William finds sympathetic, but Rowena Mayfield in *William's Television Show*, 3, manages to fill the bill: '. . . William had been pre-pared to treat her with the aloofness and contempt with which he normally treated the One Great Love of Robert's Life. But there was no doubt that Rowena was different.' She plays with Jumble, takes an intelligent interest in William's plans for

making a lagoon from a stream, building a cable railway up the sides of the old quarry, and organis-ing a circus: 'This did not, of course, commend itself to Robert, but the beloved generally had some weakness, and William was a weakness that could easily be dealt with. Robert dealt with him by the simple method of taking him by the collar and throwing him out of the room.' Of course, this does not deter William from involving himself in the relationship. Liking Rowena, he stays around to watch progress. Robert curses him at the time – ' "Good Lord! What a sight you look!" ' – but later has cause to be grateful, for it is William who gets round Rowena's irate father, Professor Mayfield, who has been the stumbling-block for Robert (and his rival in this instance, Oswald Franks).

Robert's friendships with members of his own sex are, on the whole, deeper and more stable than Ethel's with her girlfriends. His goddesses are listed below, together with his male chums, and a note of the books and chapters in which they are first mentioned.

Book	Character
26.7	Abbot, Rosalyn
11.4	Barlow, Peggy
20.6	Barron, Sheila
15.12	Barton, Lorna
4.1	Bell, Ronald
9.9	Bellairs, Miss Julia
16.7	Bellew, Clarinda
1.12	Bellew, Sydney
15.9	Bergson, Rupert
4.11	Blake, Miss
1.2	Cannon, Miss
11.4	Clavis, Dolly
11.4	Cotton, Molly
4.11	Crane, Miss
5.4	Dexter, Marion
5.14	Dobson, Miss Doreen
11.4	Donber, Betty
23.9	Dulcie (Bagshott niece)
13.10	Eleanor
9.7	Flavia, Cousin
4.11	Flower, Miss
28.5	Forrester, Dolores
11.9	Franklin, Gordon
8.7	Franks, Oswald
15.12	Gerrard, Cornelia
33.5	Green, Celia
7.8	Groves, Gloria
17.8	Hadlow, Ward
5.4	Hatherley, Marion
4.1	Jameson Jameson
2.8	Laing, Miss
2.3	Lewes, Mr
29.3	Lytton, Roxana (Elsie)
19.9	M.P.'s daughter
18.1	Macnamara, Dahlia
33.1	Masters, Diana
31.3	Mayfield, Rowena
17.10	Melissa
18.3	Mendleson, Felicia
15.6	Mercer, Honoria

Book	Character
15.3	Merton, Dorita
32.6	Monson, Hermione
14.11	Moston, Emmeline
7.8	Oldham, Gladys
21.9	Pomeroy, Philippa
33.1	Reedham, Biddy
27.7	Sally (Sunley niece)
5.11	Tompkins, Glory
7.8	Victor
8.8	a very pretty girl
8.10	a beautiful girl
9.7	a golden-haired girl
9.7	a 'Red Indian Chief'
11.9	a beautiful girl
13.10	a goddess (moved)
14.7	a girl
16.11	a belle
17.2	a girl
19.3	a dentist's daughter
37.5	a girlfriend

Romford, Mr

An admirer of Ethel who entrusts a white cat he has bought for her to William for delivery. Somehow it ends up as a ferret! (*William Again*, 6). He also appears in *William – The Bold*, 8.

Rossiter, Miss

Her family used to own the Hall; she now lives in a very ordinary house in the village. Is harassed by the horrible MRS PORKER. (*William's Happy Days*, 9)

Roundway, Mrs

One of William's few staunch and uncritical adult friends, whose main function is to supply him with

one of her home-made cookie boys whenever he comes past her cottage. He rescues her widowed sister Maggie Hemmings from the on-the-make attentions of Bert, an unpleasant suitor who, although middle-aged, has a plentiful crop of golden hair ('There isn't a woman born as can resist yellow curls'). William's intervention proves Bert's bubbly bright locks to be a wig, so Maggie marries George instead, a reliable suitor favoured for her sister by Mrs Roundway. William's assistance is not wholly altruistic, because Maggie has been staying with Mrs Roundway and, finding her garrulous and somewhat interfering with the time-honoured cookie boy routine, William determines to get Maggie remarried and out of the way (*William*, 9). Mrs Roundway also appears in *William – The Bad*, 8 (see BRETHERTON, MRS), but is quite distinct from Miss Roundway, a lady with a strong interest in genealogy who crops up in *William the Superman*, 2.

Sam

Gardener's boy to Mr French, William's temporary form-master, and a member of one of William's secret societies. See ALBERT (1). (*William Again*, 7)

Sandy Dick

A tramp con-man. See TRAMPS.

Schmitt, Fräulein

Prefers to be known as Miss Smith: started work as a 'help' at the vicarage just before the war started. Supposedly an Austrian refugee, she is 'small, shy, timid and quiveringly anxious' to express her admiration of anything British. She turns out to be an enemy agent (see SPIES and TRAMPS). (*William and the Brains Trust*, 5)

Schools

William's Primary Education
The school-related stories depict William as attending either a male-staffed boys' grammar school (where the syllabus includes Latin and chemistry) or a mainly female-staffed primary school where he learns elementary English grammar, basic history and 'simple practice'. The latter appears to have been the village (church) school (see 13.8: 'Choir Fund . . . Church Renovation Fund . . . with the Church School bazaar only just over') to which the Outlaws were sent as a result of deliberate parental policy in the hope that 'feminine influence might have a mellowing effect upon [William's] character' (2.8). Perhaps it is a pity that they did not attend the preparatory department of the grammar school. They might not then have

floundered so badly in their early grammar-school days! There is no evidence that the Outlaws attended a private elementary school such as the 'Marleigh Rational School for Children' (19.2), situated conveniently at Little Marleigh, except for a single curious remark – a narrator's slip? – that Mr Brown was 'paying the education authorities a substantial sum' (1.4). (Fees could not have been a drain on Mr Brown's resources until William started at the grammar school.) Thirty-strong classes with a wide social mix do not in any case suggest a small proprietary school.

It is self-evident from the text that the school-related stories are not chronological but in the early days move backwards and forwards between grammar school and primary school as the narrator happens to recall the events. For example, 3.7 is a grammar-school story involving Mr French, while in 5.13 ('William and Uncle George') Emmeline is said to attend the same school as William, and William and Ginger go home *together*, which would indicate that William and Ginger are still neighbours (see WILLIAM'S HOUSES) and attending the church school. The August story 'The Midnight Adventure of Miss Montagu' (6.6) presumably took place in the summer holidays before William started at the grammar school since the school acquaintances he invites to his garden auction are mixed and extremely young. In the primary-school stories William's own behaviour seems significantly more juvenile.

Three references to (different) birthdays (5.8, 12.6, 15.3) all show William at the grammar school, but once William has reached eleven every birthday is numerically the same.

William's primary-school teachers are: Miss Drew (form-mistress, English, arithmetic), Miss Jones (English grammar, history), Miss Dewhurst (another form-mistress). He also has lessons from an unnamed mathematics teacher and a 'French master' who screams (1.3) ' "Step out 'oo makes the noise!" ' This last could be a French national

teaching an unspecified subject. The plot, atmosphere and geographical circumstances of this story make it difficult to see it as an early grammar-school event.

The Grammar School and Its Staff

> . . . the muscular young men who formed the staff of the local Grammar School. (12.8)

> Uncle Charlie . . . saw himself delivering his famous Travel Talk at every public school in the country. (18.8)

> That afternoon after school William walked through the playground of the preparatory department . . . (15.3)

> 'We were boarders . . .' ('William and the Old Boy': 30.6)

These and similar remarks throughout the text indicate that the school of which the Outlaws were junior lower-stream members was a distinguished, old, independent, fee-paying grammar school. There is no reason to suppose that they were in the lowest stream. Henry in particular was an intelligent boy. Furthermore they are pursuing (unsuccessfully) a Latin course (Balbus). In 27.7 we have a lengthy description of William engaged upon his Latin homework where in his mental agitation he translates 'The Queen ruled' by 'mensam amabas'. Reggie's class exercise in 12.8 suggests familiarity with the ablative absolute. Probably this visiting prodigy has been set more advanced work by the master. Both Mr Brown and Robert surely must have attended the same school. Probably in their day it was still situated in Hadley town. The Old Boys encountered by Mr Brown – Mr Falkner and Ambrose Gilpin ('Sandie'), who addresses Mr Brown by his old nickname of 'Podger' – do not clarify the point (31.7). A radical resiting of the school might be sufficient to prompt Robert's remark, 'I'm not connected with the school in any way', in an anxious context (15.3). The greying Old Boy who encounters the Outlaws in the 1950s recalls the school as situated in the village in his day. However, like other peripheral characters he would have aged at a normal speed, while William and his close associates remained static. See DISCREPANCIES.

When William first went to the grammar school Mr Marks/Markson had not yet been appointed headmaster. The name of his predecessor is not known, but he had a daughter of sufficient maturity for Mr French to call and try to charm her (3.7). The appointment of Mr Markson took place not long before the events described in 'William and the Chinese God' (8.3). This man, who was to become an 'intellectual leader of the neighbourhood' (25.1), had been introduced to Ethel for the first time only the previous week. (His full name, incidentally, must have been Mr Marks-Markson, a name no odder than Jameson Jameson, Graham Graham or Gerald Fitzgerald but awkward enough to explain why he is called indiscriminately 'Mr Marks' and 'Mr Markson'.)

Mr Markson, a classical scholar and writer of highly respected books on Roman Britain and Roman law, in spite of his appearing to the Outlaws a roaring ogre, appears to have been quite a young man, probably in his early thirties at the time of his appointment. A shy and well-meaning man (8.3) behind the terrifying schooltime mask, we find him in 13.2 engaged to a Miss Finch, 'an extremely pretty girl with dark eyes, dimples and dark curling hair and a great expert on Red Indians, knots and caterpillars' – a kind of twenty-year-old Joan Crewe in fact. One notices, too, that at the time of his nervous breakdown (recorded in 12.8) he leaves in charge as acting head the sixth-form master Mr Ferris, a muscular young man with a keen eye, which is a severe snub to older masters unaccustomed to a youngish head.

One suspects that for some years the Second Master was 'Ole Stinks' who taught William science. As well as being clearly an experienced schoolmaster one notices that it is he who takes it upon himself to rise from the front bench and walk the length of the school hall to supervise the behaviour at the back during a lecture on orphans (11.6).

It is important to notice (3.7) that 'William's attitude to his schoolmasters was, as a rule, one of pitying forbearance, but he was, on the whole, quite kindly disposed to them'. 'Ole Stinks' quite liked William, and occasionally invited him to tea. In return William lent him his stories and plays to read (5.12). Although the Outlaws indulged in pranks – putting a hedgehog in Mr Hopkins's desk, sewing up the sleeves of the headmaster's gown – they were not bad boys. They did not seek to create trouble in class, asked merely to be left alone and at worst held up classes of inexperienced teachers by pretending not to understand (11.6). But they could be roused to counter-activity by a serious sense of injustice, whether at the hands of a regular member of staff or, as more often happened, at the hands of an unwise temporary master such as Evelyn Courtnay (5.12) who replaced 'Ole Stinks' during the period that the latter was absent with scarlet fever, or Mr Renies (13.5) who replaced William's regular history-master, a mild, elderly, short-sighted and deaf individual, who likewise fell victim to scarlet fever. It is not clear whether he is to be identified with Mr Bunker (8.1) and/or 'Old Fuss-pot' (15.5) who taught William history.

Mr Perkins ('Ole Warbeck') clearly also served in a senior capacity. The evidence is to be found in 18.2 ('Ole Warbeck couldn't be worse than he was last term') and 18.4 ('[Mr Perkins] knew William only slightly').

That William's historical understanding could be awoken by an outstanding teacher is indicated by his reaction to the wartime appearance of the otherwise retired Mr Polliter (25.6). See also WARTIME.

It is of course impossible to be categorical regarding the length of contact between William and an individual subject-master. There could be 'one of those mysterious re-arrangements of staff [which occurred] at regular intervals' (21.8) whereby the bulldog Mr Coggan ('Old Coggs') took over William's French lessons from his usual easy-going teacher (21.8). Clearly the latter was not Mr Strong (6.4), who could make himself 'extremely disagreeable over French verbs' and was ultimately responsible for the 'Williamcans' (6.4).

We cannot name William's Latin master except by his nickname 'Monkey-Face' (probably identical with 'Old Face' in 7.1). Mr Markson set William a Latin imposition (10.4), but his Latin prose classes were doubtless confined to the sixth form (11.6).

We have surprisingly few details regarding William's English and maths masters. 'Ole Potty' (Mr Potter?) said on his report that he should read more (10.1). The temporary would-be novelist Mr Crisp (32.2) may not actually have taught him. He was taught maths by 'Sparkie' (Mr Sparks?) (12.8) whose absence with influenza brought William in contact with Mr Ferris (see above) and Mr Jones who kept him in 'doing sums' on the half-holiday (i.e., Wednesday afternoon. Presumably Wednesday afternoon was optional games – the Outlaws show little sign of participating in organised school sport. They are free to attend dancing classes or a Miss-Milton-organised group at this time. Yet there is no sign of Saturday-morning school. Probably there was at one stage, but the time-table was reorganised on a Monday-to-Friday basis). Whether it was Sparkie or Mr Jones who had the courage of his convictions to write 'uniformly bad' on William's report one cannot say.

Mr Parkinson, 'one of the Junior form-masters' (12.2), and Miss Carter, 'mistress of the second form' (4.14), both appear to be attached to the 'prep' school. When in 30.7 Douglas remarks

anxiously, ' "Don't get [Ethel] teachin' in our school," ' he must be thinking of the preparatory department. The senior school clearly has an all-male staff even during the war when the most senile of old men have to be employed (25.6).

The study of William's form-masters is on the whole an easier problem. His first known form-master was the peaceful and long-suffering MR CREMER (3.7) whose illness brought William into temporary contact with the aggressive MR FRENCH who later was to play a considerable part in his life. On the return of Mr Cremer, Mr French retired to his fifth form. But the first encounter had been a turbulent one ('William's Secret Society'). At some stage Mr Cremer was replaced by Mr Strong (see above). At this early date Mr French was presumably one of the muscular young men on the staff. His total absence from the text at the relevant period suggests that he was of an age to serve with the armed forces during the war. He must have been approaching retirement age when in 37.5 he became engaged to a 'pleasant-faced, middle-aged woman' (Milly), an event which in 38.3 causes the Outlaws to acknowledge that 'beneath the hostility . . . lay a . . . half-reluctant affection' towards Mr French and they decide to give him their personal wedding present. After the war Mr French (not in the best of health, apparently) assumed a more senior position on the staff, perhaps that of second master. He takes his place with the headmaster and chairman of the governors in 28.3 and is very much the head's mouthpiece in 37.5. Mr French appears to have been a historian who assisted, when required, with junior maths as he taught both subjects to the Outlaws as well as serving as their long-standing form-master. His absence on two occasions to undergo operations brought William into contact with two temporary masters, the appalling Mr Vastop ('Old Fathead') (29.3) and the 'progressive' Mr Mostyn (35.4). A whole term's absence suggests a serious operation.

Mr French in 3.7 lives in a road 'through which

[William] did not often pass'. During his absence in hospital his house is occupied by Mr Vastop – probably the same address as in 3.7. In 37.5 he has moved out of the village and drives to school from a place unknown to the Outlaws in a small red car. By 38.3 he has taken Willow Cottage by the medieval bridge, presumably in readiness for marriage and possibly with a thought to retirement.

The names of the two school governors are known: Mr Steadman (17.3) and Augustine Potter (13.2). (K.C.W.)

Secret Societies

With William's flair for drama, and his conviction that the grown-ups who concoct the rules for society have little empathy with him, it is inevitable that he should occasionally resort to forming secret societies. An early example of this is recorded in *William Again*, 7 (see ALBERT (1)). This 'Down wiv tyrants!' society gets out of hand because William has to enrol some unscrupulous (and money-grabbing) young toughies. The clandestine group which he forms with Ginger, Henry and Douglas, however (in *William and the Tramp*, 7), for the purpose of putting down 'crim'nals' simply fizzles out after its first abortive exercise.

The trappings of such groups (passwords, the signing of names in blood, and so on) appeal to William & Co. as much as their actual activities. At a deeper level the Outlaw group itself can be seen as a clandestine one. Theirs is a secret-from-adults world: 'The ill-timed and tactless interference of parents had nipped in the bud many a cherished plan, and by bitter experience the Outlaws had learned that secrecy was their only protection . . .' Of course their families know that William, Ginger, Henry and Douglas are special friends, but there is little indication that they think of these stalwarts as any kind of regular group, let alone a named one. There are, for instance, comments in the stories by Mr Brown about Ginger or Henry or Douglas being 'one of his younger son's friends', but never as being one of the Outlaws.

A feature of the juvenile secret activity (or place) is that generally even the nearest and dearest adults are unaware of it. Thus, when the Outlaws arrange for a show to take place in William's bedroom (timed for when his mother is out, and his father is having his post-luncheon snooze on the library sofa) they have few qualms that William's parents will find out. This is in spite of the fact that the show is widely advertised amongst the local children, because strict orders of secrecy are given: 'The threats of what the Outlaws would do if their secret were disclosed had kept many a child awake at night.' See also OUTLAWS, THE. (*Just – William*, 5)

Sedley-Mortimer, Mrs

An earnest and officious lady who travels around the country setting up branches of her terribly killjoy Youth on the Prow movement. When she visits William's village she is lionised by Mrs Bott, who naïvely dreams that support of this youthwork will bring her at least an O.B.E. Through the intervention of Violet Elizabeth, Mrs Sedley-Mortimer innocently gives her inaugural lecture (on the horrors of cosmetics) with her face plastered in green paint and red tile-polish, to the delight of her juvenile audience and the disgust of the adults who,

convinced that Drink must be her Weakness, resolutely decide to bar Youth on the Prow from the
village. (*William and the Brains Trust*, 9)

Selwyn, Mr Tertullian

See OLYMPIC GAMES.

Servants

For the first two decades of their popularity, the
William stories appeared when it was common-
place for fairly comfortably off families to have at
least a maid of all work, and very possibly also a
cook and a parlour-maid. The Brown family were
well equipped with domestic servants: the first

books mention both Ellen and Emma as maidser-
vants (though it is not clear whether these are two
separate people, or, like other stereotyped characters in the saga, interchangeable). Cook is a force
to be reckoned with from *Just – William*, 2,
onwards. Robert is planning a picnic with the beauteous Miss Cannon, and nervously spends the preceding week 'suggesting impossible dainties of
which the cook had never heard. It was not until
she threatened to give notice that he reluctantly
agreed to leave the arrangements to her.' (The
Browns' cooks do move on, and change from time
to time.)

They have a gardener (unnamed) from *Just –
William*, 4, and later they also have a charwoman,
Mrs Hobbin(s), who is first mentioned in *William –
The Rebel*, 11. It seems that she is replaced eventually by Mrs Peters 'the daily' who is mentioned in
William's Television Show, 7. She has come in specially to help with the refreshments for Mr and Mrs
Brown's wedding anniversary party, and is
'spruced up for the occasion in a dress of purple
silk with an osprey in her hair'. Alas, she deterio-
rates after a few years of service with the Browns:
in *William the Lawless*, 1, she is described as having a 'long thin face' and an 'air of gloomy suspicion'. (It is true that William has just dropped a tin
of green paint from an upper window-sill on to her
head: ' "It was a rotten ole hat an' that splodge of
green paint in the front made it look as good as
new. It *improved* it. They ought to have been *grateful* to me." '

By this time the daily domestic is the only 'help'
that the Browns have, for during the war they lost
their cook to the A.T.S. and later their maid (or
maids) to other work, and learnt to manage without
full-time replacements. Hopefully, like other
housewives up and down the country, Mrs Brown
would have managed to equip herself with a reasonable range of labour-saving devices during the
1950s and 1960s, so that she would be less depen-
dent on the labour of others.

This might have saved her a lot of stress, for William often manages to be a focus for any hostility and resentment that servants, both in the Brown household and elsewhere, might be feeling:

The maid who answered the door said that Mrs. Macnamara was in. She looked at William with the disfavour with which all domestics were wont to regard him, and admitted him grudgingly, ordering him to wipe his boots, and, for goodness' sake, try to get some of that mud off.
(*Sweet William*, 1)

Other Named Servants

Book	Character
11.6	Annie (Clarence Mapleton's aunt's maid)
12.3	Bates (Lanes' gardener)
14.6	Binks (Hall gardener)
5.12	Eliza (Courtnays' maid)
13.5	Ellen (Renies' maid)
26.1	Emily
30.1	Flossie (Claytons' maid)
28.2	Hannah (Golightlys' maid)
26.7	Hobbins (jobbing gardener)
14.4	James (chauffeur)
1.6	Jane
10.8	Jane (housemaid)
14.1	Jenkins (Botts' butler)
12.9	Jenkins (Hall butler)
7.8	Jenkins (gardener)
7.6	Jenkins, Old (gardener)
21.4	Johnson (chauffeur)
4.14	Johnson, Mrs
24.4	Marie (Botts' maid)
11.10	Mary (a housemaid)
14.4	Molly (Jane's maid)
1.3	Mr Biggs (butler)
26	Mump, Fanny (cleaner)
18.4	Percival
18.4	Syd
3.5	Thomson (butler)
28.1	Tonks (chauffeur)

Simpkin, Arabella

A long-standing challenger of the Outlaws, who doesn't think their shows are worth the penny or halfpenny that they charge, but always tries to attend (and to get back her entrance fee). She is usually burdened with her two-year-old brother, Fred, and sometimes with a little sister, and/or the baby George Thomas (*William and the Tramp*, 6). She is described as sharp-featured and pugnacious. Her first appearance is in *William – The Gangster*, 5, and she is mentioned in some fourteen of the stories, ending with *William the Lawless*, 4.

Smith, Farmer

A young farmer whom William rather likes, because he doesn't seem to regard boys as natural enemies. He allows William to go round his farm and make friends with his animals. Most of all, when Farmer Jenks is trying to have Jumble put down for sheep-worrying, Smith befriends William and helps to save his precious pet (*William and A.R.P.*, 5). Farmer Smith is mentioned in six stories altogether, ending with *William and the Pop Singers*, 5.

Societies and Social Attitudes

William's world is essentially an ordered one, of manners and fashions that are subject to change but never to revolution. The between-the-wars books have a colourful crop of formidable ladies who are 'massive jewel-bedecked mountains' sporting lorgnettes and pince-nez; of slum-dwellers and 'toffs' (*William Again*, 5, etc.); of city sophisticates and country yokels such as the 'old man sitting at the door of his cottage . . . making passes at a fly with his ear-trumpet' (*Sweet William*, 9); of resolutely escapist 'flappers' whose only comment on the League of Nations is that it seems 'just too cute for words'. In the 1940s, despite the depredations of the Second World War, the mood is still one of optimism and – in the main – of thinking the best of people. In *William and the Evacuees*, 1, the village's Committee of Residents for the Entertainment of Evacuees are also knitting for the little darlings and horrors, and Miss Milton insists on helping, despite, as Mrs Monks points out, the fact that her garments always turn out to be elephantine and shapeless: ' "Of course, she *means* well," she added hastily, remembering her rule to Believe the Best of everyone . . .' The opposite of believing the best of people is often bitchiness, and how this can develop between ladies with too

much time and leisure on their hands is well shown in *William Carries On*, 7, when Mrs Bott and Miss Milton are engaged in a pointless feud, and 'each had given a small tea-party purposely in order not to invite the other'.

There is no doubt that the tone and tempo of life in William's village reflect the overall placidity of English life before the Second World War – although William often inadvertently shatters the mood. In *William – the Fourth*, 4, disguised as a grizzly bear and unable to remove his head-dress, he calls at the vicarage, where his mother is attending a meeting, to ask for her assistance. To his amazement, 'The entire mothers' meeting, headed by the vicar's wife and the vicarage cook and housemaid, were dashing down the main road of the village, screaming as they went.'

William's own standards and values are frequently at odds with those that are conventionally accepted. He will lie (although to him this is a process of imaginative interpretation rather than

untruth), listen unashamedly at keyholes, read other people's letters and do little that does not further his own interests: ' "Do you mean to tell me you want to be paid for doing a little thing like that?" "Yes," replied William simply.' There are even occasions when, to make some point or other, he will deliberately set out to steal. Despite his direct and simplistic approach to life, he has an 'almost oriental' dislike of losing face; appropriately, he provides similarly elaborate justification and explanation for unsympathetic behaviour on the part of his various heroes: in *William and the Evacuees*, 6, he builds up an entirely erroneous image of the bravery of his father's timid and tetchy visitor from Africa, MR TICEHURST, and nothing can shatter this: 'He made several attempts at conversation as they went towards the old barn, but Mr. Ticehurst did not respond. [He is actually preoccupied with a fear of getting his feet wet.] His lack of response, however, only increased William's respect for him. Silent, reserved, resolute . . . The stuff of which heroes were made.'

Chapter 1 of the same book tells us that, although possessing an abundance of initiative, William 'was always inclined to be a fatalist and to let things take their course. And he wasn't a boy to retreat, if he could help it, from any position he had once taken up.' Nevertheless, he acknowledges to MISS ROSSITER that he does sometimes have worries, although the things that concern him would seem silly to other people. When pressed, he says that these are ' "when windows keep gettin' in the way of my arrers an' cats go sticking their fur in Jumble's mouth an' things like that . . . I don't mean that I worry a *norful* lot about them." '

As well as these important personal preoccupations, William is often intrigued by the aims and activities of some reforming society or other in the village; indeed, he often throws in his lot – and his gusto – with these. They cover a wide range – from the Church Lads' Brigade to Psychical Research; from the Women's Institute to the Reformed Bolshevists; from the Open Air Holiday Association to the Society of Ancient Souls. A pretty full list is given here but with only the first mention of the more common, such as the Women's Institute and the Dramatic Society.

Book	Society
37.5	Adventure Society
31.3	Amateur Dramatic Society
7.2	Anti-Vivisection
27.4	Anti-Vivisection
8.1	Archaeological Society
36.5	Art Club and various
1.7	Band of Hope
11.7	Band of Hope
16.1	Beekeepers' Guild
5.14	Bible Class
38.2	Brighter Thought Movement
16.8	Children's Guild
19.3	Church Lads' Brigade
24.7	Committee of Church Rooms Canteen
22.1	Committee of Residents for the Entertainment of Evacuees
3.10	Dramatic Society
19.8	Educational Play Guild
4.10	Encouragement of Higher Thought
5.7	Encouragement of Higher Thought
38.5	Extra Dimension Community
14.2	Football Club
14.11	Football Club
15.3	Football Club
7.1	Geologist Society
18.3	Hadley Amateur Dramatic Society
31.2	Hadley Dramatic Society
28.5	Hadley Thespian Society
30.4	Hadley Women's Guild
13.3	Helicon Literary Society
16.2	Kindness to Animals League
34.3	League of Animal Friends
16.1	League of Nations Union

20.1	League of Perfect Health
17.7	League of Perfect Love
9.2	Literary Society
28.1	Literary Society
28.2	Literary Society
33.5	Literary Society
13.3	Marleigh Temperance Society
32.6	Mellings Field Club
6.2	New Era Society
14.4	New Era Society
14.6	New Thought Circle
17.1	Open Air Holiday Association
29.7	Over Sixty Club
35.4	Over Sixty Club
20.10	Providence Club
10.4	Psychical Research
18.8	Punishment Insurance Society
4.1	Reformed Bolshevists Society
38.1	Residents Association
3.8	School Dramatic Society
18.4	School Historical Society
3.7	Secret Society of Vengeance
15.7	Sick and Poor Fund
34.1	Society for the Abolition of the Conventional in Life and Art
18.6	Society for Educating Future Citizens in the Responsibilities of Citizenship
20.5	Society for Giving Decent Grown-Ups a Good Time
35.5	Society for the Preservation of Animal Life
20.10	Society for Providing Comforts for Sick Pets
2.13	Society of Ancient Souls
20.1	South London Boys' Guild
8.5	Study of Psychical Philosophy
5.2	Temperance Society
16.6	Temperance Society
19.10	Tennis Club
11.5	Thought Mastery Movement
9.9	Total Abstinence
8.7	Twentieth Century Poets
32.1	Under 30 Club
11.8	Village Boys' Cricket Club
11.1	Village Football Club
16.8	Village Women's Guild
24.7	War Working Party
25.8	War Working Party
13.6	Women's Guild
18.2	Women's Guild
15.7	Women's Institute
37.1	Women's League
38.4	Young Wives
25.9	Youth on the Prow

Solomon, Mr

The long-suffering superintendent of the Sunday school at the Browns' church whose pupils have included Robert and William. He comes into three

of the stories: *William – In Trouble*, 9; *William – The Rebel*, 12; and *William – The Outlaw*, 4. His horror of William is just about balanced by his tremendous admiration for Ethel who, as *William – The Outlaw* tells us, is not above encouraging his attentions when she is in the 'for her, very rare position of being without a male admirer on the spot . . . Mr Solomon was not of course a victim worthy of Ethel's bow and spear, but he was better than no-one. Therefore she gave him tea and smiled upon him. He sat, blushing deeply and gazing in rapt adoration at her blue eyes and Titian hair . . .' Unfortunately for Mr Solomon, William is never far away on the occasion of these delicious *tête-a-têtes*. See also CHRISTMAS and CHURCH AND RELIGION.

Solrun

A girl from Iceland who is homesick: William tries to make her feel better by producing a 'hot geyser' for her in Mrs Bott's air-raid shelter. It misfires, but at least gives her a jolly good laugh. (*William and the Evacuees*, 5)

Sparkie

A maths-teacher at William's school. (*William's Happy Days*, 8)

Spies

William's ever present fascination with spies and secret agents naturally reaches new heights in wartime. In *William and the Brains Trust*, 5, he indirectly helps Finch (a British intelligence agent disguised as a tramp) to round up two spies: 'Miss Smith', who is actually Fräulein Schmitt, supposedly an Austrian refugee (who has been working at

the vicarage for some time), and her colleague, an unnamed military-looking man 'with a white moustache and a limp' (see SCHMITT, FRÄULEIN and TRAMPS).

Spin-Offs

For a character who has been so popular for so long, the number of commercial spin-offs from William have been thankfully few. What few there are at least make any collection of them containable within a small cupboard, and give that added edge of scarcity which is nectar to the enthusiast. Paradoxically, there is nothing more boring for the collector than to be able to walk into a shop and buy just what he is looking for. (What he or she wants is the chase: the excitement of only just missing out; the joy of seeing something in the shop window on Sunday when the shop is closed, and the agony of finding it gone on rushing back at nine o'clock on Monday morning. Many a collector has lost heart the moment he has found that last elusive item, and suddenly has nothing to look for any more.)

Collectors will therefore be delighted to know that the list of William spin-offs is incomplete. Several items of interest have turned up in the last year or two, some within only months of the *Companion* going to press. Doubtless there will be more. The chance of finding something 'unknown' is still a real possibility; but here, at least, is a list with which to begin.

Just William – The Book of the Film (1939) is a 2s 6d hardback collection of the six stories that went to make up the film of the same name (not the book *Just – William*), along with the script of the film itself.

Just William's Luck: The Story of the Film in the Making (1948), priced at 1s 6d, includes a foreword by Richmal Crompton as well as a multitude of photographs and bibliographical detail of the actors and production team involved.

The 'Just William Card Game' (1953) by Pepys (who published thirty-seven other card games at the time) was advertised on the dustwrappers of William books. It comprised forty-four cards by Thomas Henry depicting scenes from ten stories. If you're stuck with a Violet Elizabeth card, you can't win!

There are at least two 'early' jigsaws (probably around 1950): 'Milking Time' by Thomas Henry, 14 inches x 9 inches on cardboard, 240 pieces, published by Wiltoys of London in their Peter Pan series, and a wooden jigsaw (also 14 inches x 9 inches and by Thomas Henry – publisher's details not known) showing William, Ginger and Violet Elizabeth hanging out the washing and using a garden roller to 'iron' it. The Thames Television series of 1977–8 spawned four jigsaws featuring photographic scenes, and the witty 'Just William Game' by Palitoy where certain jobs ('Take tadpoles out of bath') have to be done around the Browns' cardboard constructional house, which players can avoid by applying one of William's excuses ('Learnin' to be a Brain Surgeon – must protekt hands'). There were also some William toffees, a William wigwam and two annuals (1978 and 1979).

Some 'Gooseberry Eyes' were manufactured to coincide with Macmillan's launch of the current series of William reprints, and a map of William's village, painstakingly devised by Kenneth Waller using every topographical detail in the saga, is due for publication in this centenary year.

A very scarce item is the 'Just William Puppet Theatre' from (probably) 1949, based on the film of that year *William Goes to the Circus*. Published under the trade-name Good-win, the game includes puppet cut-outs controlled by stiff wires and a full script for the actors to follow.

Another item that is almost impossible to obtain is *The Just William Magic Painting Book*, containing sixteen pictures by Thomas Henry and probably published around 1950 (by B.B. Ltd). Finding one at all requires a stroke of tremendous luck; finding one with none of the paintings done requires a small miracle.

William and the Artist's Model, published by J. Garnet Miller Ltd in 1956 at 2s 6d, is a play by Richmal Crompton based on her story 'Violet Elizabeth Wins' (*William – The Bold*, 1). Two other plays, *Just William* (1950) and *More Just William* (c. 1950), written by Alick Hayes (the producer of the radio series), and based on Richmal's characters, were published by MacDonald & Young, followed in 1960 by *William's Half Holiday*.

Just William's Painting Book illustrated by Lunt Roberts appeared in 1957, and *Just William's Cookin' Book* in 1977 (an Armada paperback).

Those old enough to remember Saturday-morning pictures and the ABC Minors Club may have a little 'cigarette' card of *Just William's Luck*, a hand-coloured scene from the film of 1948.

Thomas Henry, in his own right, produced several series of postcards, and at least two cards featured a William cartoon.

Woman's Own (1947–62) is collectable for the William strips by Thomas Henry, and for those by Henry Ford from 1962 to 1969. In 1977 'Look-In' (the junior *TV Times*) also had some William strips by Arthur Ranson.

Doubtless there are others: copies of *Radio Times* for the radio series (1945–52), or the television series (1962–3); the sheet music for the radio theme tune, published at 1s by B. Feldman & Co.

in 1946; photographs from the film sets; a programme from *Just William* at the Granville Theatre, London, 1946; a William story that hasn't been published . . . You never know what might turn up next if you search long enough. (D.S.)

Sports

Generally speaking the Outlaws are not avid enthusiasts of organised sport, preferring games of their own invention. However, on several occasions they lust after – and manage to acquire – a new football, and at least one of their football matches is described (in *William – The Rebel*, 10). They are playing on a vacant plot of land in Marleigh, and there is amongst them an unorthodox approach to the game: 'The Outlaws considered four to be the ideal number for a football match.' In fact they spend more time retrieving their ball from adjacent gardens than actually playing: ' "I don't think there's a single place left to play in England that hasn't got a house next to it, all ready to make a fuss the minute your ball goes into its garden. Sometimes I feel I don't care how soon the end of the world comes." ' This reflection – from William – in the early 1930s is a particularly sad one to come from a country boy: one wonders how much more the children of the cities must have suffered this restriction of sporting places!

It is shortage of money rather than of space that curtails their sporting endeavours in *William – The Good*, 4. They have suddenly developed a passion for cricket: 'They had, of course, partaken in the pastime in previous years, but listlessly and with boredom' because the game had been organised through the school and was 'therefore devoid of either sense or interest'. For their private cricketing sessions they desperately require a set of stumps, because those chalked on a conveniently placed tree-trunk have the drawback that 'bowler and batter are seldom agreed' as to when one of these

static stumps is hit. The Outlaws waste so much cricketing time in settling such disputes by single combat that 8*s* 6*d* for movable stumps seems to be essential, if elusive.

The most interesting of their 'organised' sports is hockey. The Outlaws are fascinated by the sight of the girls of Rose Mount School careering around a field in pursuit of a small ball, armed with strangely shaped sticks, and after struggling with the feeling that this might be a sport suited only to 'inferior [feminine] beings' with inferior powers they succumb unashamedly to the ecstasies of hockey. Of course their version is rougher and more tumbly than that of the girls. They use their sticks (walking-sticks 'borrowed' from their fathers) not only to hit the ball but also to trip up each other: impartial observers might consider it 'more suggestive of a permanent rugger scrimmage than anything else', but the Outlaws emphatically declare that it is 'a jolly good game'.

Stinks

'Ole Stinks', chemistry-master. See SCHOOLS.

Strange, Miss Rubina

See AUTHORS.

Strange, Mr Vivian

See AUTHORS.

Sunday School

Very much part of William's life, particularly because Mr Brown said that he 'might as well go into an asylum straight off' if he couldn't get a little peace from 'that boy' on Sunday afternoons. See also CHRISTMAS, CHURCH AND RELIGION, LOMAS, MISS and SOLOMON, MR. (*William – The Conqueror*, 8)

Sunny Mag

Sunny Mag first appeared in July 1925 as a 'sister' magazine to the *Happy Mag*. From the point of view of content, it is difficult to tell the two magazines apart, each being a happy blend of fun and fiction. No William stories were published in the *Sunny Mag*, although it did carry two stories by Richmal Crompton in August 1929 and March 1932: 'A Lesson for Uncle John' and 'Out for the Afternoon' respectively, both illustrated by Thomas Henry. Conversely, no stories by Richmal Crompton other than William were published in the *Happy Mag*.

On 2 December 1925 the (only) *Sunny Mag Christmas Extra* was published. Inside were four full-colour presentation plates of William, each one a Thomas Henry classic. 'The Man in

Possession', 'Company Coming' and 'Too Good to be True' were reprinted by Halcyon Press Ltd in 1988. The fourth, 'Something MUST be Done!' is interesting, because it was used as the dustwrapper for *William's Happy Days* six years later, but completely repainted, and with the mistletoe and the caption omitted.

Six other issues carried full-colour William covers:

> January 1927: 'William's Christmas Box'
> April 1927: 'Darling, Can You Guess What I'm Going to Say Next?'
> November 1927: 'The Fifth – and Last!'
> January 1928: 'His Christmas "Heave"!'
> April 1929: 'Further Outlook – Showery!'
> October 1930: 'Darling, How Can I Tear Myself Away?'

Newnes's own file copy shows, interestingly, that the postcard rights for the April 1927 cover (William sliding down the banister towards the unsuspecting couple) were granted to Francis & Mills in June of the same year. This and at least one other William postcard were produced.

The issue of *Sunny Mag* for April 1933 was the last. The magazine, which had incorporated the *Gaiety Mag* in February 1928, was itself swallowed up by the *Happy Mag* for the issue of May 1933. (D.S.)

Sweets and Sweetshops

From the early days of the saga (*Just – William*, 1) sweets have played an important part (as indeed they are likely to have done in the lives of William's readers). We are told that 'in the matter of sweets, William frankly upheld the superiority of quantity over quality', and although his stomach could stand up to large amounts of 'Gooseberry Eyes and garden soil in fairly equal proportions'

the 'horrible sweets' are too much for Joan who is 'very sick' after accepting some from William. Other favourite sweets of William and the Outlaws appear to be bulls'-eyes, which are often mentioned. In *William – The Fourth*, 8, Joan seems to be made of stronger mettle, happily accepting a coconut lump from William, an aniseed ball from Ginger and a peardrop from Henry. In return she offers each of them a liquorice treasure. Not to be outdone, Jumble begs for treacle toffee, but does not get any on this occasion because William has just eaten it all.

In *Just – William*, 10, William experiences the ultimate fantasy-fulfilment of managing a sweetshop. Mr Moss, who owns it, takes New Year's Day off to go and propose to the woman whom he has been asking for ten years, but who has so far

turned him down. ('She must be a softie,' comments William. 'Does she *know* you've got a sweetshop?') Mr Moss's nephew is supposed to be coming to mind the shop, but because he is late William is asked to hold the fort until his arrival. In fact the nephew is ill, so William is in charge of the shop for the whole morning. He swaggers, and indulges in roseate dreams, and liberally samples the stock of butter balls, cokernut kisses, pineapple crisps, liquorice all sorts, nutty footballs, mixed dewdrops, toasted squares and fruity bits. A 'very dainty' nine-year-old girl comes in: she is dressed fetchingly in a white fur coat, and she has blue eyes, velvety rosy cheeks and 'golden curls'. William is smitten (he is noticeably more susceptible to ringleted blondes in the early stories – *before* he meets Violet Elizabeth – than later on). He plies her with as many sweets as she can carry: 'Things is awful cheap today.' The little girl staggers off under their weight murmuring '*Sank* you! Sank you ever so!', while William leans against the door 'in the attitude of the good-natured, all-providing male'.

Next Ginger and Henry call, and he makes them stuff their faces (and their pockets). They have an acid-drop-throwing battle with a gang of street-boys, and William begins to feel anxious on two counts. Despite a very evident depletion of the stock, he has taken only a few pennies from customers. Also he is beginning to feel extremely sick. Fortunately for him, Mr Moss – whose beloved has at last accepted him – is too happy to notice anything.

William helps the kindly sweetshop-owner again in *William – The Fourth*, 8. Mr Moss, who always gives the Outlaws good measure, is under threat of having to close his business because Mallards, a new 'big company' sweetshop, has opened in the village and is under-selling him. William decides that the solution is to advertise Mr Moss's wonderful wares at a very important sale of work, which is to be opened by no less a personage than His Grace the Duke of Ashbridge. The Outlaws promenade around the sale, carrying home-made sandwich-boards exhorting people to get their Treekle Toffy, Munky Nuts and Fruty Bits from Mr Moss; unknowingly His Grace is also promoting Moss's cause, because William has affixed a Have You Tryd Mosses Cokernut Lumps card to the back of his coat. He sportingly talks things over with William and his friends, treating them all to ices, and making the village 'gasp' by spending 'almost the entire afternoon' with them, 'discussing pirates and Red Indians, and telling them stories of big game hunting'. (Having been 'bored almost to tears by the vicar's wife and the committee', he has recognised and responded to this much 'more entertaining company'.) The Duke invites them to walk to the sta-

tion with him. On the way, he calls at Mr Moss's shop, tastes his cokernut lumps, and orders a monthly supply. The villagers, of course, immediately switch their allegiance from Mallards back to Moss's. Within a week or two, Mallards has to close down. Such is the power of William – abetted by a title.

Thomas

A small boy who comes into the stories before Violet Elizabeth Bott and who threatens to 'scream an' scream an' scream' if William doesn't take off his boots and stockings and go into the pond to fetch watery creatures for him. (William starts off

by trying to be helpful: he is wearing his Scout uniform – something that rarely happens!) (*More William*, 9)

Thompson, Miss

A pleasant lady who seems helpful to all and sundry; she enters the saga in *William and the Tramp*, 3, and appears altogether in thirteen books, ending with *William the Lawless*, 4.

Thompson Twins, Geraint and Launcelot

See KNIGHTS.

Tit-Bits Summer Annual

Published by Newnes from 1920 to 1930, the *Tit-Bits Summer Annual* was a high-spirited bumper collection of cartoons, jokes and (mostly) humorous stories that really set the format for the *Happy Mag* and *Sunny Mag* which began in 1922 and 1925 respectively. This joyful procession of holiday-making, belly-laughing, quick-witted, rib-tickling magazines was the stuff that had the 1920s roaring:

From Will Owen:

'So Hobson's pretty secretary has left him. What was the trouble?'
    'She caught him kissing his wife.'

From Thomas Henry:

MOLLY: 'I do love the sandy coves in Devon.'
MOTHER: 'Molly, I will not allow you to talk about men in that vulgar manner.'

From Lunt Roberts:

DOG FANCIER (to prospective buyer): 'Intelligent? I should just think he is! Why, 'e only bites the postman when 'e's bringin' bills!'

And from many, many others.

Bonuses for William fans are numerous. Two full-colour William covers by Thomas Henry (1924 and 1926), a double-page William cartoon adventure, 'William's Holiday at the Seaside is a Great Success – for William' (1924), and the first appearance in print (1924) of the story 'An Afternoon with William' (*Still – William*, 10), with an additional illustration (not in the book) of Ginger feeling sick in the boat.

> William looked at him with interest. 'You're lookin' a bit pale,' he said, with over-cheerful sympathy, 'p'raps it was the crab.'
>
> Ginger made no answer.
> 'Or it might have been the liquorice,' said William, with interest.
> 'I wish you'd shut up talkin' about them,' snapped Ginger.

In the issue of 1928 is another of the articles 'By William' (written by Richmal Crompton), twelve of which appeared in the *Happy Mag* between 1926 and 1933. This contribution is entitled 'My Day in London', illustrated (as always) by Thomas Henry, and it gives a personal account of William's day in the metropolis with an aunt:

> 'If any of you are thinking of going to the British Museum, I can jolly well tell you it's not worth going to. It's full of great huge broken statues and nothing else. You'd think they'd have got someone to mend them up a bit, wouldn't you? Or else thrown them away and got some new ones . . . I soon had enough of going round with my aunt and my aunt saying the date they were made and who made them and things like that and soon I met another boy going round with *his* aunt and *his* aunt telling him the date they were made and who made them and that sort of thing.'

Three more articles 'By William' (rediscovered in July 1989) appeared in the *Tit-Bits Summer Annual*. 'Commonsense about Holidays' in 1927; 'Picnics' in 1929; and 'My Summer Holiday' in 1930. A full list of these articles from all sources may be found in Appendix 4. (D.S.)

Tompkins, Glory

Sometimes spelt Tomkins. See ROBERT AND HIS FRIENDS.

Torrance, Sir Gervase

See V.I.P.s.

Tramps

Gentlemen of the road are presented unsentimentally in the stories, and William's encounters with them are often infelicitous. Nevertheless he retains tremendous respect for tramps, and hopes to become one at some stage of his career.

In *William Again*, 14, he and Joan are playing Robinson Crusoe by the river. 'Erbert 'Ammond, a tramp whom William tries to co-opt as Man Friday, makes off with William's clothes. In *William's Crowded Hours*, 8, the Outlaws stumble upon Sandy Dick 'cooking something over a smoky fire' in the woods. He convinces them that they can only become tramps in adult life if they pay him more or less straight away the necessary entrance fee of two shillings each. After various abortive attempts to raise this money they do so by selling Ethel's old photographs from boyfriends (see FUNFAIRS AND FÊTES). Fortunately just as they are about to hand over their entrance fees the police move in on Sandy Dick. However, he crops up again in *William – The Dictator*, 8.

In *William Carries On*, 8, 'Honest Jim' cons William into buying from him a so-called Abyssinian Retriever (which has been stolen). Fortunately, however, the reward money for its return comes to the same amount as the purchase-price paid by William.

In *William and the Brains Trust*, 5, William's determination to take up tramp-ing as a career is at

its most concentrated after a picturesque tramp turns up at a forces canteen which is temporarily in William's charge:

> William went to the door and watched him wistfully as he took his way over the fields in the direction of Marleigh, his rags fluttering in the breeze. The attractions of every other imaginable career paled in comparison. After all, he considered, brightening, once he was twenty-one, no one could stop him being a tramp if he wanted to . . .

In this case, the tramp who is so inspiring turns out to be a Mr Finch of the Secret Service, who is disguised as a tramp in order to observe and apprehend a couple of German agents (see SPIES).

In *William – The Bold*, 1, Archie has difficulty in portraying a tramp in a country scene, so the Outlaws go out and find him a real live one as a model. It is only Violet Elizabeth's interfering and managing ways that stop the tramp from taking off with Archie's valuable silver teapot. Yet another

unnamed tramp turns up in chapter 3 of the same book. He makes off with what William thinks is a good-quality coat of Robert's, but which turns out to be one that Robert had put aside for jumble some time earlier.

In *William and the Tramp*, 1, the eponymous man of the road is colourfully engaging, but light-fingered (see BUMBLEBY, MR). He goes under a variety of names: Marmaduke Mehitavel, 'Harchibald' Mortimer, Horatio Grimble, and so on.

University Allegiances

In *William and the Pop Singers*, 5, Cedric, a Protest Marcher from Newlick University, asks William if he has heard of it. William answers that he hasn't: ' "Me an' Ginger are Oxford and Cambridge turn and turn about for the boat race . . ." ': that, apparently, is the totality of their interest in the world of the universities. (The name of the seat of learning attended by Robert, who is of course a perpetual student, is not disclosed, but William probably would not support this anyway.) Cedric refers to Oxford and Cambridge as 'Those moth-eaten decayed relics of antiquity!' and is convinced that the key to the future lies only in the newer universities. William doesn't take up this point, presumably because his wide-ranging and often varied ambitions never include academic achievements.

Vastop, Mr

Called 'Ole Fathead' by William, Vastop is relieving Mr French, William's form-master for one term. (Mr French, because of having William in his form, seems to require quite a lot of longish sick-leave!) Roxana gives Robert a large and lurid American tie, and asks him to wear it at her forthcoming party. William can't resist 'borrowing' it and taking it to school to show his friends, but the slimy sarcastic Vastop confiscates it, and will not return it even when William explains that it is Robert's. William and Ginger fortunately catch Vastop out in a situation which shows him as a coward and a cheat; they say that they might have a memory-lapse over this if Robert's tie could be returned to them. It is. (*William and the Moon Rocket*, 3)

Verity, Sir George and Lady

Snooty short-term tenants at the Hall who never join in any of the village fun, although the local inhabitants are nevertheless 'vaguely proud of them'. She has 'the most paralysing way with a pair of lorgnettes'; he has 'one of the finest collections of miniatures in England'. William saves these from the clutches of a burglar, who, at a bazaar for the Church schools, masquerades as a Prominent Political Personage. William, on stilts for one of his shows, falls on top of the burglar-cum-politician, and two gems from Sir George's collection of miniatures fall from his pocket. (*William's Happy Days*, 4)

Victims

Although William can be arrogant, pugnacious and self-willed, he is rarely malicious. However, that does not prevent his path being strewn with innocent victims who endure dark and dire buffeting as the result of his various brainwaves, fantasies and ambitions. Two examples occur in *William Again*. In chapter 10, inspired by the local Dramatic Society production which featured a Great Detective, William determines to become a sleuth. Hearing his mother talk about a recent spate of burglaries in the village, he notices a man coming from the station, carrying a black bag. This is James Croombe, a harmless merchant in the City. William shadows him relentlessly, convinced that he is a jewel-thief carrying his 'swag'. The wretched Mr Croombe, who turns out to be very suggestible, keeps catching glimpses of the not very attractive face of a boy (William) who seems to be haunting him, in the street, in his home and in other people's houses. He is driven to believe in spiritualism; he wonders if he is hallucinating; his wife, Marie, persuades him to try psycho-analysis, and altogether he has a thoroughly miserable time until the very tangible juvenile ghost is laid.

In chapter 13 William's victim is another eminently respectable and hard-working man of fixed habits: Mr Porter, who has been commuting to the same office for thirty years. On his way from the station one night, in pleasurable anticipation of his regular routine of warm fire, comfortable slippers, well-cooked dinner, good wine, excellent cigar and the evening paper, Mr Porter is stopped by William, who tells him that 'the lady wot' he is 'in love with is in deadly danger', and that he must go to her at once. (William is trying to gather copy for his writer friend Vivian Strange, who has run out of inspiration about how his characters might behave in certain circumstances.) The baffled Mr Porter, fearing that his wife might be in danger (' "What was Mary thinking of. . .?" '), and with his frustration at being kept from his slippers, supper, wine and so on increasing at every step, follows William on a labyrinthine path through streets and gardens. He ends up incarcerated in a coal-shed, and transformed from a restrained and respectable member of society into a savage and screaming seeker of violent retribution, whose torrent of foul language surprises even himself.

Village

See WILLIAM'S VILLAGE.

V.I.P.s

The recurring V.I.P.s in the saga tend to be titled men and women who support local causes, open fêtes, and judge baby- or pet-shows. Several of them are targets for Mrs Bott's social-climbing aspirations, but generally speaking they know how to get out of a situation gracefully, and to save their energies for good works, or the fulfilment of their own cherished plans and projects.

LADY ATKINSON is no public benefactor but a self-centred woman who patronises (in the worst sense of the word) her underlings. In *William and the Space Animal*, 4, thanks indirectly to William, Mrs Bott finds herself being proposed by the Honourable Mrs Everton-Massinger and Lady Barnham for the Committee of the Women's Guild. In *William – The Fourth*, 8, the Duke of Ashbridge opens the sale of work (*and* helps to save Mr Moss's sweetshop from closure: see SWEETS AND SWEETSHOPS). Mrs Bott is stalking the toffs more zealously than ever in *William – The Pirate*, 1; she has given 'a staggering subscription' for the rebuilding of the Marleigh Cottage Hospital, and its chairman, Lord Faversham, is coming down from London to attend a party at the Hall: 'The expression of boredom on his Lordship's face intensified almost to agony as Mrs. Bott led him to the gothic armchair in the middle of the front row . . .'

Sir Gerald and Lady Markham are popular and long-standing local figures, who are adept at the business of opening fêtes, etc. (They are also, of course, very kind to Archie Mannister when he greatly needs a sympathetic commission in *William and the Witch*, 5.) Another pleasant and helpful titled pair, who come into the stories rather later than the Markhams, are Sir Gervase and Lady Torrance (*William – The Explorer*, 7; *William and the Witch*, 5; and *William and the Masked Ranger*, 5).

Wakely, Chief Constable

A friend of Henry's father who, on his way from the station to play chess with him, is waylaid by the Outlaws and a motley collection of children from the village. They see Mr Wakely as 'the King's representative' and feel that by making him agree to their demands they can be sure of the agreement of the whole government. (Their demands are restoration of the 'privileges' of sweeping chimneys and working in coal-mines which were taken away from children in the nineteenth century. William and his friends consider that the subsequent legislation for universal compulsory education was a retrograde step.) Far from being angry with the children, who lock him up in a garage, Chief

Constable Wakely is pleased enough with events to give William a ten-shilling tip, because the garage contains evidence which incriminates COLONEL MAIDSTONE, a racketeer whom Scotland Yard have been after for some time (*William – The Bold*, 2). He is mentioned again in *William – The Explorer*, 7, and *William and the Pop Singers*, 2.

Wartime

Some of the most amusing and atmospheric of the William stories are those which were written during the Second World War, and collected in the four books *William and the Evacuees*, *William Does His Bit*, *William Carries On* and *William and the Brains Trust*. Although social changes *did* occur in the saga during the 1920s and 1930s, there was a timelessness about the between-the-wars stories, a sense that William's village with its manor house, workmen's cottages, church hall, tiny shops and well-tended gardens was deeply rooted in the meadows, woods, hills and valleys which surrounded it, and that the quality of life there was unshakeable. However, the mood and tempo altered appropriately during the period of the war; many of the ladies who had been taken up with Higher Thought or Perfect Love or Psychic

Phenomena turned their attentions to knitting and sewing for soldiers and evacuees, and helping out in canteens; well-ordered families (including the Browns) were disrupted by the departure of cooks or housemaids into munitions factories or the women's services; irate and conservative farmers had to come to terms with the loss of manpower and the acceptance of land-girl labour; firmly retired civil servants and military men recharged their energies in the A.R.P. or the Home Guard; previously work-shy bright young things suddenly surprised themselves and everybody else by taking on serious jobs in industry, or as medical auxiliaries. (Even the frivolous Ethel, after two decades of staying at home and looking decorative, went to work with surprising vigour – in A.R.P., then the A.T.S. and as a V.A.D.) Most of all, of course, life on the Home Front changed because of the exodus into the armed forces of almost all of the village's able-bodied young men.

Like real-life children up and down the country William and the Outlaws collected paper and scrap-iron for salvage, were irritated by the shortages of sweets and favourite foods, collected shrapnel and fragments from fallen aircraft for souvenirs, cherished fantasies of catching a Nazi spy, and earnestly endeavoured to 'do their bit' to help the nation's war effort. The stories provide indelible vignettes of William shoving a saucepan on his head as a makeshift steel helmet, and using a tin-tray as a shield when trying to tackle a suspected unexploded bomb. As well as involving himself in physical acts of derring-do, of course, William plunges into socially challenging activities, such as evacuation and rehousing.

At first the war is a nuisance rather than a stimulus to the Outlaws. In *William and the Evacuees*, 5, we are told that 'the war had distinctly curtailed their activities. Farmers, laying out more land for vegetable growing, were impatient of trespassers. Land army girls, imported from towns, showed scant sympathy with William and his concerns.

"I can't be bothered with you," was the response of all grown-ups to their claims. "There's a war on . . ." ' Undeterred, William and the Outlaws make the best of things, using the Botts' luxurious underground air-raid shelter as a place in which to play submarines, for example, and taking advantage of the relaxation of discipline at school 'as the result of a gradual infiltration of women teachers' (*William Carries On*, 5), and, in chapter 2 of the same book, getting the better of a pompous and over-zealous air-raid warden.

Just as in real life, the wartime mood of the books shifts from patriotic endeavour to cussed resistance of officialdom and restrictions, and of course some dabbling in the black market. (The Botts, for instance, use their money to good effect to insulate themselves against at least some of the difficulties of wartime shortages: *they* manage to get hold of fancy cakes and chocolate biscuits, for instance, while the Outlaws are having to bemoan the loss of bulls'-eyes and slabs of milk chocolate, as well as pistol caps, and so on.)

William plays a part in the apprehending of at least two spies (*William and the Evacuees*, 3, and *William and the Brains Trust*, 5). This, however, is not enough. Robert is now a second lieutenant in one of the less famous regiments, and William is determined to make him into a hero (*William Carries On*, 5). William (who is now temporarily on almost friendly terms with Hubert Lane) boasts about Robert's supposed daredevil achievements: according to William, 'It was Robert who had conquered the Italians in Africa . . . who was solely responsible for the sinking of the Bismarck . . . It was Robert who had captured Rudolf Hess . . .' Hubert's worm of credulity turns at this point, and he manages to go one better by claiming that his mother's second cousin Ronald has captured Hitler! (Actually Ronald has a friend, Lieutenant Orford, who, proud of his resemblance to the Führer, 'cultivates the moustache and forelock'.)

Robert continues to do his bit, but remains a

reluctant hero, despite all William's prodding and prompting. He turns his attention to Ethel's situation in *William and the Brains Trust*, 6, when she is home on forty-eight hours' leave from the A.T.S. Mrs Brown is afraid that things will be very dull for Ethel as everyone of interest to her is away on war service. 'William thought of Ethel in pre-war days, moving always with a crowd of young men and maidens . . . from tea dance to dinner dance, from tennis court to swimming pool . . . on the river, in cars, on pillions . . . always with the same crowd of young people or with the chief boy friend of the moment in close attendance. Both girl friends and boy friends had now vanished from the village . . . "There's not a man in the place but the Vicar and General Moult," said Mrs. Brown, "and they both bore her to death." '

William hits on the idea of his wonderful, elderly relief history-master (Mr Polliter) enlivening Ethel's evening with some of his compelling stories. (Polliter is about the only teacher who ever really manages to enthuse William with his subject.) Despite his mother's objections, William concocts an elaborate plan to bring Ethel and Mr Polliter together. (The history-master thinks he is being asked to give Ethel some coaching; from William's description he gathers that the girl must be retarded.) All's well that ends well: Polliter's handsome, strapping, army-major son is spending his short leave with his father and, because of a Williamesque misunderstanding, he crosses Ethel's path and becomes her admiring temporary companion.

Welbecker, Mr

The 'Old Boy' from William's school who gives the Shakespeare lecture and prize each year (except on the occasion when William hogs the stage as Hamlet: see LANE, DORINDA). (*William – The Pirate*, 2)

William

Described in Richmal Crompton's own words:

He is, of course, the 'bad boy' of all the ages, but he isn't as black as he's painted. His insatiable curiosity may put the refrigerator out of action, immobilise the Hoover, fuse the electric lights, but it is the spirit of the inventor and pioneer that inspires his work of destruction. He explores unknown stretches of country, plunging into ditches, climbing trees, doing battle with his enemies and comes home a sight to break his mother's heart, but his courage and initiative are the stuff of which heroes are made.

He has sudden and spasmodic impulses to 'help' his family. He 'helps' wash up and leaves a trail of broken crockery in his wake; he 'helps' get in the coal and covers hands, face and kitchen floor; he 'helps' bring in the deck chairs and becomes inextricably entangled with each one; he puts in a spot of gardening and no one can ever use the secateurs again. It is not always easy to remember how laudable his intentions were.

Beneath his tough exterior, he is sensitive, generous and affectionate and, despite his outrageous appearance and behaviour, he has a sense of dignity that you affront at your peril. I have been touched to learn from some parents that the

William stories have helped them understand the maddening creatures with whom they have to deal. Honesty, however, compels me to add that others have found William's activities so unedifying that they have forbidden him the house.

(From 'Puppet Pulls the Strings', *Books and Bookmen*, December 1957)

William in Performance

William saw himself as a great thespian and a master playwright; it is therefore appropriate that some of his exploits should have been transferred from the printed page to performance on stage, screen, radio and television. An outline of William's involvement in these media is provided here. (Detailed cast-lists can be found in *William : a Bibliography* by W. O. G. Lofts and Derek Adley, published privately at South Harrow, Middlesex.)

On the Screen

Just – William was released in August 1939. As the very first William film it caused considerable excitement amongst William's many fans. Redolent of the 1930s and the between-the-wars sense of security which many children then had, this film's release, rather ironically, coincided with the uneasy run-up to the beginning of the Second World War.

Its distinguished cast included Dicky Lupino (nephew of the celebrated comedian Lupino Lane) as William, Roddy McDowell (before he achieved Hollywood fame) as Ginger, Fred Emney as an over-sized blustering Mr Brown, and the quizzically comic Basil Radford as 'Mr Sidway'. Richmal dedicated her 1939 book *William and A.R.P.* 'to Dick Lupino, Roddy McDowall, Peter Miles, Norman Robinson – the William, Ginger, Henry and Douglas of the screen'.

Just William's Luck was released in December 1947, with William Graham playing William Brown, and Garry Marsh brilliantly portraying the slightly irascible Mr Brown. The distinguished veteran actor A. E. Matthews played the tramp, and the glamorous Hy Hazell was perfectly cast as Gabrielle (Gloria) Gaye (the film-star to whom William tries to marry off Robert). The plot of this film was more carefully rounded out than that of the 1939 production. Written by Val Guest, who also produced the film, it delved more deeply and atmospherically into the Brown household than the earlier film or, indeed, some of the books.

Richmal adapted it, under the same title, in 1948; it is the only William book which is a full-length novel rather than a collection of short stories. It gives interesting insights into the characters of Ethel and Robert, and quite a lot of information about William's home. Emily ('the Browns' maid') is played in the film by Muriel Aked and has an important rôle. Echoing this, Richmal suggests in the book that Emily has been with the family for many years. One therefore has to presume that Emma (one of their prewar maids) is in fact synonymous with Emily, and that – whether or not she temporarily left the family to participate in war service – by 1947 (in the film) and 1948 (in the book) Emily has been promoted from the rôle of a rather dim housemaid to that of family friend or companion which Emily seems to occupy briefly in the more liberal postwar period. See also SERVANTS.

William Comes to Town (also sometimes rather confusingly called *William Goes to the Circus*) was released in December 1948, with the regular characters played by the same actors as in *Just William's Luck*.

On the Stage

In 1946 a play called *Just William* was produced at the Granville Theatre. William was played by John Clark (the first radio William) and, surprisingly, the very lean laughter-maker Charles Hawtrey was cast as the overweight Hubert Lane. This, of course, was a professional production. A one-act play for amateur production, *William and the Artist's Model*, was published by J. Garnet Miller Ltd in 1956. It was an adaptation by Richmal of the story 'Violet Elizabeth Wins', which formed chapter 1 of *William – The Bold*.

On the Radio

There were five series of radio dramatisations between 1945 and 1952. William was played by John Clark in the first two series which, at their peak, achieved listening figures of 18 million. In 1947, Julian Denham took over; then, in 1948, David Spenser. Andrew Ray, son of the famous fast-quipping comedian Ted Ray, portrayed William in the fifth and last radio series in 1952.

It is interesting to note that Violet Elizabeth was played by another offspring of a distinguished comedian: Anthea Askey – the daughter of Arthur, of course – lisped her way fetchingly through the 1948 productions.

On Television

William didn't hit the home screen until 1951, when Joy Harington (who produced the Bunter television series the following year) produced a one-off *Just William* play for BBC television with Robert Sandford in the title rôle. Later in the 1950s, Keith Crane played William in one or two BBC TV productions. In 1962 the BBC transmitted six programmes. Dennis Waterman achieved the distinction of becoming the first regular television William, and when a further series began in 1963 (with Denis Gilmore as William) it seemed that perhaps the world of the Outlaws and the Brown family would regularly reappear on the screen. However, this was not to be.

A long gap followed, until London Weekend Television transmitted thirteen half-hour episodes in 1977, and fourteen later on in that year, running into 1978. Each episode was adapted by Keith Dewhurst from a well-chosen Richmal Crompton story; for the first time William and the Outlaws and their environment were screened in colour. In both series William was played by Adrian Dannatt (a boy from Westminster School who is now a journalist). He conveyed the character adeptly, despite the fact that he was perhaps a little plumper than the generally accepted image of William. Hugh Cross was a perfect spiky-cum-complacent Mr Brown, Diana Fairfax was compelling (if perhaps just a little too young and attractive) as Mrs Brown, Diana Dors was Mrs Bott 'to a T', with just a little extra warmth and knowingness thrown in, and Bonnie Langford, though far too old to be the authentic seven-year-old Violet Elizabeth, nevertheless conveyed the spirit of the character with panache. Both series had a 1920s setting, which worked extremely well.

Records

In 1982 Kenneth Williams recorded *William Stories* and *More William Stories* (Decca Records). In 1990 the BBC distributed an audio cassette collection called *Just William*, comprising Martin Jarvis's radio readings of ten William stories.

William's Houses

William's Birthplace (the Old House)

The text shows that William and Ginger were born next door to one another in a semi-detached house (2.14). Their front gardens were separated by a railing. William's back garden was surrounded by a high wall, in part ivy-clad, up which William would climb to converse with his neighbour on the other side, the young Joan Clive. These houses were downhill from, but in easy walking distance of, the village centre. Since the 'new house' to which the Browns subsequently moved could not have been built much after 1905–10, the old house must have been at very least mid-Victorian. The rooms were large and numerous. Since William in 3.11, to accommodate Grandfather Moore and Aunt Lilian, is sleeping on the third storey, it seems reasonable to suppose that the servants' rooms in the attic were on the *fourth* storey. When in 32.5 Mrs Brown says of The Hollies, 'Oh, it's quite small,' she is speaking relatively. In the new house, after all, two guests, in separate rooms, were the maximum and caused domestic reorganisation. At the old house one Christmas, besides the entire Brown family, there were three prim aunts and two small children to be accommodated (2.1).

In the case of the old house there is insufficient detailed information in the text for a precise house-plan to be feasible, but it is adequate to show significant differences between the old and new houses. In the walled garden of the old house there is a disused stable and a coal-*house* with 'a little window high up' (2.6). Somewhere among the rhododendrons, roses and raspberries William grows his own Virginia stock 'which he doesn't give to *anyone*' (1.2).

Downstairs the drawing-room in front has a view of both the front gate and the side gate (1.6). The front gate can also be seen from the landing window. The library, in which Mr Brown relaxes and Robert shows off his new rifle to a friend, is at the back of the house (2.3). Also downstairs are the dining-room, kitchen, scullery and larder. The house has a cellar in which William locks the cook (1.6). William's favoured exit is by the bathroom window and scullery roof. The Sunday-school children visiting William's bedroom for the show make their way by the garden wall and the scullery roof (1.5) while Aunt Emily sleeps in the guest-room next door. William's bedroom is evidently on the second storey, as is Ethel's. The latter is at the back of the house and has a balcony (1.6). One may surmise that Grandfather Moore (3.11) is accommodated in William's room. Possibly William is sleeping in his 'play-room' (2.6). This is a reminder that William's earliest years were spent here. (Ginger's 'nursery' is similarly referred to elsewhere.) In 3.11 William is still young enough to be 'despatched to bed at half-past seven as usual'.

At least one of William's bedroom windows faces over the wall to Joan Clive's bedroom window with 'only about five yards between them' (2.14).

On one half-term holiday (seemingly his last at the junior school) William's family moved to The Hollies, as the new house was called (9.7). The description of the move is to be found in 2.10. However, the stories in the books do not always represent the strict chronological order of publication, nor is the narrator's memory of William's adventures strictly chronological. In the early books there is consequently some overlap between

THE HOLLIES
GROUND FLOOR

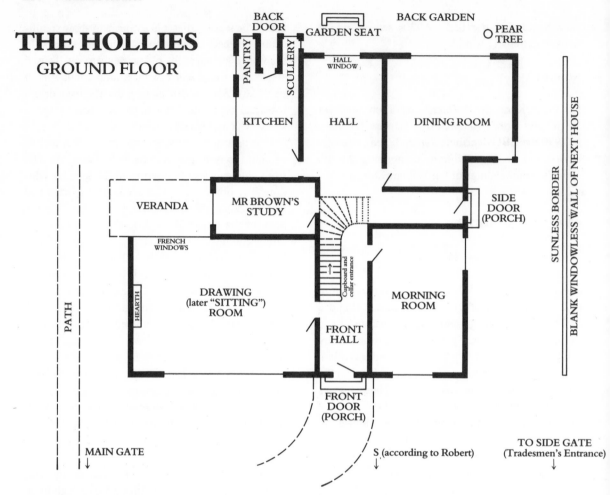

LINES OF SIGHT

1. It is possible to see into the dining room from a crack in the drawing room, looking between the lowest banisters.
2. The hall window is visible from the front door area, looking under the rising staircase as it disappears into the upper floor level.
3. The side door is visible from the area of the kitchen door.
4. The drawing room hearth is visible from the lowest stairs.

THE HOLLIES
FIRST FLOOR

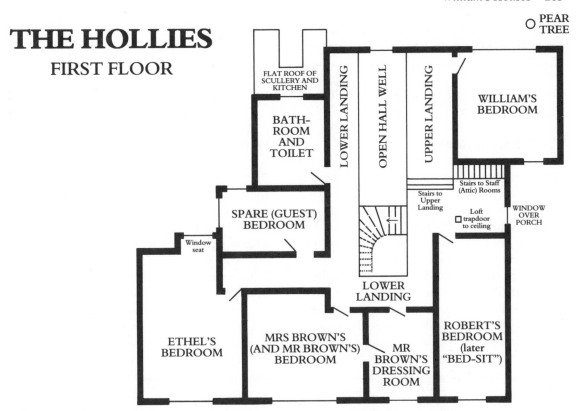

○ PEAR TREE

FLAT ROOF OF SCULLERY AND KITCHEN

LOWER LANDING

OPEN HALL WELL

UPPER LANDING

WILLIAM'S BEDROOM

BATH-ROOM AND TOILET

Stairs to Staff (Attic) Rooms

Stairs to Upper Landing

Loft ☐ trapdoor to ceiling

WINDOW OVER PORCH

SPARE (GUEST) BEDROOM

Window seat

←

LOWER LANDING

ETHEL'S BEDROOM

MRS BROWN'S (AND MR BROWN'S) BEDROOM

MR BROWN'S DRESSING ROOM

ROBERT'S BEDROOM (later "BED-SIT")

FIRST FLOOR

Above ground floor level there is some form of decoration around the house (except the back and kitchen walls) sufficient to prevent William climbing upwards.

The house is red brick. If the decoration is not a narrow band, presumably the upper part of the wall is covered with pebbledash, stucco or tiling.

Ethel's room and the guest bedroom probably overhang the veranda.

ATTIC FLOOR
(not illustrated)

(a) Cook's room at the top of the attic stairs – later (after Cook's departure) converted into a box-room. This has access to a nearby roof.

(b) One or more attic rooms formerly inhabited by maid(s), later probably lumber-rooms.

These attic rooms (a and b) are set back over the rear section of the house, with windows looking out to the front. They are probably on a second gable looking over a lower front gable which covers the cisterns and hot-water system situated over the main front bedrooms (access by loft ladder).

old-house stories and new-house stories. Occasionally they cannot be certainly assigned. Usually internal evidence gives firm evidence of the house in mind. Thus 2.7 is the first certain 'new house' story (see below), while stories as late as 5.1 and 5.13 refer to the old house.

The Hollies (the New House)

Since The Hollies, though large, was a less capacious house, the move must have been for the sake of the convenience of a more modern house and perhaps also for a better view. Although the view from the front windows of The Hollies was dull (15.11), the view from the back over fields, woods and hills towards Upper Marleigh would have been delightful (32.5). The removal was recorded in 1920. The Hollies was not brand new at the time. The eponymous holly-bushes were no longer much in evidence. Furthermore on the day of the removal William climbed up the ivy on the house wall, which must have taken some time to establish itself sturdily enough to permit this. A building date of *c.*1910 seems reasonable. The house was of red brick and of 'uncompromisingly modern appearance' for those days (2.7). Since Robert was a keen collector of local maps (25.3) we may accept his assertion (26.2) that the house faced south. The back garden was fenced and not walled, with a hedge (through which the Outlaws made a convenient hole) at the far end and a back gate to the field beyond the house. The next-door house to the east was much older. Although the garden was fenced at the back, the front gardens were separated by a wall which formed the boundary of the passageway of the tradesmen's entrance to The Hollies from the side gate (14.5), round to the back of the house. Although there was little space to the east, on the west there was ample room between the wall of the house and the neighbour's fence (see below).

The main gate was on the west and could be seen from way down the back garden in the area near

the tool-shed (9.3). The drive curved towards the front door, and a path led along the left-hand side of the house between lawn and kitchen garden. When the garage was finally built in the 1950s it must have been on the left of the drive.

At the front and sides of the house there was probably an overhang which effectively prevented William from attempting upward climbing. On the one occasion he performs such a climb, arguably from the study to the guest-room (see note on 2.7), he finds it difficult. This may suggest that the guest-room jutted out over the study below. Over the front bedrooms there was a low parapet with coping and a flat or sloping roof, leading back to the attic windows over the centre of the house (see below).

The front garden had rose- (and other flower-) beds in an expanse of lawn surrounded by laurels and a surviving holly-bush. There was a front garden seat which gave a view of the side gate (20.3). Possibly Mr Brown's bird-bath and bird-table (27.4) were also in the front garden. The immaculate lawn (7.6) and flower-beds of the back garden were tended in pre-war days by a succession of gardeners. Ethel would occasionally intervene even in those days, and irritated the gardener by building a rockery (23.2). In the 1920s and 1930s the Browns had their own hard tennis-court (9.7) and organised tennis-parties (14.3, 14.7) One wonders whether Mr Brown, eventually obliged to do all his own gardening and clearly under greater financial restraints than he once was, sold or leased some of his land, perhaps to Farmer Smith whose cow Daisy could be heard from the air-raid shelter at the end of the garden (23.7). In 32.8 we are told that the lawn was not a large one and did not require a large mowing machine. But perhaps this merely means more flowers and vegetables and less grass. The garden seat in the back garden could not be seen from the road or from Ethel's bedroom (9.6).

Of the outhouses, the tool-shed (with a window in the roof) was beyond the kitchen garden near the back gate on the extreme west. The coal-shed was 'just beyond' the tool-shed. The summerhouse, like the greenhouse, seems to have been on the opposite (eastern) side of the back garden 'at the end of a path' (6.3). We know that to get to the greenhouse Moyna Greene in all her fourteenth-century glory (7.6) came out through the drawing-room (french) windows, 'crossed the lawn and disappeared behind the trees . . . '

In the prewar period the front door was largely reserved for the reception of visitors (e.g., General Bastow: 9.3). 'A spare key was always kept under the edge of the mat in the porch' (21.1). The status of the front door was reduced in the postwar period, and it was regularly used for domestic comings and goings. The front door opened into what a hyper-critical visitor (32.5) described as 'rather a poky little hall'. Its impression of narrowness and darkness would have been increased by the dominant position of the staircase to be described below. The first door on the left (31.7) upon entering was the drawing-room, a room large enough when 'turned out' to accommodate dances (6.12) and large parties, such as the Browns' wedding anniversary party (31.7). The front windows overlooked the front lawn, encircled by laurel-bushes with 'an extremely dull stretch of country road' beyond the hedge (15.11). French windows on the opposite side of the room gave a partial view of the back garden (15.11, 26.10). A step down led on to a veranda and the section of lawn where the late-afternoon sun could be enjoyed (26.10). Reserved in the prewar period for the reception of visitors, it replaced the morning-room as the family relaxation room in the postwar period, and from 27.2 onwards (1949) is always referred to as the 'sitting-room'.

Facing the front garden on the other side of the hall was the morning-room. A little additional light entered through a window at the other end of the room on the side wall through which Mr Brown viewed the results of William's gardening in the sunless strip by the neighbour's wall (14.5). In this room in prewar days the family gathered and Mr Brown had his favourite chair (14.5). A conjuror performed here (6.11), and Robert entertained Honoria Mercer with disastrous consequences (15.6). When William achieved his ambition to dial 999, the telephone was in the morning-room (22.3). Later it appears to have been moved to the hall. The morning-room is not mentioned after 22.3. The demotion of the drawing-room to the status of morning-room in later years is underlined in 36.1 (1966) when the Outlaws are left alone in the house by Mrs Brown to play with jigsaw puzzles and model kits in the 'sitting-room'. The door of the morning-room was in the right-hand wall of the hall and was passed by anyone going from the drawing-room to the dining-room (21.6).

From the lowest steps of the staircase it was possible to see the drawing-/sitting-room hearth (37.6). The lowest banisters must have been so placed that William, peering through the crack in the drawing-room door, could see Ethel removing a bottle from the dining-room sideboard (9.1). A door under the stairs led down steps to the cellar (with a grating and a window) where ginger ale (16.6), potatoes and coal (21.1) and the like were stored. The use of the cellar as a wartime air-raid shelter was considered (21.1) but later abandoned in favour of a shelter in the garden (23.7).

A second door in the staircase was that of the cupboard under the stairs, which contained brooms (27.7) and Mrs Brown's bag of household mending (32.8). The staircase itself could not have been L-shaped as William was in the habit of sliding down the banisters from top to bottom (29.7). A C-shaped lower curve fits the known facts. Some sense of the size of the front hall can be deduced from 37.6 where William, using his father's walking-stick as a jumping-pole, 'tries to leap the gulf that separated the end of the hatstand from the bottom step of the staircase'. From the hatstand one could see down the hall to the hall window at the back of the house (26.7, etc.) which was clearly large (openable: 26.6) and was the main source of light to the much more roomy section of the hall between the stairs and the back of the house. Behind the staircase leading into the back section of the hall was Mr Brown's study (19.3, 22.6) with a bookcase containing at least one family heirloom (25.6). On the west of the house beyond the study was the kitchen with scullery and pantry. Mrs Brown's assertion that the larder 'gets the sun all day unfortunately' (26.2) cannot be literally true, but it would certainly catch the force of the afternoon and evening sun. The back door into the kitchen was used at times by William in the days of domestic staff but was used much more by the family after their departure (33.6, etc.). The staff toilet which must have existed near the back door goes unmentioned in the text. By leaning out of the kitchen door one could see across the hall and along the passage to the side door which ran between morning-room and dining-room (14.5). In prewar days William would tend to enter and exit by the side door. Mrs Brown likewise on occasions going shopping used the side door and the tradesmen's entrance to the side gate into the lane. The side door, like the front door, had a porch (11.9). There is no reference to the side door in later books. Presumably once the domestic staff (who had the side and back doors under observation) had gone it was deemed wiser to use the front door for normal ingress and egress. Food from the kitchen had to be carried across the hall to the dining-room (26.5). Downstairs there were parquet floors (15.2). The hall was partially carpeted, with linoleum near the kitchen door (32.5). It seems probable that the hall between kitchen and dining-room was partially overlapped by the upstairs landing.

The dining-room, which could seat a considerable party, was lit by windows on the north side, overlooking the back garden, and a window on the south side which gave a view of the side porch and, more important, of William working in his sunless border (14.5). Windows on the east side would

have had little purpose as they would have directly faced the windowless wall of the next-door house a few feet away (14.5).

Since part of the dining-room seems to have been situated under the area of the 'upper landing' (see below) it is likely that the ceiling was raised some eighteen inches higher than the kitchen ceiling opposite, which would enhance the appearance and lighting of the room.

It seems clear from the text that in the days when the side door was much used the family hung their coats in the wider (back) hall and that the hatstand in the front hall was used mainly by visitors entering by the front door.

The disposition of the upstairs rooms is fairly clear. In 11.9 William 'as he was going upstairs glanced into Robert's bedroom'. From the road outside Robert can be seen brushing his hair (27.3). Mrs Brown's bedroom overlooks the drive and is next to Ethel's room (26.12), which is the door on the left after the guest-room (32.5). William's bedroom is situated at the back of the house above the dining-room. In 11.2 Robert accuses William of bringing down 'a great lump of plaster from the ceiling' in the dining-room and asks whether William is keeping an elephant in his bedroom above.

Putting all the evidence together, we learn the following. The C-shaped staircase reaches its head on the east side of the house over the side-door passage. Robert's room is immediately on the right and large enough (situated as it is over the morning-room) for Robert 'to transform his bedroom into a bed-sitting-room' (31.7). Its principal windows overlook the front garden (27.3). Continuing along the 'lower landing' (see below), one passes the door of Mr Brown's dressing-room (27.6, 29.8) and then Mrs Brown's bedroom. There seems to be a certain amount of delicacy here. Mr Brown's *bedroom* is mentioned only rarely (e.g., 26.14). Presumably one may assume that Mr Brown's bedroom is identical with Mrs Brown's and that there is an internal door (not mentioned in the text) which connects with Mr Brown's dressing-room. Ethel's room must consequently be at the west side of the house over at any rate part of the drawing-room. We are told in 9.6 that 'Ethel's room did not happen to overlook the garden'; yet in 32.5 Mr Brown working in the back garden sees Aunt Susan framed in the window of Ethel's room. The explanation is not difficult to see. There is no view of the garden seat or the main part of the back garden from Ethel's window. She does, however, have a limited view over the western extremity of the garden, looking out over the potato patch and presumably the kitchen garden in general, and can enjoy the distant view (presumably from her window-seat: 13.8) over the 'lovely view of the hills and woods beyond' which so much delights Aunt Susan (32.5). It cannot be proved (but it may very well be) that this north-facing window of Ethel's room juts out over the veranda below. The nearby guest-room ('spare-room') may well have a similar overhang for reasons explained below.

On emerging from her bedroom, Ethel stands in a short (windowless) corridor which terminates to her left within a few steps with a blank wall which forms part of the window-seat area of her bedroom. Against this wall stands an article of furniture described variously as a chest of drawers and a wardrobe (21.6). A few steps to her right in the opposite wall is the door of the guest-bedroom (32.5). From the guest-bedroom Aunt Florence can see the fields behind the garden where William and Ginger organise their 'bull-fight' (33.2) and the tree in the distance near Henry's house where Violet Elizabeth's silhouetted figure recalled that of a Greek soldier (33.2). There are, however, no south-facing windows in the guest-room, as Mr Bennison discovers to his cost (see below). Walking past the guest-room door to the main landing one reaches the bathroom door (over the kitchen) with a mat outside (26.1). The north-facing bathroom window overlooks the flat roof of

the scullery, a route by which William enters in 32.5.

There is no short cut from bathroom to William's bedroom. One has to pass the parental bedroom and Robert's room *en route*, round three sides of a rectangle. Story 2.7 is noteworthy; its particular difficulties will be discussed later. Running from the guest-room in the direction of his own, William charges into the guest's boots, his father's boots and Robert's boots in the landing passage in that order. The word 'passage' confirms that the landing was not 'open plan' and one could not look down into the hall beneath. Yet from below one could apparently look upwards towards a ceiling (probably with a window) which was also the floor of the attic. Since the other bedrooms are said to be on the 'lower landing' (2.7) one may presume that William's bedroom was on the 'upper landing'. The situation appears to be as follows. Standing at the top of the stairs, one faces an open landing area lit by a large window above the side door below. Diagonally to one's right is the door to Robert's bedroom virtually on the corner. The evidence that it is on the open landing side is finely balanced with the evidence that it is on the landing-passage side: (a) one can see into Robert's bedroom before reaching the top of the stairs (11.9); (b) peeping out from his own bedroom, William can see a light under Robert's door (26.14); (c) William tiptoes 'past Robert's door' as he makes for the stairhead; (d) running from the guest-room (2.7), he sends Robert's boots flying (see above). In the ceiling of the open landing is a trapdoor to the loft (26.14, 33.5) over the front bedrooms, which houses the boiler (14.6), the cistern (19.8, etc.) – which always leaks into the front bedrooms (14.6, 33.5) – and provides the exit to the roof (19.8) over the coping of which Mrs Brown is horrified to see William's small soot-covered face in 2.10.

Two or three steps up to the left of the stairhead would create the 'upper landing' which the text of

2.7 seems to indicate. From the upper landing a staircase ascended to the staff bedrooms at attic level, and further along the upper landing was the door to William's bedroom. That William's bedroom jutted out with a window facing south is evident because (a) he discomfits the chauffeur of a Rolls-Royce by pulling faces at him from his bedroom window (19.4), and (b) Mr Bennison in 4.13 is compelled to go to William's bedroom to point out the constellation Leo, which would be visible in the south or south-eastern sky at the beginning of the spinning-top season (April or May). However, when William 'insisted on finding all the other constellations mentioned in the book' he no doubt used the more extensive window-space which looked northwards over the back garden, which also allowed one by looking left to see the fields where the 'mooverers' pitched their tents (9.3). Through this same window William would lean to address his imaginary brigand lieutenant, who would lean out of the corresponding window of the empty house next door (14.5), and through it William would climb to make his descent by the pear-tree.

The staff bedrooms on the top floor consisted of Cook's room, presumably the 'small bedroom at the top of the stairs' which William tries to enter from the roof in 2.10 and which after the departure of Cook into the A.T.S. (23.7) was later converted into the box-room (33.6), together with the room(s) of the live-in housemaid(s). These rooms being over the back half of the house, their windows would be well back from the coping mentioned above. From the corner of one of these attic windows the steps and porch of the house next door were just visible (14.5).

Note on 'The Ghost' (2.7)

Although 'The Ghost' (2.7) precedes 'The Helper' (2.10), in which the removal to The Hollies is described, 2.7 clearly refers to the 'new house'

with its 'uncompromisingly modern appearance'. 2.10 was originally published in *Home Magazine* in April 1920 and 2.7 several months later (see Appendix 2). According to the text of 2.7, Cousin Mildred is sleeping in the room *above* William's bedroom, which would mean that she is sleeping in the servants' quarters! Later we learn that Robert and his parents are sleeping on the same floor as Mildred – on the 'lower landing'. Later still, an angry Mr Brown awoken during the night demands of William whether he was 'down on the lower landing just now'. The confusion is self-evident, but the solution fairly clear. In 27.6, when the decorators are in, William sleeps on a camp-bed in the dining-room. In 9.7 it is hard to see how both Flavia and Uncle Frederick were accommodated unless Flavia occupied the guest-room and Uncle Fred William's room (although we are not told this), the displaced William presumably sleeping downstairs on the camp-bed. Less disorganisation would be caused to the household if the camp-bed were placed in the study (beneath the guest-room) rather than in the dining-room. If in 2.7 'William's bedroom' means 'William's *temporary* bedroom' beneath the guest-room, his climbing *up* to Mildred's room is explained. Presumably some other unmentioned guest is occupying William's room. The story then works perfectly until Mr Brown asks if William had been 'down' on the lower landing, which would only be accurate if William were occupying his normal room. One presumes that Mr Brown's brain was still a little befuddled with sleep. (K.C.W.)

William's Village

It was Richmal Crompton's intention that William's village should be anonymous and situated nowhere in particular but in easy reach of London. For almost fifty years she described an unplanned and sometimes inconsistent landscape with an ad hoc geography designed to fit the story of the moment. Yet from time to time she wrote into the text small unconscious clues which clearly suggest the location of the fantasy village and strongly imply its name. One notes, for example:

(1) The counties of Surrey, Berkshire (and Hertfordshire) are specifically ruled out by passing remarks in the text such as when Lady Walton (16.8) invites Mrs Bott down to her place in Surrey.

(2) When the Outlaws have already walked several miles towards London in their quest for 'Pensions for Boys' (18.9) they are warned that they still have over fifty miles to go, which places the village some fifty-five miles from London.

(3) An American tourist travelling by car from London on a projected visit to Stratford-upon-Avon arrived by accident in the village having lost her map (6.5). Unless she planned to 'take in' Oxford, her natural route was by the A41 via Bicester and Banbury. Bicester was then $53\frac{1}{2}$ miles by train from Paddington.

(4) In 13.3 a belated temperance lecturer arrives in Marleigh (the next village beyond William's) explaining that 'he had got into the wrong train at Paddington'.

(5) In 25.1 the Vicar remarks when Professor Knowle does not arrive by the expected train: 'It's just possible that he's not coming from London . . . A train from Birmingham gets in shortly after the London one . . .' As recently as 1967 trains ran from Birmingham (New Street) to Paddington calling at Banbury and Bicester. The Bicester–Paddington route was not long after rerouted into Marylebone ($54\frac{3}{4}$ miles). One may suggest, then, that 'Hadley' corresponds with Bicester and 'Fellminster' with Banbury.

Summing up all the evidence scattered through the thirty-eight books, one may fairly conclude that William's village is situated in a fantasy landscape near Bicester, off the road to Banbury, rising from the generally flat countryside as abruptly as the village of Somerton actually does. Somerton, with its adjoining aerodrome, in several respects resembles Marleigh. Interestingly enough, Mrs Bott once stayed (37.3) at the 'Somerton Arms' in Marleigh.

One may say with considerable confidence that Mr Brown commuted daily for most of his working life into Paddington, taking the branch line from the village station and changing on to the main line at Hadley, and in his later years, after rerouting, into Marylebone, continuing his journey into London by the Bakerloo line.

The statement in 4.14 that the village was more than a hundred miles inland, if taken literally, would place the village somewhere in the Midlands too far for daily commuting to London. The statement would be true enough if one measures from the east or the west coast. From the village to the south coast the distance would be something more in the order of eighty miles as the crow flies.

The Name

William's village is stated to be in the parliamentary constituency of Hadley. It is in his village that Hadley celebrates the centenary of its charter. When Miss Taverton (31.2) on her errand to an address in *Hedley* (which, as Robert points out, is in the far north of England) arrives by mistake in *Hadley* she is met by the Outlaws at the station and led up Hadley hill, through the village past the post office as far as the Old Barn and later back at least as far as the Browns' house. She must *en route* have seen signposts and the village name clearly displayed. Yet at no time does she protest that the boys are taking her out of her way. Given that the full name of the Northumberland village is Hedley-on-the-Hill, all problems are resolved if William's village were called Hadley-on-the-Hill. One may surmise that Robert has heard of Hedley from his father, who makes regular business-trips to an unspecified destination in the north of England, and that Mr Brown has noted the close resemblance of the two names while in Consett or Newcastle. This seems to throw some light on the nature of Mr Brown's business.

Thus it is that the villagers speak constantly of going into Hadley just as the inhabitants of Harrow-on-the-Hill speak of going into Harrow.

The Map

Although the geography of the village was constructed haphazardly by the author, a close reading of the text (together with a little determined ingenuity) can produce a very fair degree of consistency. The later books are fortunately more ordered than the early books. Furthermore in the later ones a chronology is often clearly established and the time-gap between the events of one story and another expressly stated. The earlier stories, especially those clustering around the removal described in 'The Helper' from the house where William was born to the house subsequently referred to as The Hollies and William's transferral from co-educational primary school to single-sex grammar school, have no such precise chronology. They are much more in the story-telling tradition of 'Did I ever tell you about the time when William . . .' There is consequently some overlap between the two houses and the two schools, with the result that stories that depict William at an all-boys grammar school may appear before others that show his schoolfellows as mixed and highly diminutive. Furthermore, although William never attains a twelfth birthday, he does enjoy two birthdays in the course of the text and his babyhood is referred to. Some stories may be presumed to refer to the days before William reached his eleventh birthday.

There are other discrepancies that require explanation. In early stories the vicarage and church room are located near the church. Later they face across to the Old Barn field. Since the church and the Old Barn cannot have moved, a rebuilt vicarage and church room are indicated. At one time Miss Milton's cottage is backed directly by a field suitable for military manoeuvres but later by a railway embankment. The obvious conclusion is that in her later years she moved from Jasmine Villas into a cottage more suitable for her changed circumstances. Perhaps the most serious discrepancy is contained in the story where Mrs Bott in alarm over a supposed unexploded bomb opposite her gates hurries to 'the nearest house, which happened to be the Browns' '. This juxtaposition contradicts all other references and is explicable only as a dramatic abbreviation by the narrator of the fact that in her panic she ran half-way round the village to interview Mr Brown! There is similarly a problem when William is taken home separately in a police car near the end of 'Just William's Luck'. The route is feasible only if the approach is made from the direction of Applelea and William persuades the driver to enter into the joke at the expense of Hubert Lane at some point *before* the turn-off to William's house opposite Green Lane.

The map (published by Macmillan, 1990) has been constructed from the evidence of all thirty-eight books. Where the text provides no evidence, no attempt has been made to locate a specific residence. In any case in fifty years people come and go. Even house-names may be altered. No map can fully cover a half-century of change.

Topography and History (as deducible from the text)

William's native village extends over a considerable area of rising hillside overlooking the confluence of a river (unnamed in the text) and a minor tributary into which several wandering streams ultimately flow as it winds south towards Hadley. Farm land and common land combine with extensive tracts of mixed deciduous woodland in which evergreens such as holly also thrive. The soil is an acidic loam over a sticky clay subsoil favourable to a large variety of flora, including plants as calcifugous as rhododendron and common tormentil (*Potentilla erecta*). The farming is generally confined to animal husbandry, the road from Hadley to Upper Marleigh representing a clear divide between cattle on the lower (westward) side towards the river and sheep on the higher and generally rougher ground towards the east. Behind and above the village rise the summits of Bunkers Hill and Ringers Hill, providing an extensive view not only over the village but also over a broad expanse of field and meadow to the west of the river in the direction of Steedham. The alleged volcanic origin of Ringers Hill makes it a source of unique geological interest in south-east England. Professor Fremlin, the geologist, has shown it to have been the haunt of Stone Age man from earliest times. Various local excavations, including that by the late Professor Porson of a substantial Roman villa on the hillside not far from the church, and the work of Monson and the Mellings Field Club, give a good indication of the extent of Roman occupation.

The medieval settlement grew up between the junctions of the route from Hadley to Upper Marleigh and the tracks that ran eastward to the Mellings and westward to Steedham. The Steedham road still descends the hill and crosses the river by a fifteenth-century bridge. This area is represented today by the village green with its pond and cluster of hostelries (the White, Red and Blue Lions), the village hall and a number of ancient cottages. The situation of the small Norman church with its 'majestic tower set among immemorial elms' below the village on the Marleigh road suggests a willingness to accommo-

date the convenience of the local nobility rather than that of the villagers who still make their way to church downhill across the common. Visitors to the church should notice the gallery which survives in spite of the depredations of death-watch beetle. The small community at the top of Hadley hill at the road junction leading off towards Eastbrook Farm (the East Brook in question presumably being the stream that crosses the farm and continues across the grammar-school playing-fields) is clearly also ancient, complete as it is with the only forge to survive until William's day, the village forge proper seemingly having been converted into a garage.

Little of the Elizabethan era survives in the immediate locality of the village. One wing of Marleigh Court (where Elizabeth I is said to have stayed) remains intact. The gabled frontage of Marleigh Manor (the residence of Sir Gerald Markham), sometimes known locally as 'Marleigh Hall', has been replaced by a pseudo-Palladian facade, and Applelea Court has been reduced to a building of 'Tudor influence with Jacobean additions'. The Hall itself, occupied for centuries by generations of the Rossiter family, was a pretentious multi-gabled Victorian rebuild even before undergoing further alterations to suit the capricious tastes of *nouveaux riches* occupants such as Mrs Porker and the Botts.

A few thatched cottages (including Rose Cottage and Mrs Maloney's cottage) survived into the twentieth century. Honeysuckle Cottage was much favoured by writers and artists for its picturesque qualities. A few Georgian houses such as Meadowview in Green Lane remained intact. The latter part of the nineteenth century saw the construction of capacious Victorian houses with large gardens, stables and coach-houses particularly in the area near the station and on what was presumably leased glebe-land to the south of the Steedham road and land leased from the Hall to the north of it. It was in two such adjoining houses that William and Ginger were born. The Hollies, to which the Browns subsequently moved, dates from the period immediately preceding the First World War.

In the 1920s the village grew considerably. Attempts to move with the times are exemplified by the short-lived picture-palace. Mallards, the confectionery chain, tried unsuccessfully to establish a foothold. Most important, the insanitary old cottages in the vicinity of the village green in which the inhabitants lived in Dickensian squalor were demolished early that decade, making possible the construction, among other things, of a new vicarage and church room. The inhabitants of the old cottages, where not employed as agricultural labourers, seem to have found employment in the local quarries. Of these there were two, one below the Hadley road and behind The Hollies, the other at Little Marleigh, off the Marleigh road near Briar Lane. Both quarries seem to have ceased production by the early 1920s, and their derelict and overgrown state afforded the village boys exciting adventure-playgrounds. Although the text gives no clear indication, the likelihood is that the quarries produced clay for a local brick-industry. The Hollies, a house of red brick and in 1920 still of 'uncompromisingly modern appearance', was probably constructed of bricks from this source.

By the 1930s the picturesque nature of the village and its environs was attracting a regular series of camping holidaymakers from London. The opening of the Regina guest-house in 1934, perhaps in emulation of the Cedars Hotel in Marleigh which was already drawing a celebrity clientele, represented a first tentative move towards a more commercial approach. It was not until the post-1945 period that amenities such as the new local golf-course were developed, and even then most established residents preferred to remain faithful to the golf-course which adjoined Hadley Common.

By 1938 a new housing estate was rising between the road and the river not far from the Hall grounds. But, more significantly, the late 1960s development of a council house estate on the Upper Marleigh road at the most northerly point of the Borough of Hadley was indicative of changing times and led to a certain influx of Londoners, some at least stemming from Poplar. Fortunately for the Outlaws, their fear that the Old Barn field itself was earmarked for housing development in 1966 at the time of the centenary celebrations of the granting of the Hadley charter proved unfounded.

In the 1950s the stable population had still been fourfold: (1) farmers and farm labourers, (2) commuting businessmen with offices in London, most of whom had their roots in the village, (3) a considerable number of retired people, some of whom had returned to the scenes of their early life, (4) a small residue of local aristocracy, all with their families and dependants. As late as 1964 the Outlaws could still with reasonable justification describe their village as 'small and remote' although in 1962 increasing traffic on the Upper Marleigh road had induced Mr Brown to add his name to a petition for a 30 miles per hour speed-limit through the village.

The text indicates that before the Second World War the main communications included: a regular half-hourly double-decker bus service from the village station into Hadley, and a through service from Hadley, stopping outside the grammar school and in the centre of the village, and continuing to Upper Marleigh. Some buses presumably continued northwards to Fellminster, others turned left at the Green Dragon in Upper Marleigh down to Marleigh village and station. There are indications of an occasional bus service to Marleigh village from William's village station along the Marleigh road via Bassenton. Buses also ran to Steedham post office, child fare 8d each way.

William's village station survived the Beeching cuts. It was on a branch line from Hadley via Applelea, which no doubt continued beyond Steedham to Oxford. London-bound passengers changed on to the main line at Hadley, travelling to Paddington until the line was eventually rerouted to Marylebone. The Outlaws' collection of tickets from discontinued lines may suggest that the branch line that ran from Hadley to Marleigh (stopping presumably at East and West Melling) succumbed to the Beeching axe.

As tended to be the case in prewar villages, relatively few local roads had specific names, Well Lane, Briar Lane (which petered out into the woods behind Little Marleigh), Emstead Lane and Green Lane being exceptional. This last (as can be paralleled in other villages) had no connection with the village green but ran down from the south-west corner of the village between green meadows almost to the riverside. It should be noted that the Marleigh road properly speaking was not the one over Hadley hill but the ancient lane that wound its leisurely way from Hadley, bypassing Applelea, across Hadley Common, then along the riverside past the village church and Hall gates, and so on through Bassenton, representing a total journey of some five miles from William's village to Marleigh church. Pedestrians on the Marleigh road preferred to take the direct footpath to Marleigh church through the woods, thus reducing the journey to roughly two miles. Following the bus route from the village green through Upper Marleigh (about 1½ miles), where the wartime aerodrome was located – somewhat dangerously, it would seem – behind the hill, down into Marleigh village entailed a total journey of three miles. Not unnaturally, the higher and shorter route to Marleigh favoured both by public and private transport was often loosely referred to as the 'Marleigh road', especially if the speaker was standing in the vicinity of the post office or the Old Barn.

Similarly, the term 'village street' in the text is occasionally ambiguous. The village centre was T-shaped round two sides of the green with the Steedham road ('West Street', so to speak) running into 'North Street', i.e., the road from Hadley to Upper Marleigh. The latter is usually the 'village street' of the text as it represents the direct route from The Hollies to the Old Barn. William rarely has business in 'West Street' since when leaving the Old Barn to go, say, to Ginger's house he favours either the lane downhill past the Hall gates or the field route. But there are some instances where the term 'village street' must refer to 'West Street'.

Schools

The uniforms (changed to navy blue in the 1960s) of Rose Mount Girls' School (headmistress Miss Priscilla Golightly) were a familiar sight in the village. Most village children attended the co-educational school situated near the church and which appears to have been the Church school. There was an infants' department, and most children remained there until school-leaving age. Although Mr and Mrs Brown at one stage gave serious thought to sending William away to a boarding-school, the Outlaws' parents made the decision to send their sons to the village school for their primary education in the hope that female company might have a mellowing effect. The fact that the feud with Hubert Lane does not seriously develop until the Outlaws and the Laneites find themselves together at the grammar school implies (hardly surprisingly) that the Lanes made a very different decision where Hubert was concerned. There was the added advantage that when William, Ginger and Henry were small the village school was close by. Any financial contribution made by Mr Brown to the village school must have been at most a very small one. Fees were only a consideration once the Outlaws had started at the grammar school. The textual assertion that Mr Brown was known to protest over the fees paid to what must have been the primary school authorities must be an error on the narrator's part.

The grammar school to which the Outlaws transferred at the age of eleven was a school of importance, under the headship of a distinguished classical scholar and writer on Roman law, Mr Marks/Markson, known to the boys as 'Ole Markie'. (The inconsistency over the headmaster's name is easily explained if its full form was similar to that of Mrs Bruce Monkton-Bruce (or even Jameson Jameson), i.e., Mr Marks-Markson or Markson-Marks, with the result that he was known both as Mr Marks and Mr Markson.) The school had a prep department and took boarders. Its sixth form attracted boys from a large area. Since many would have left rapidly at the end of the day to catch buses or trains homeward, the local geography was not always very well known to them. The presence of a school of such standing in the village suggests that Hadley Grammar School, probably a sixteenth- or seventeenth-century foundation, had by the 1920s outgrown its original buildings in the market-town of Hadley and moved into larger buildings with large playing-fields two miles or so up the hill in the village of Hadley-on-the-Hill, where it was well served by local buses and trains.

Health and Welfare

The local workhouse, high on the eastern extremity of the village, was operative until the 1920s. A house called The Manor (not to be confused with Marleigh Manor) was opened as an old people's home in the 1960s. Medical services were available at Hadley General Hospital and at Marleigh Cottage Hospital. Dr Bell, the Browns' family doctor, also practised surgery at the Hadley Nursing Home. There were also establishments such as the osteopathic 'Nature Cure' clinic on the northern outskirts of Marleigh patronised by Mr Bott.

Hadley

The fire service, local newspaper (*The Hadley Times*) and policing above local village level were all based in Hadley. Since apart from the post-office-cum-general-store, a cobbler, a barber, a butcher, one or two confectioners and the odd junkshop there were few opportunities for shopping in the village the inhabitants very frequently slipped down into Hadley. The walk downhill by road or by field-path, less than a mile, was easy. But returning on foot on a hot day meant a tiring uphill journey. A visit to Hadley was essential for serious shopping, to buy fish or clothes, to visit Woolworth's, the library or the swimming baths, or for entertainment. Before 1939, Hadley had more than one cinema. The Grand Hotel in Hadley was known for its tea-dances during the war and by the 1960s was advertising 'West End cuisine'. The opening of the Hadley New Theatre in 1966 lent further cultural distinction to a market town aiming at higher standards of sophistication. (K.C.W.)

Willingham, Patsy

A little girl living on the outskirts of the village to whose charms Douglas has heavily fallen victim. ' "He's turned into a sort of *slave*," said William bitterly. "He doesn't seem *yuman* any longer . . ." ' Fortunately for the solidarity of the Outlaws the Willinghams leave the neighbourhood pretty soon, but not before Douglas has abandoned the Outlaws on several occasions to be with Patsy. There is a dogged defiance about him, even after William and the others have held a pretty tough post-mortem with him on the whole affair. They are extremely contemptuous that he has actually been 'pushin' an ole girl on a swing' and on her tricycle. Douglas still sighs deeply that 'it was a great experience'. (*William and the Masked Ranger*, 4)

Woman's Own

By 1947 recovery from the war was in full swing, and it was a busy time again for Richmal Crompton. Her new William stories were now first being published in *Home Notes*. She had already been offered a contract to write about a new child character (Jimmy) for the *Star*, and the film *Just William's Luck* had been conceived by Val Guest, with Richmal involved in working his screenplay into a full-length story for the book of the same name. Already William on the radio was into his second series, with his creator providing every third script, and it was in this period of great activity that the editor of *Woman's Own* requested a William strip cartoon to appear in the magazine each week. Richmal Crompton agreed, Thomas Henry agreed, and the first one appeared on 7 February 1947.

The strips were without captions, although the occasional speech-bubble or noticeboard was used to emphasise the (very mild) joke.

Richmal Crompton's complete trust in Thomas Henry's ability to maintain William's character had been established many years before in the *Happy Mag*, where his double-page William adventures in cartoon form had appeared from time to time. It was only when the artist was put under editorial pressure in *Woman's Own* to introduce ideas that would have made William too delinquent that he wrote to Richmal asking for her support. The support was rapidly forthcoming, and the affair was settled to everyone's satisfaction.

Thomas Henry continued to provide the strips for the rest of his life, another fifteen years. Another artist, Henry Ford, took over (closely watched by Richmal), and was soon illustrating the remaining books as well. The last cartoon appeared on 5 April 1969, just a few months after Richmal Crompton's death. (D.S.)

Xenophobia

William's brand of xenophobia is simplistic; foreigners don't have the same standards and values as he does, so, if they want any relationship with him, *they* must mend their ways. Moreover, they should abandon those ghastly languages which it is torture for a small boy to learn: ' "I don't wanter talk to *any* French folks, an' if they wanter talk to me they can learn English. English's 's easy 's easy to talk. It's *silly* havin' other langwidges. I don' see why all the other countries shun't learn English 'stead of us learnin' other langwidges with no *sense* in 'em. *English's* sense." ' (*William – The Conqueror*, 4)

'Yubear'

See HART, MRS AND SUSIE.

Zevrier

A classical violinist hired to entertain at the lavish
party which Mrs Bott is holding at the Hall for
Lord Faversham (and the entire neighbourhood).
William befriends Mr Manelli (a Punch and Judy
man who has fallen on hard times) and his brilliant
performing dog, Toby. He takes it upon himself to
invite them to perform in the marquee at the party;
all he then has to do is to waylay Zevrier (what a
good thing that so many distinguished speakers
and performers coming to the village use the railway and Shanks's pony rather than the door-to-
door car!) and keep him from attending the party.
Zevrier wants some soulful anecdote about how he
has fired some young person with his performance
– and he doesn't like Mrs Bott anyway because she
writes to him as 'Mr Zebra'. So he spends the afternoon in a haystack playing to William ('the most
unmusical boy in the British Empire'), while
Manelli has wild success with his show at the party
– and in getting future bookings. (*William – The
Pirate*, 1)

Addendum: The entry for the Outlaws makes the
point that neither Henry nor Douglas is given a surname in the William stories. However, since *The
William Companion* was first published, a letter
written by Richmal Crompton to a schoolboy has
come to light revealing that their names were
Henry Bates and Douglas Frinton.

APPENDIX 1: THE WILLIAM BOOKS

	Title	*First published*
1	*Just – William*	May 1922
2	*More William*	Dec 1922
3	*William Again*	June 1923
4	*William – The Fourth*	Apr 1924
5	*Still – William*	Apr 1925
6	*William – The Conqueror*	Mar 1926
7	*William – The Outlaw*	Oct 1927
8	*William – In Trouble*	Mar 1927
9	*William – The Good*	May 1928
10	*William*	Mar 1929
11	*William – The Bad*	Mar 1930
12	*William's Happy Days*	Oct 1930
13	*William's Crowded Hours*	June 1931
14	*William – The Pirate*	May 1932
15	*William – The Rebel*	Apr 1933
16	*William – The Gangster*	May 1934
17	*William – The Detective*	July 1935
18	*Sweet William*	Aug 1936
19	*William – The Showman*	July 1937
20	*William – The Dictator*	June 1938
21	*William and A.R.P.*	May 1939
	(reprinted as *William's Bad Resolution* in 1956)	
22	*William and the Evacuees*	May 1940
	(reprinted as *William – The Film Star* in 1956)	
23	*William Does His Bit*	Apr 1941
24	*William Carries On*	May 1942
25	*William and the Brains Trust*	Apr 1945
26	*Just William's Luck*	Apr 1948
27	*William – The Bold*	July 1950
28	*William and the Tramp*	Sept 1952
29	*William and the Moon Rocket*	Sept 1954
30	*William and the Space Animal*	Sept 1956
31	*William's Television Show*	Sept 1958
32	*William – The Explorer*	Sept 1960
33	*William's Treasure Trove*	Sept 1962
34	*William and the Witch*	Sept 1964
35	*William and the Pop Singers*	1965

Title	**First published**
36 *William and the Masked Ranger*	1966
37 *William the Superman*	Nov 1968
38 *William the Lawless*	1970
*Just William – The Book of the Film**	Aug 1939

* The script plus the six selected stories on which it was based.

NOTE: Although *William – In Trouble* was originally published before *William – The Outlaw*, the numbering of books both above and throughout the *Companion* has been maintained to match Newnes's own sequencing of the titles.

(D.S.)

APPENDIX 2: The William Stories in Date Order of Magazine Appearance

Title in Book	Magazine	When Published		Book	Original Title (if different)
Rice-Mould	Home Magazine	Feb	1919	2.2	
The Outlaws	Home Magazine	Mar	1919	1.8	
William Goes to the Pictures	Home Magazine	Apr	1919	1.1	
Jumble	Home Magazine	June	1919	1.12	
The Show	Home Magazine	July	1919	1.5	
William Joins the Band of Hope	Home Magazine	Aug	1919	1.7	
William's Burglar	Home Magazine	Sept	1919	2.3	
William the Intruder	Home Magazine	Oct	1919	1.2	
William and White Satin	Home Magazine	Nov	1919	1.9	
William's Christmas Eve	Home Magazine	Dec	1919	2.14	
The Best Laid Plans	Home Magazine	Jan	1920	1.11	
William and the Smuggler	Home Magazine	Feb	1920	2.11	
The Rivals	Home Magazine	Mar	1920	2.6	
The Helper	Home Magazine	Apr	1920	2.10	
The Circus	Home Magazine	May	1920	3.11	
The Ghost	Home Magazine	Aug	1920	2.7	
The Fall of the Idol	Home Magazine	Oct	1920	1.4	
The Revenge	Home Magazine	Nov	1920	2.9	
A Busy Day	Home Magazine	Dec	1920	2.1	
William's New Year's Day	Home Magazine	Jan	1921	1.10	
The Knight at Arms	Home Magazine	Feb	1921	2.4	
William's Hobby	Home Magazine	Mar	1921	2.5	
William and the Ancient Souls	Home Magazine	Apr	1921	2.13	
The May King	Home Magazine	May	1921	2.8	
The Weak Spot	Home Magazine	June	1921	4.1	
A Question of Grammar	Home Magazine	July	1921	1.6	
William and Photography	Home Magazine	Aug	1921	4.2	
The Reform of William	Home Magazine	Sept	1921	2.12	
Enter the Sweep	Home Magazine	Oct	1921	6.1	
The Fête – and Fortune	Home Magazine	Nov	1921	4.3	
William all the Time	Home Magazine	Dec	1921	4.4	
Aunt Jane's Treat	Home Magazine	Jan	1922	4.5	
William Below Stairs	Home Magazine	Feb	1922	1.3	
Kidnappers	Home Magazine	Mar	1922	4.6	
The Great Detective	Home Magazine	Apr	1922	3.10	
The Cure	Home Magazine	May	1922	3.2	
The Native Protégé	Home Magazine	June	1922	3.8	
That Boy	Home Magazine	July	1922	3.3	

Title in Book	*Magazine*	*When Published*		*Book*	*Original Title (if different)*
What Delayed the Great Man	Home Magazine	Aug	1922	3.1	
William the Reformer	Home Magazine	Sept	1922	3.4	
Not Much	Ladies' Home Mag	Oct	1922	3.5	
Just William's Luck	Happy Mag	Dec	1922	3.9	
William and the White Cat	Happy Mag	Jan	1923	3.6	
William Sells the Twins	Happy Mag	Feb	1923	3.12	
William's Helping Hand	Happy Mag	Mar	1923	3.13	
William's Secret Society	Happy Mag	Apr	1923	3.7	
William Gets Wrecked	Happy Mag	May	1923	3.14	
William's Evening Out	Happy Mag	June	1923	4.7	
William Advertises	Happy Mag	July	1923	4.8	
William and the Black Cat	Happy Mag	Aug	1923	4.9	
The Bishop's Handkerchief	Happy Mag	Sept	1923	5.1	
William the Showman	Happy Mag	Oct	1923	4.10	
A Dress Rehearsal	Happy Mag	Nov	1923	4.14	
William Enters Politics	Happy Mag	Jan	1924	4.12	
Henri Learns the Language	Happy Mag	Feb	1924	5.2	
William's Extra Day	Happy Mag	Mar	1924	4.11	
William Makes a Night of It	Happy Mag	Apr	1924	4.13	
The Sweet Little Girl in White	Happy Mag	May	1924	5.3	
A Bit of Blackmail	Happy Mag	June	1924	5.5	
William Turns Over a New Leaf	Happy Mag	July	1924	5.4	
An Afternoon with William	Tit-Bits Summer Annual		1924	5.10	
The Cat and the Mouse	Happy Mag	Aug	1924	5.12	
William the Money-Maker	Happy Mag	Sept	1924	5.6	
The Haunted House	Happy Mag	Oct	1924	5.7	
William and Uncle George	Happy Mag	Nov	1924	5.13	
William the Match-Maker	Happy Mag	Dec	1924	5.8	
William's Truthful Christmas	Happy Mag	Xmas	1924	5.9	
William Spoils the Party	Happy Mag	Jan	1925	5.11	
William and Saint Valentine	Happy Mag	Feb	1925	5.14	
A Birthday Treat	Happy Mag	Mar	1925	6.2	
The Leopard Hunter	Happy Mag	Apr	1925	6.3	
William Leads a Better Life	Happy Mag	May	1925	6.4	
William and the Early Romans	Happy Mag	June	1925	8.1	
William and the Lost Tourist	Happy Mag	July	1925	6.5	
The Midnight Adventure of Miss Montagu	Happy Mag	Aug	1925	6.6	
The Mysterious Stranger	Happy Mag	Sept	1925	6.7	

Title in Book	Magazine	When Published	Book	Original Title (if different)
The Sunday-School Treat	Happy Mag	Oct 1925	6.8	
William the Philanthropist	Happy Mag	Nov 1925	6.9	
William the Bold Crusader	Happy Mag	Dec 1925	6.10	
The Wrong Party	Happy Mag	Xmas 1925	6.11	
William Starts the Holidays	Happy Mag	Jan 1926	6.12	
Revenge is Sweet	Happy Mag	Feb 1926	6.13	
William and the Fairy Daffodil	Happy Mag	Mar 1926	8.2	
William and the Chinese God	Happy Mag	Apr 1926	8.3	
All the News	Happy Mag	May 1926	8.4	
William's Mammoth Circus	Happy Mag	June 1926	8.5	
The Magic Monkey	Happy Mag	July 1926	8.6	
William Among the Poets	Happy Mag	Aug 1926	8.7	
William at the Garden Party	Happy Mag	Sept 1926	8.8	
The Terrible Magician	Happy Mag	Oct 1926	7.2	
William to the Rescue	Happy Mag	Nov 1926	8.10	
William and the White Elephants	Happy Mag	Dec 1926	7.5	
William Joins the Waits	Happy Mag	Xmas 1926	8.9	
William Plays Santa Claus	Happy Mag	Jan 1927	7.4	
Finding a School for William	Happy Mag	Feb 1927	7.6	
The Stolen Whistle	Happy Mag	Mar 1927	7.7	
William Finds a Job	Happy Mag	Apr 1927	7.8	
Georgie and the Outlaws	Happy Mag	May 1927	7.3	The Perfect Little Gentleman
William's Busy Day	Happy Mag	June 1927	7.9	
William is Hypnotised	Happy Mag	July 1927	7.10	A New Page in History
William and the Archers	Happy Mag	Aug 1927	9.3	William the Bold Archer
William – The Money Maker	Happy Mag	Sept 1927	9.4	
William – The Outlaw	Happy Mag	Oct 1927	7.1	No More School
William – The Avenger	Happy Mag	Nov 1927	9.5	
William – The Good	Happy Mag	Dec 1927	9.1	
Parrots for Ethel	Happy Mag	Xmas 1927	9.6	
William – The Great Actor	Happy Mag	Jan 1928	9.2	
One Good Turn	Happy Mag	Feb 1928	9.7	William's Good Turn
William's Lucky Day	Happy Mag	Mar 1928	9.8	
The New Game	Happy Mag	Apr 1928	10.2	William's New Game
A Little Adventure	Happy Mag	May 1928	9.9	William on the Trail
William and the Waxwork Prince	Happy Mag	June 1928	10.4	William the Waxwork Prince
William's Double Life	Happy Mag	July 1928	10.3	

Title in Book	*Magazine*	*When Published*	*Book*	*Original Title (if different)*
William the Showman	Happy Mag	Aug 1928	10.5	
The Mystery of Oaklands	Happy Mag	Sept 1928	10.1	
The Outlaws Deliver the Goods	Happy Mag	Oct 1928	10.6	Ten Pounds Wanted
Fireworks Strictly Prohibited	Happy Mag	Nov 1928	10.7	Fireworks Strictly Forbidden
William and the Prize Pig	Happy Mag	Dec 1928	10.10	
The Outlaws Fetch the Holly	Happy Mag	Xmas 1928	10.8	Fetching the Holly
The Sentimental Widow	Happy Mag	Jan 1929	10.9	
The Knights of the Square Table	Happy Mag	Feb 1929	11.1	
William and the Little Girl	Happy Mag	Mar 1929	11.2	William Falls in Love
William Adopts an Orphan	Happy Mag	Apr 1929	11.6	
The Pennymans Hand on the Torch	Happy Mag	May 1929	11.10	William and the New Neighbours
William, Prime Minister	Happy Mag	June 1929	11.3	
William and the Prize Cat	Happy Mag	July 1929	11.5	William's Prize Cat
William and the Sleeping Major	Golden Arrow	Aug 1929	13.9	
William and the Campers	Happy Mag	Aug 1929	11.7	William and the Good Little Boys
The Outlaws and the Cucumber	Happy Mag	Sept 1929	11.8	William and the Prize Cucumber
William Gets His Own Back	Happy Mag	Oct 1929	11.4	
A Little Interlude	Happy Mag	Nov 1929	11.9	William the Bold Pirate
William Goes Shopping	Happy Mag	Dec 1929	12.1	
The Christmas Truce	Happy Mag	Xmas 1929	12.3	William's Christmas Truce
William and the School Report	Happy Mag	Jan 1930	12.2	William's School Report
William and the Cow	Happy Mag	Feb 1930	12.5	William's Afternoon Out
William's Birthday	Happy Mag	Mar 1930	12.6	
William Helps the Cause	Happy Mag	Apr 1930	12.4	William's Star Turn
The Outlaws and the Hidden Treasure	Happy Mag	May 1930	12.7	William and the Buried Treasure
William the Superman	Happy Mag	June 1930	12.8	William the Mesmerist
William and the Twins	Happy Mag	July 1930	12.10	
William Puts Things Right	Happy Mag	Aug 1930	12.9	
William and the Spy	Happy Mag	Sept 1930	13.1	
The Plan that Failed	Happy Mag	Oct 1930	13.2	William the Martyr
The Outlaws and Cousin Percy	Happy Mag	Dec 1930	13.4	William and the Clever Cousin
William and the Snowman	Happy Mag	Xmas 1930	13.10	
William and the Young Man	Happy Mag	Jan 1931	13.3	William Stays to Tea

Title in Book	Magazine	When Published		Book	Original Title (if different)
The Outlaws and the Tramp	Happy Mag	Feb	1931	13.8	William and the Wonderful Tramp
William and the Temporary History Master	Happy Mag	Mar	1931	13.5	William Gets His Own Back
A Crowded Hour with William	Happy Mag	Apr	1931	13.6	William the Hero
The Outlaws and the Missionary	Happy Mag	May	1931	13.7	William and the Missionary
Aunt Arabelle in Charge	Happy Mag	June	1931	14.10	William's Busy Fortnight
William Holds the Stage	Happy Mag	July	1931	14.2	William the Star Actor
The Outlaws and the Triplets	Happy Mag	Aug	1931	14.3	William and the Lost Babies
William and the Eastern Curse	Happy Mag	Sept	1931	14.4	
William and the Musician	Happy Mag	Oct	1931	14.1	Invited by William
The New Neighbour	Happy Mag	Nov	1931	14.5	William's Next Door Enemy
Mrs Bott's Hat	Happy Mag	Dec	1931	14.6	William in Disguise
William and the Princess Goldilocks	Happy Mag	Xmas	1931	14.7	
Their Good Resolution	Happy Mag	Jan	1932	14.8	William's Rescue Party
William's Invention	Happy Mag	Feb	1932	14.9	William the Great Inventor
William and the Drug Trafficker	Happy Mag	Mar	1932	15.9	William the Star Detective
April Fool's Day	Happy Mag	Apr	1932	15.10	
A Little Affair of Rivalry	Happy Mag	May	1932	14.11	William and the Rivals
William's Wonderful Plan	Happy Mag	June	1932	15.7	
William and the Fisherman	Happy Mag	July	1932	15.8	William Goes Fishing
The Outlaws and the Penknife	Happy Mag	Aug	1932	15.5	A Present for William
A Rescue Party	Happy Mag	Sept	1932	15.2	William and the House of Mystery
Three Dogs and William	Happy Mag	Oct	1932	15.1	William's New Dog
Mistakes Will Happen	Happy Mag	Nov	1932	15.3	
William and Cleopatra	Happy Mag	Dec	1932	15.4	
William and the Watch and Chain	Happy Mag	Xmas	1932	15.6	
William Makes Things Hum	Happy Mag	Jan	1933	15.11	William's Bad Bargain
It All Began with the Typewriter	Happy Mag	Feb	1933	15.12	William and the Typewriter
Three Cheers for Sweetikins	Happy Mag	Mar	1933	16.2	William and the Dear Little Dog
The Plan that Failed	Happy Mag	Apr	1933	16.4	William's Weekend
Only Just in Time	Happy Mag	May	1933	16.5	William Runs a Night Club
William and the Love Test	Happy Mag	June	1933	19.10	

Title in Book	*Magazine*	*When Published*		*Book*	*Original Title (if different)*
William the Sleep-Maker	Happy Mag	July	1933	16.6	
William and the Russian Prince	Happy Mag	Aug	1933	16.7	
William Clears the Slums	Happy Mag	Sept	1933	16.8	William the Philanthropist
William – The Gangster	Happy Mag	Oct	1933	16.1	
The Outlaws and the Fifth	Happy Mag	Nov	1933	16.9	William's Prize Guy
William 's Christmas Eve	Happy Mag	Dec	1933	16.10	
William and the Real Laurence	Happy Mag	Xmas	1933	16.3	William the Imposter
A Night of Mysteries	Happy Mag	Jan	1934	16.11	William's Night of Mysteries
Waste Paper Wanted	Happy Mag	Mar	1934	17.8	
William and the Monster	Happy Mag	Apr	1934	17.10	
William and the Nasties	Happy Mag	June	1934	17.6	
William and the Campers	Happy Mag	Hol	1934	17.1	William and the Lion
William the Invisible	Happy Mag	Oct	1934	17.2	
William the Rat Lover	Happy Mag	Nov	1934	17.4	First Prize – William
A Present from William	Happy Mag	Xmas	1934	17.11	
William the Conspirator	Happy Mag	Feb	1935	17.3	
William and the Tablet	Happy Mag	Apr	1935	17.5	William Sweeps the Chimney
William and the League of Perfect Love	Happy Mag	May	1935	17.7	William and the League of Love
William the Persian	Happy Mag	June	1935	17.9	
(not published in the books)	Happy Mag	July	1935	–	William on the Trail
William and the Wonderful Present	Happy Mag	Aug	1935	18.1	
William and the Perfect Child	Happy Mag	Sept	1935	18.2	
William Helps the Cause	Happy Mag	Oct	1935	18.3	William the Money Maker
William and the Bugle	Happy Mag	Xmas	1935	18.4	William Gets a Job
William and the Policeman's Helmet	Happy Mag	Jan	1936	18.5	William Plays Policeman
William the Reformer	Happy Mag	Feb	1936	18.6	William the Governor
St. Mars' Day	Happy Mag	Mar	1936	18.7	
Uncle Charlie and the Outlaws	Happy Mag	Apr	1936	18.8	William and the Good Uncle
Pensions for Boys	Happy Mag	June	1936	18.9	
A Spot of Heroism	Happy Mag	Hol	1936	18.10	William the Hero
William to the Rescue	Happy Mag	Aug	1936	19.3	William the Spy-Hunter
William and the Sea-Side Show	Happy Mag	Sept	1936	19.1	William the Showman
William and the Little Strangers	Happy Mag	Oct	1936	19.2	
A Few Dogs and William	Happy Mag	Dec	1936	19.4	Other People's Dogs

Title in Book	Magazine	When Published		Book	Original Title (if different)
The Outlaws go A-Mumming	Happy Mag	Jan	1937	19.5	William the Dragon
William Starts the New Year	Happy Mag	Feb	1937	19.6	William the Benefactor
William the Film Star	Happy Mag	Mar	1937	19.7	
William the Globe-Trotter	Happy Mag	Apr	1937	19.8	
Coronation Gala	Happy Mag	May	1937	19.9	William Plays the King
He Who Fights	Happy Mag	July	1937	20.1	William and Lucinda
Agnes Matilda Comes to Stay	Happy Mag	Hol	1937	20.3	William and the Awful Child
What's in a Name	Happy Mag	Aug	1937	20.2	William the Dictator
A Question of Exchange	Happy Mag	Sept	1937	20.4	Unfair Exchange
Aunt Florence and the Green Woodpecker	Happy Mag	Nov	1937	20.5	William and the Woodpecker
William and the Ebony Hair Brush	Happy Mag	Dec	1937	20.6	William Helps the Police
Aunt Louie's Birthday Present	Happy Mag	Jan	1938	20.7	William's Christmas Shopping
William and the Dentist	Happy Mag	Mar	1938	20.8	William Visits the Dentist
The Holewood Bequest	Happy Mag	May	1938	20.9	William the Collector
William and the Old Man in the Fog	Happy Mag	June	1938	20.10	William and the Phantom Legacy
William's Good-Bye Present	Happy Mag	July	1938	21.2	
William's Day Off	Happy Mag	Hol	1938	21.3	William and the Piebald Mouse
William and the Badminton Racket	Happy Mag	Sept	1938	21.8.	William's Day Off
Portrait of William	Happy Mag	Oct	1938	21.4	
William the Dog Trainer	Happy Mag	Nov	1938	21.5	
William and the Vanishing Luck	Happy Mag	Dec	1938	21.6	
William's Bad Resolution	Happy Mag	Jan	1939	21.7	
William and the Begging Letter	Happy Mag	Apr	1939	21.9	William the Beggar
William and A.R.P.	Happy Mag	May	1939	21.1	
William Tries the Films	Happy Mag	June	1939	22.2	
William and the Man from Africa	Happy Mag	July	1939	22.6	
William and the Unfair Sex	Happy Mag	Sept	1939	22.4	
William Gets his Own Back	Happy Mag	Nov	1939	22.8	
William – The Highwayman	Happy Mag	Dec	1939	23.2	
(not published in books)	AR Peggio	Dec	1939	–	William's Unlucky Day
William and the Air Raid Shelter	Happy Mag	Jan	1940	22.5	William Shares a Secret
William and the Black-Out	Happy Mag	Feb	1940	22.7	

Title in Book	*Magazine*	*When Published*		*Book*	*Original Title (if different)*
William and the Bird Man	Happy Mag	Apr	1940	22.3	William and the Bird Lover
William and the Evacuees	Happy Mag	May	1940	22.1	William Takes Charge
Boys Will be Boys	Modern Woman	Aug	1940	23.3	
William – the Fire-Fighter	Modern Woman	Sept	1940	23.4	
William Does His Bit	Modern Woman	Oct	1940	23.1	
William Gets a Move On	Modern Woman	Nov	1940	23.9	
William Makes a Corner	Modern Woman	Dec	1940	23.5	
William – The Salvage Collector	Modern Woman	Jan	1941	23.7	
The Outlaws and the Parachutist	Modern Woman	Feb	1941	23.6	
William Helps the Spitfire Fund	Modern Woman	Mar	1941	23.8	
Claude Finds a Companion	Modern Woman	Apr	1941	23.10	
Too Many Cooks	Modern Woman	May	1941	24.1	
William and the Bomb	Modern Woman	June	1941	24.2	
William's Midsummer Eve	Modern Woman	July	1941	24.3	
Joan to the Rescue	Modern Woman	Aug	1941	24.4	
Reluctant Heroes	Modern Woman	Sept	1941	24.5	Reluctant Hero
Guy Fawkes – with Variations	Modern Woman	Nov	1941	24.6	
William Works for Peace	Modern Woman	Dec	1941	24.7	
William Spends a Busy Morning	Modern Woman	Feb	1942	24.8	
A Present for a Little Girl	Modern Woman	Apr	1942	24.9	
Hubert's Party	Modern Woman	June	1942	24.10	
Mrs. Bott's Birthday Present	Modern Woman	Aug	1942	25.2	
William and the Mock Invasion	Modern Woman	Oct	1942	25.3	
William and the Tea-Cake	Modern Woman	Jan	1943	25.5	
Entertainment Provided	Modern Woman	May	1943	25.6	
William's War-Time Fun Fair	Homes & Gardens	June	1943	25.4	
William and The Brains Trust	Modern Woman	Aug	1943	25.1	
Soldiers for Sale	Modern Woman	Feb	1944	25.8	
The Outlaws' Report	Homes & Gardens	May	1944	25.7	
Youth on the Prow	Modern Woman	May	1944	25.9	Youth at the Prow
Feasts for Heroes	Modern Woman	Oct	1944	25.11	
William Goes Fruit-Picking	Modern Woman	Apr	1945	25.12	
Aunt Florence, Toy-Maker	Homes & Gardens	Nov	1945	25.10	
The Battle of Flowers	Modern Woman	May	1946	27.5	The Pageant
A Witch in Time	Home Notes	31 Jan	1947	27.4	William and the Witch
William and the Brown Check Sports Coat	Home Notes	14 Feb	1947	27.3	William Scares the General
William and the Tramp	Home Notes	10 Oct	1947	28.1	William and the Homeless
William and the Four-Forty	Home Notes	28 May	1948	27.7	
Violet Elizabeth Wins	Home Notes	7 Jan	1949	27.1	

Title in Book	Magazine	When Published	Book	Original Title (if different)
Esmeralda Takes a Hand	Home Notes	16 Dec 1949	27.6	
William Meets the Professor	Home Notes	10 Feb 1950	28.2	
William – The Bold	Home Notes	7 Apr 1950	27.2	William the Rebel Leader
Cats and White Elephants	Home Notes	26 May 1950	27.8	
William Beats the Record	Home Notes	29 Dec 1950	28.3	
William and the Returned Traveller	Home Notes	4 May 1951	28.4	
William and the Haunted Cottage	Home Notes	30 Nov 1951	28.5	
William and the Pets' Club	Home Notes	25 Jan 1952	28.6	
William's Secret Society	Home Notes	11 Apr 1952	28.7	
A Helping Hand for Ethel	Home Notes	28 Nov 1952	30.7	
Archie has a Party	Home Notes	9 Jan 1953	28.8	
William and the New Game	Home Notes	26 Mar 1953	29.2	
William and the American Tie	Home Notes	23 July 1953	29.3	
William and the New Elizabethan	Home Notes	24 Sept 1953	29.6	William Goes Patriotic
William and the Over-Ten Club	Home Notes	31 Dec 1953	29.7	
Archie on the Run	Home Notes	29 Apr 1954	29.4	William in Charge
William and Little Yubear	Home Notes	22 July 1954	29.5	William's New Friend
These Little Mistakes Will Happen	Home Notes	9 Sept 1954	29.8	William's Mistake

(D.S.)

APPENDIX 3: Characters Not Listed Individually in the A–Z Section

First	Last	Character	First	Last	Character
26.11		Abbot, Miss (Rosalyn's aunt)	33.1	34.3	Barton, Jimmy
36.3		Abbott, Mrs	18.10	28.2	Beacon, Mrs
36.2		Abdullah (Boy Wednesday)	6.1		Bell, Mrs (Joan/Mary's mother)
22.4		Adela	14.4		Bellews, Mrs
3.10		Agatha (a Croombe cousin)	20.10		Bellfield, Miss
16.10		Alex, Aunt (Blakes')	14.6		Belson's (circus?)
10.3		Algernon (William as)	8.1		Benson Minor
26.7		Alistair	19.3		Bentley
34.1		Amanda	15.9		Bergson, Rupert
36.3		Anderson, Mr	21.3		Bert
32.5		Angela	3.5		Bertram
34.3		Angelique (Forrester)	23.7		Beverton, Bella
25.11		Ann	23.7	23.8	Beverton, Mrs
19.7		Appleton, Miss	31.4		Bill (Higgs's cousin)
13.10		Archie	1.10		Bill (Mr Moss's nephew)
27.1		Archie's Aunt Georgina	18.1		Bill (bearded burglar)
35.1		Argonauts, The	16.8		Billy (twin)
33.3		Arnold	21.8		Black, Mrs, old
21.8		Ashtead, Dr Horace	16.9	16.10	Blake, Major
38.4		Aunt Emma (Thompson)	23.7		Blake, Miss
20.4		Aunt Fanny (Bott)	16.9	16.10	Blake, Miss Diana
5.13		Aunt Ferdinanda	2.10		Blake, Mr
18.6		Aunt Flossie (Ellen's)	18.4		Blinks Major
34.2		Aunt Josephine (Bott)	6.10		Bobbie, Frampton's nephew
20.4		Aunt Maggie (Bott)	24.4		Borinsky, Princess (alias)
30.1		Aunt Phoebe	8.7		Boston, Mr Eugene
13.9		Badlow, Mrs	22.7		Brading, Claude
13.9		Badlow brother	2.14		Brent, Johnnie
13.9		Badlow twins (John)	11.7		Brewster, Betty
23.9		Bagshott, Mr	15.11		Brewster, Farmer
32.4		Bailey, Mr	11.4		Brewster, Gladys
22.1		Baker, Polly	17.7		Brewster, Mrs
22.4		Bannister, Sir Gerard	4.11		Brooke, Mr
5.8		Barker, Gladys	–		Brown, James*
10.6		Barmer, Mrs	22.7		Bruces, The
28.7		Barnet, Mrs	30.1		Bruster, Milly
30.4		Barnham, Lady	30.1		Bruster, Mrs
20.6		Barron, Mr	21.4		Bryce, Miss
35.3		Barrows, Miss	38.3		Buller

First	Last	Character
31.3		Burnham, Miss
19.5		Burwash, Mrs
1.8		Butler, baby
21.3		Camp, Mr and Mrs
17.7		Cassock, Sir Marmaduke
17.7		Cassock, Sir Marmaduke's son
29.2		Cecil, Patsy's cousin
31.7		Charles
12.1		Charlie
14.11		Charlie (Emmeline's cousin)
11.2		Charlie (lunatic)
13.9		Charlie/Charles
21.6	25.8	Clavis, Mrs (Claris in 25.8)
30.1		Clayton, Billy (the Gryphon)
35.4		Clayton, Peter
30.1		Clayton, Peter (baby)
31.3		Clements (builders)
4.9		Cliff, Miss
35.5		Constantia
22.1		Cookham (old man)
27.3		Cooper, Mr
4.3		Craig, Rev. P.
29.4		Crumbs, Mr (local carrier)
38.5		Cuthbert, Miss
4.6		d'Arcey, Lord and Lady
28.6	37.1	Dakers, Frankie
35.2		Dakers, Frankie's sister
11.5		Dakers, Freddie
38.1		Dakers, Mrs
9.6		Daphne
20.2		Darlington, Mr
20.2		Darlington, Sally
3.8		Dawson's mother
23.10		Dayford, Mrs (child psychologist)
1.7	2.6	de Vere Carter, Mrs
2.2		Delia
24.1		Devizes, Mr (editor)
33.5		Devon, Miss Alicia Virginia
34.3	37.1	Dexter, Bobby
37.1		Dexter, Mr

First	Last	Character
16.8		Dickie (twin)
35.5		Dolores
35.5		Dopey
16.10		Dorita (Blakes' cousin)
26.6		Doune, Mr
3.6		Drew, Mr
29.6		Ducrasne, Mrs
23.2		Durant, Mr (geologist)
32.2		Ellison, Dr
32.2		Ellison, General (deceased)
24.10		Emmy, Aunt (Hubert's)
1.4		Eric
31.6		Eric
12.1		Ermyntrude
27.6		Esmerelda (dummy)
23.10		Eustace, Uncle (Dayford)
38.6		Exton
7.1		Face, Old (teacher)
5.9		Fairly, Mr
38.6		Fatty
35.4		Faversham, Amos (Jenks's labourer)
21.4		Faversham, Mr
35.4		Faversham, Mrs
9.2		Featherstone's sister
9.2	26.11	Featherstone, Miss Alice
36.1		Felicia, 'Aunt' (friend)
35.3		Fellowes, Mr (deceased)
22.1	30.1	Fellowes, Mrs
30.1		Fellows, Micky
36.3		Fenella
35.5		Ferdinand
32.8		Field, Agatha
32.8		Fields, The
25.5		Finch – a 'tramp'
7.2	15.12	Fitzgerald, Mrs Gerald
15.5		Flavia (writer about 'Michael')
19.3		Fletcher, Mr
9.2		Fleuster, Mr
22.4		Folkat, Miss
9.2		Formester, Miss

First	Last	Character	First	Last	Character
34.3		Forrester, Lady	30.2		Gervase, Sir
36.2		Forrester, Major	29.2		Gilbert, Mrs
29.8		Forrester, Miss	29.2		Gilbert, Patsy
16.6		Forrester, Mr	19.2		Gillespie, Miss Marcia
28.6		Forrester, Peregrine (Albert)	31.7		Gilpin, Miss Agatha
31.4		Fortescues, The	31.7		Gilpin, Mr Ambrose ('Sandy')
22.1		Foster, Jimmy	8.2		Gladys
23.3		Foulard, Mr	22.2		Godwin, Miss
29.7		Fountain, Miss	35.2		Golightly, Thomas
6.1		Fox, Miss	8.2		Grace, Miss
6.1		Fox, Mr Arnold	3.9		Graham, Monkton (writer, alias)
9.6		Foxe, Lucy	32.4		Granter, Miss Lucy
23.6		Foxton, Billy (blacksmith)	32.4		Granter, Miss's sister Erica
6.10		Frampton, Miss (spiritualist)	21.7		Great-Aunt Sarah (Lane)
15.3		Frances, Herbert	2.14		Green, Fisty
15.3		Frances, Herbert's mother	31.8		Green, James
9.3		Francis, John	2.2		Green, Mrs
10.6	34.3	Franklin, Mrs	33.5		Green, Mrs
5.9	31.3	Franks, Mr	37.4		Green, Mrs
5.14	8.7	Franks, Mrs	2.2		Green, baby
31.2		Franks, young brother	17.5		Greene, Johnny
7.7		Freddie	7.6		Greene, Moyna
5.13		Frederica	2.4		Greene, Mr
5.13		Frederica's mother	7.4		Greene, Mr (curate)
12.10		Freedom, Elissa (psychic)	17.5		Greene, Mrs
7.1		Fremlin, Professor (geologist)	2.4		Greene, Priscilla
38.3		French	9.2		Greene-Joanes, Miss
9.9		Frenshams, The	15.11		Greg, Mr
30.6		Frisky – a man	30.6		Gregson
38.4		Fulham, Mr	35.2		Gregson, Mr (deceased)
31.8		Furnace, Mr	18.1		Gregsons, The (dance)
15.5		Fuss-pot (history-teacher)	24.4		Gretchstein, Baroness (alias)
37.7		Galloway, Mrs	26.9		Greyston, Valerie
9.3		George (a small Outlaw archer)	24.1	24.9	Griffin, Miss Lavinia
18.6		George (red-faced man)	7.8		Groves, Gloria
4.11		George (very very old)	7.8		Groves, Mr (artist)
12.1		George (window-shopper)	4.14		Groves, Mr John
23.3		Georgie	9.2		Gwladwyn's nephew
23.3		Georgie's mother	9.2		Gwladwyn, Miss
19.6		Gert	25.12		Hallowes, Mrs
29.2		Gertrude, Patsy's cousin	25.7		Hamilton, Major

First	Last	Character
32.2		Hampshire, Miss
14.3		Hanshaw, Mrs
36.4		Harts, The
9.1		Hawkins, Betty
3.5		Hawkins, Christine
9.1		Hawkins, Mrs
22.6		Hayes, Jimmy ('Human Tornado')
16.4		Hedley-Smith, Mrs
4.11		Helbert (gipsy)
4.11		Helbert's mother
5.4		Helm, Mrs
37.6		Hemlock, Mrs
9.2		Hemmersley, Miss Georgine
–		Hemming, Bill*
10.9		Hemmings, Pete
5.7		Henks, Colonel (deceased)
19.4		Herbert
12.9		Herbert ('Erbert)
12.9		Herbert's mother
8.5		Heron, Mrs
36.5		Herriot, Mrs
29.6		Hetherley, Mrs
5.14		Hinlock, Laurence
22.1		Hinton, Major
9.3		Hodges, Farmer
9.5		Holding, Mr and Mrs
20.9		Holewood, Colonel
3.5		Holmes, Elbert
32.4		Honiton, Mr (sunbather)
30.3	37.4	Hopkins, Miss
30.3		Hopkins, Miss's sister
7.10		Hopkins, Mr (teacher)
7.2		Hopkins, Mrs
3.5		Horatia
16.7		Horner, Theo(dore/dosius)
36.5		Hoskins, Mr (bell-ringer)
10.6		Hoskins, Mrs
31.6		Hugo
9.3		Hunter, Mr (magistrate)
16.3		Jack, little

First	Last	Character
19.1		Jacko's master
11.10		Jakes (shepherd)
6.13		Jam (Marmaduke)
15.2		James
5.13		James (medical student)
17.3		James, Crazy (station cabbie)
13.9	38.1	Jameson, Mr
13.9	38.1	Jameson, Mrs
1.12		Jarrow, Mr
1.12		Jarrow, Ninette
38.5		Jenkins, Miss
35.4		Jenkins, Mr
5.6	31.8	Jenks, Mrs
13.6		Jenks's youngest daughter
14.6		Jim (lorry driver)
24.8		Jim, Honest (tramp)
25.11		John (Squadron Leader)
25.11		John's wife
7.4		Johnnie
35.1		Johnny (an Argonaut)
2.10		Johnson, Mr
4.14		Johnson's boy
5.13		Jonathon (a curate)
9.1		Jones, Blanche
23.5		Jones, Miss
21.6		Jones, Miss (Hadley)
1.6	3.12	Jones, Miss (teacher)
2.10		Jones, Mr
6.7		Jones, Mr
14.4		Jones, Mr
23.5		Jones, Mr and Mrs (bomb-dodgers)
14.5		Jones, Mr (teacher)
32.1		Jones, Mr Aloysius
2.11		Jones, Mr Percival
32.1		Jones, Mr, Senior
9.2		Jones, Mrs
31.6		Jones, Mrs
32.5		Jones, Mrs
9.1		Jones, Mrs (Blanche's mother)
22.1		Jones, Mrs (Carolina's mother)

First	*Last*	*Character*	*First*	*Last*	*Character*
21.6		Jones, Mrs (Marleigh)	14.1		Manelli, Signor
3.8		Jones, Reverend Habbakuk	14.9		Manes, Miss
27.7		Jones, Sergeant (policeman)	12.10	27.1	Mannister, Auriole
23.5		Jones, the builder, and Mrs	27.1		Mannister, Euphemia
24.7		Keith, Douglas	11.6		Mapleton, Clarence ('John')
24.7		Keith, Flight Lieutenant	5.8		March, Mr George
24.7		Keith, Mrs	13.8		Marlow, Mrs
24.7		Keith, Susan	14.4		Marlow, Old (deceased)
24.7		Keiths' Aunt Lucy	6.13		Marmaduke (Jam)
24.7		Keiths' Uncle Herbert	32.3		Marmaduke, Roxana's Uncle
37.3		Kennal, Mrs (hotel manageress)	12.7		Marsden, Peggy
22.4		Lady Cynthia	6.9	28.3	Marsh, Mr
15.11		Laetitia	6.9		Marsh, Mr's mother
2.8		Laing, Miss	18.6		Martha
13.6		Lane, Dorinda's father	11.3		Martin, Mr
14.2		Lane, Dorinda's mother	25.8		Martin, Mr
6.12		Langley, Harold	14.10		Martin, Mrs (writer)
6.12		Langley, Mrs	3.11		Mary
24.2		Leicester, Mr (kinematograph)	25.4	25.5	Mason, Mrs
32.7		Len	25.4		Mason, Percival
2.3		Lewes, Mr	33.1		Masters, Diana
8.8		Lewes, Master (vicar's son)	22.4		Masters, Lucy
38.6		Leylam	33.1		Masters, Mrs
20.8		Limpsfield, James	26.5		Maurice, Miss
33.4		Limpsfield, Mr (superintendent)	8.10		Maylands, Mrs and family
1.8		Litton, Farmer	12.9		Meddows, Mrs
31.2		Lorrimer, Eric	37.7		Medlar, Mrs
3.6		Loughton, Mr	12.6		Medlow, Clarence
20.1		Lucinda	14.7		Medway, Mr
16.3		Lucy, little	35.5		Meggison, Mr
31.3		Lupton, Mr	17.10		Melissa
8.6		Luton, Farmer	36.2		Mercer, Arnold J. (headmaster)
5.2	23.8	Luton, Mr	35.6		Merrivale, Alec (writer)
19.5		Luton, Mrs	15.3		Merton, Georgie
30.4		Lytton, Mr	10.6	32.1	Merton, Mrs
32.3		Lytton, Mrs	11.5		Messiter, Miss
18.1		Macnamara, Mrs	30.2		Mexton, Mrs
16.3		Maddox, Charles	7.2		Miggs, Miss
16.3		Maddox, Mrs	17.3		Miggs, Miss
16.3		Maddox, Mrs's mother	35.2		Miggs, Mr (caretaker)
6.5		Maloney, Mrs	16.8		Miggs, Mrs (caretaker)

First	Last	Character	First	Last	Character
18.1		Millers, The (dance)	17.9		Nichol, Mrs and mother
37.5		Milly	34.3		Nobby (burglar)
21.3		Milton, Miss (sister of)	7.8		Oldham, Gladys
19.7		Minster, Jimmie (film-star)	25.8		Oldham, Miss
29.7		Mirabel, Miss (London)	24.9		Paget, Miss (little girl)
38.6		Misty (head teacher) and wife	24.9		Paget, Mrs
4.12		Moffat, Mr	19.5	37.1	Parker, Freddie
26.8		Monkton, Bruce	31.7		Parker, Mr Edgar
14.7		Monkton, Trevor	22.1		Parker, Mrs
32.6		Monson, Hermione	30.1		Parker, Susie
32.6	38.3	Monson, Mr	28.2		Parkers, The
20.1	31.5	Montague, Ralph ('Ronty')	12.2		Parkinson, Mr (teacher)
9.2		Montgomery, Cuthbert	35.2		Parkinson, Mrs
18.3		Montgomery, Edmond	4.14		Parks, Mrs
5.7		Moote, Mrs	4.14		Parks's boy
14.5		Morall, Miss	33.6		Parsons, Grandfather
7.7		Morgan, Charles	33.6		Parsons, Grandmother
1.1		Morgan, Jack	33.6	38.1	Parsons, Mrs
7.9	9.4	Morlan, Dr	6.10		Paula
7.9		Morlan, Mrs	6.7		Paulovitch (burglar)
5.4		Morrison, Mrs	23.9		Peabody, Colonel
4.12		Morrisse, Mr	34.1		Peaslake, Mr
19.5		Morrow, Girlie	2.11		Peggy (holiday)
31.3		Morrow, Martin (pseudonym)	29.8		Pelham, Mrs
19.5		Morrow, Mrs	11.10		Pelleas (Pennyman nephew)
28.1		Mortimer, Archibald (alias)	13.4		Penhurst, Percy
9.1		Morton, Dolly	25.6		Perkins (schoolboy)
35.4		Mostyn, Mr (teacher)	10.5		Perkins, Miss (journalist)
16.11		Moyna	8.9		Perkins, Misses
3.8		Mugg, Theophilus	19.9		Perkins, Mr (butcher)
21.4		Muggeridge (keeper)	21.1		Perkins, Sergeant (police)
2.3		Mulroyd, Mr	11.1		Perrivale, Montmorency
7.3		Murdoch, Mrs	27.4		Perrott, Miss
2.14		Murford, Mrs	35.1		Pete (an Argonaut)
2.14		Murford, Sadie	26.8		Peter
10.3	25.9	Murgatroyd, Miss	3.9		Peter
36.2		Nassir, Mr	27.4		Peters, Miss
12.9		Nelson (and his dog Toby)	10.5		Peters, Mr
25.12	26.9	Netherby, Mr	21.9		Peters, Mr
37.6		Newgate, Mr	10.6		Peters, Mrs
37.6		Newgate, Mr (No. 2)	28.5	38.1	Peters, Mrs (daily)

First	Last	Character	First	Last	Character
34.2		Petersham, Mr (reporter)	33.1		Reedham, Mrs and family
26.7		Petworth, Kay	12.8		Reggie
30.6		Philips	32.7		Reggie (thief)
38.5		Philmore, Miss	13.5		Renies, Mr (teacher)
38.6		Piggy	19.10		Richard
32.2		Pinchin, James	31.7		Richard
8.2		Pink, Miss	32.2		Richards, Mrs
32.2		Pink, Miss (teacher)	31.6		Risborough, Miss
18.4		Polkington, Mrs Lucy	38.3		Roberts
7.5		Poll, Miss Gertie	34.3		Robinson (burglar)
25.6		Polliter, Major (the son)	7.10	9.2	Robinson, Mrs
7.9		Polliter, Miss	38.6		Rocky
37.1		Polliter, Miss (next door)	17.1		Roderick
12.9		Pollitt, Sir Charles	4.11		Roke, Bertram
8.10		Polluck, Mr	24.5		Ronald (Lane cousin)
21.9	35.2	Pomeroy, Lieutenant Colonel M. H.	28.1		Rose, Mr (tramp)
			28.2		Rosemary
14.7		Pongo	37.2		Roundway, Miss
22.1		Poppleham, Mrs	31.2		Rushton-Smythe, Marmaduke
12.7		Popplestone, Mr Socrates	31.2		Rushton-Smythe, Mrs
8.1		Porson, Professor	10.9		Sadie
3.13		Porter, Mr	27.7		Sally (Sunley niece)
31.8		Porter, Mrs	20.3		Sam, Fat (tramp)
3.13		Porter, Mrs Mary	30.4		Sanderstead, Osbert
13.2		Potter, Mr Augustine (governor)	25.7		Sarky, Old (teacher)
10.1		Potty, Old (teacher)	30.6		Saunders
3.7		Pugh, Reverend Cuthbert	32.4		Saunders, Mr
33.3	38.1	Radbury, Professor Miss	11.8		Seales, Ben
38.5		Radley, Miss	9.8		Seed, Miss
35.6		Raglan, Mr (writer)	33.6		Serena
24.10		Ralph	2.14		Sheila
8.8		Randall, Frankie	21.4		Shoreham, Freddie
1.7		Randalls, The (of Herts)	21.4		Shoreham, Mrs (Freddie's mother)
8.3		Rawlings			
38.2		Reading, Major	21.4		Shoreham, Mrs (Freddie's great aunt)
30.3		Redditch, Mr			
16.3		Redwood, Laurence	11.4		Sikes, Ann
16.3		Redwood, Sybil	5.7		Simky, Miss
33.1	33.5	Reedham, Biddy (and as Needham)	27.2		Simpkin, Arabella's baby
			21.1		Simpkin, Arabella's sister
33.1		Reedham, Miss (aunt)	29.7	38.4	Simpkin, Fred

First	Last	Character	First	Last	Character
28.6		Simpkin, George Thomas	16.8		Terry
20.4	38.4	Simpkin, Mrs	38.5		Theo
7.9		Simpkins, Frank	13.7		Theobald, Mr (hairdresser)
7.2		Simpkins, Galileo	4.11		Thomas
7.9		Simpkins, Mrs	21.1		Thompson, Miss Louisa
30.8		Sir Claud	2.2		Thompson, Mr
27.6		Slater, Miss	21.8		Thorpe, Johnnie
5.7		Sluker, Miss	11.9		Tibblets, Mrs (housekeeper)
7.1		Smith (classmate)	30.6		Tillinson
8.1		Smith Minimus	18.4		Timpkins/Tompkins
8.1		Smith Minor	26.5		Toad Face (boss)
22.8		Smith, Daniel (cross-eye)	22.2		Tomlinson, Miss
18.3	31.7	Smith, Johnny	26.5		Tonks (Monkey-Face)
24.4		Smith, Mary (alias)	38.6		Tony
25.5		Smith, Miss (alias)	32.7	34.5	Torrance, Lady
10.1		Smith, Mr	12.10		Tosher (bearded man)
10.10		Smith, Mr	19.4		Tressider, Miss
29.2		Smith, Mrs	30.7		Tufton, Miss
36.2		Smith, Mrs	22.4		Twemlow, Miss (teacher)
6.2		Smith, Professor	34.4		Tyrral, Miss
22.8		Smith, Rube	18.8		Uncle Charlie (Hubert's)
13.1		Smithers, Miss	20.4		Uncle Charlie (act)
13.1		Sommerton, Professor	5.13		Uncle George
		(geologist)	17.11		Uncle Josiah (Carrol)
4.11		Sophia	21.2		Uncle Paul (Lane)
4.8		Spence, Miss	24.4		Vereton, Lady Vere (alias)
6.1		Spencer, Geoffrey	10.5		Verney, Clarice (actress)
38.6		Spiky	10.5		Verney, Rosemary
11.2		Stacey, Mrs	7.4		Vernon, Rudolph
35.4		Stanton, Miss	7.8		Victor
17.3		Steadman, Mr	6.3		Wakefield, Hon Percy
6.4		Strong, Mr (teacher)	16.8		Walton, Lady
34.1		Summers, Arnold	35.2		Wansford, Hugh
23.3		Summers, Colonel	18.2	18.4	Warbeck (teacher – Perkins)
27.7		Surley, Miss	1.11		Ware, Dr
38.6		Swanky (teacher)	38.3		Warren
21.3		Syd	20.3		Warrender, Agnes Matilda
26.14		Syd	20.3		Warrender, Mr and Mrs
38.6		Syd	27.6		Warwick, Mrs
31.2		Taverton, Miss	22.1		Weller, Toby
35.1		Ted (an Argonaut)	7.5		Weston, Miss

First	*Last*	*Character*
27.4	35.2	Westonbury, Mr
5.7		Whatte, Miss
1.7		Wheeler, Teddy
38.3		White
2.3		Wilkinsons (Todfoot)
36.4		Willingham, Mr and Mrs
33.3		Winterton, Dr
33.3		Winterton, Dr's daughter
36.1		Winterton, Professor
23.6		Winton, Major (special P.C.)
30.6		Worfield, James Aloysius (Porky)
21.5		Wortleton, Miss

See also the lists in ETHEL AND HER FRIENDS, THE OUTLAWS, RELATIONS, ROBERT AND HIS FRIENDS, SERVANTS.

* See 'William on the Trail', *Happy Mag*, July 1935, reprinted in the William Bibliography by W.O.G. Lofts and Derek Adley, privately published in 1977.

(D.S.)

APPENDIX 4: Articles 'By William' (by Richmal Crompton)

First Publication	Date	Caption
Happy Mag	Xmas 1926	I'll Tell You What's Wrong with Christmas*
Happy Mag	Jan 1927	New Year's Day*
Happy Mag	Sept 1927	School is a Waste of Time*
Happy Mag	Dec 1927	The Job I'd Like Best*
Happy Mag	Xmas 1927	William's Christmas Presents*
Happy Mag	Xmas 1928	When is A Treat not A Treat?
Happy Mag	Xmas 1929	William Writes a Play
Happy Mag	Xmas 1930	Brighter and Better Pets
Happy Mag	Jan 1932	New Rules for December 25th
Happy Mag	Xmas 1932	Christmas Day with William*
Happy Mag	Hol 1933	Something Like a Change*
Happy Mag	Xmas 1933	Home for the Holidays*
Tit-Bits Summer Extra	1927	Commonsense About Holidays*
Tit-Bits Summer Extra	1928	My Day In London*
Tit-Bits Summer Extra	1929	Picnics
Tit-Bits Summer Extra	1930	My Summer Holiday*
Not Known	1931?	How I Would Improve the Seaside
Eltham College Junior Magazine (*The Discoverer*)	Xmas 1965	Our Christmas Play (see *Happy Mag*, Xmas 1929)
Macmillan	1990	What's Wrong with Civilizashun.

NOTE Those items marked with an * are collected in the above-listed 1990 Macmillan book *What's Wrong with Civilizashun*.

(D.S.)